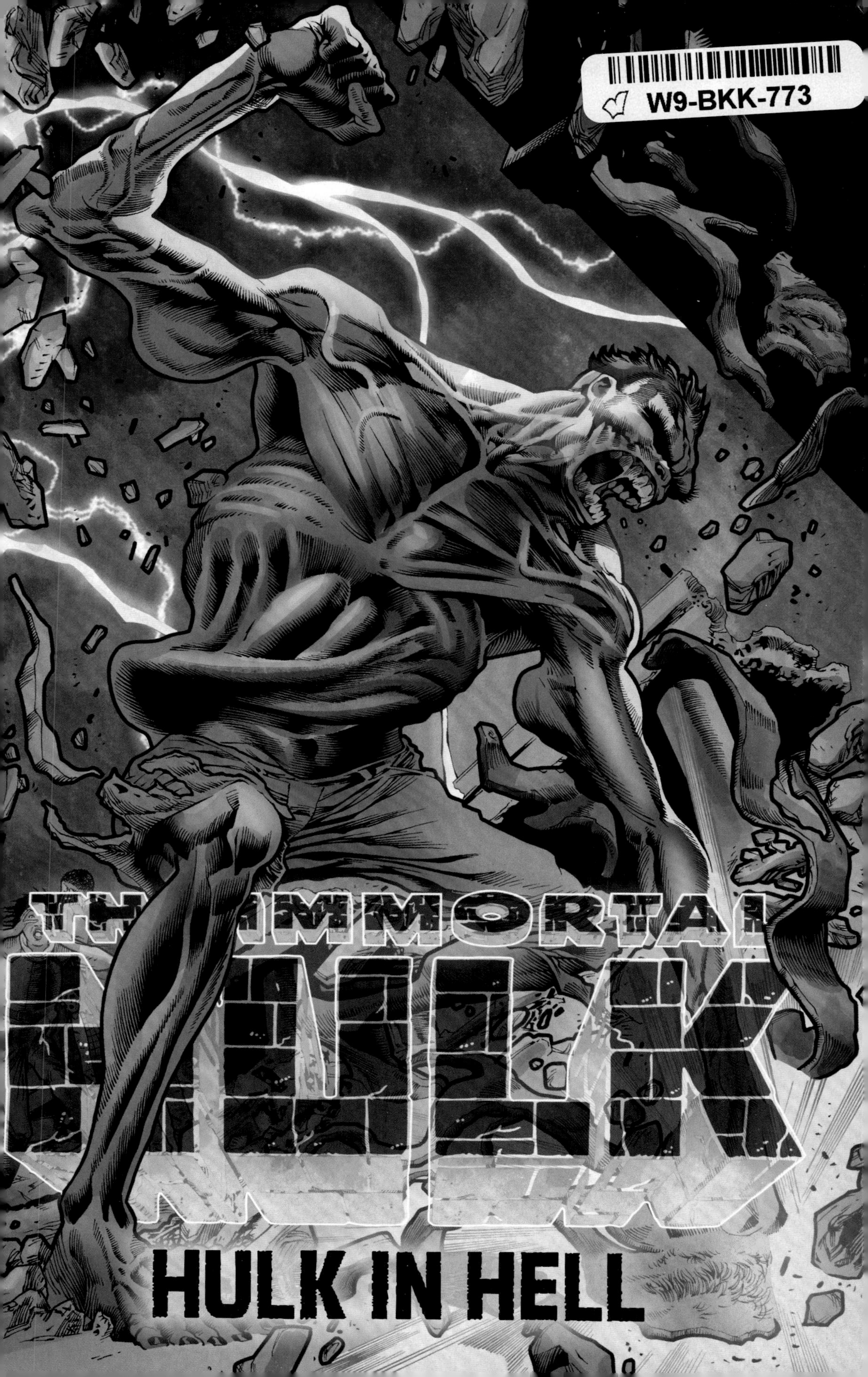
THE IMMORTAL
HULK
HULK IN HELL

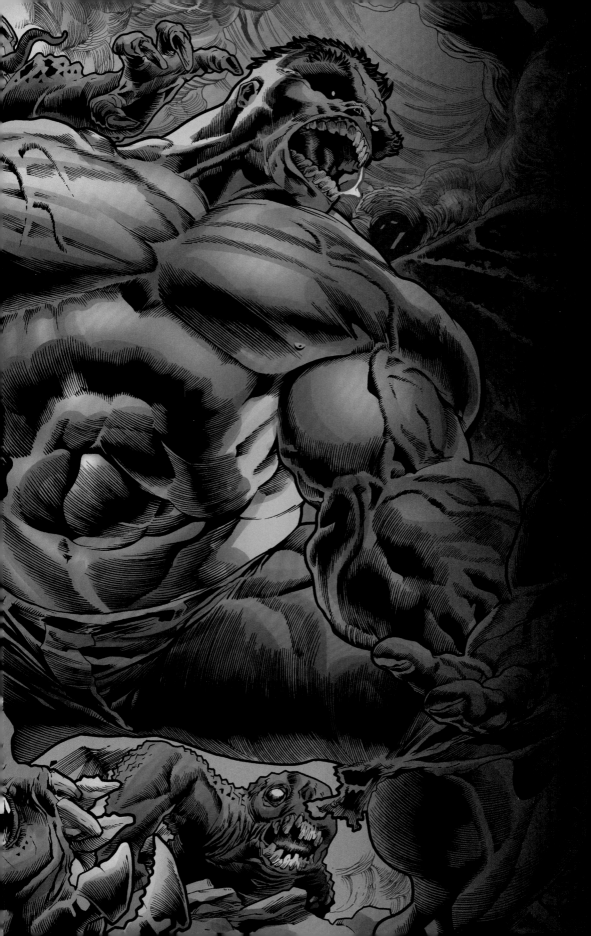

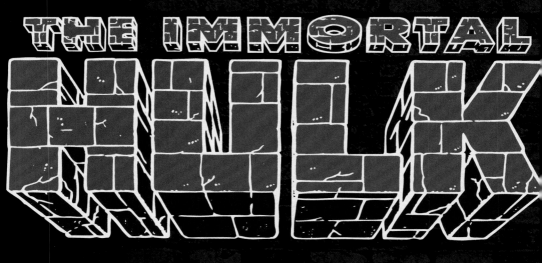

THE IMMORTAL HULK

HULK IN HELL

AL EWING
WRITER

JOE BENNETT
PENCILER [#11-13 & 15]

RUY JOSÉ [#11-13 & 15] WITH
BELARDINO BRABO [#13] & **RAFAEL FONTERIZ** [#13]
INKERS

ERIC NGUYEN
ARTIST [#12 FLASHBACKS]

KYLE HOTZ
ARTIST [#14]

PAUL MOUNTS
COLOR ARTIST

VC's CORY PETIT
LETTERER

ALEX ROSS
COVER ARTIST

SARAH BRUNSTAD
ASSOCIATE EDITOR

WIL MOSS
EDITOR

TOM BREVOORT
EXECUTIVE EDITOR

COLLECTION EDITOR: **MARK D. BEAZLEY**
ASSISTANT EDITOR: **CAITLIN O'CONNELL**
ASSOCIATE MANAGING EDITOR: **KATERI WOODY**
SENIOR EDITOR, SPECIAL PROJECTS: **JENNIFER GRÜNWALD**
VP PRODUCTION & SPECIAL PROJECTS: **JEFF YOUNGQUIST**
BOOK DESIGNERS: **ADAM DEL RE** WITH **STACIE ZUCKER**

SVP PRINT, SALES & MARKETING: **DAVID GABRIEL**
DIRECTOR, LICENSED PUBLISHING: **SVEN LARSEN**

EDITOR IN CHIEF: **C.B. CEBULSKI**
CHIEF CREATIVE OFFICER: **JOE QUESADA**
PRESIDENT: **DAN BUCKLEY**
EXECUTIVE PRODUCER: **ALAN FINE**

HULK
CREATED BY
STAN LEE &
JACK KIRBY

IMMORTAL HULK VOL. 3: HULK IN HELL. Contains material originally published in magazine form as IMMORTAL HULK #11-15. First printing 2019. ISBN 978-1-302-91506-3. Published by MARVEL WORLDWIDE, INC., a subsidiary of MARVEL ENTERTAINMENT, LLC. OFFICE OF PUBLICATION: 135 West 50th Street, New York, NY 10020. © 2019 MARVEL No similarity between any of the names, characters, persons, and/or institutions in this magazine with those of any living or dead person or institution is intended, and any such similarity which may exist is purely coincidental. **Printed in Canada.** DAN BUCKLEY, President, Marvel Entertainment; JOHN NEE, Publisher; JOE QUESADA, Chief Creative Officer; TOM BREVOORT, SVP of Publishing; DAVID BOGART, Associate Publisher & SVP of Talent Affairs; DAVID GABRIEL, SVP of Sales & Marketing, Publishing; JEFF YOUNGQUIST, VP of Production & Special Projects; DAN CARR, Executive Director of Publishing Technology; ALEX MORALES, Director of Publishing Operations; DAN EDINGTON, Managing Editor; SUSAN CRESPI, Production Manager; STAN LEE, Chairman Emeritus. For information regarding advertising in Marvel Comics or on Marvel.com, please contact Vit DeBellis, Custom Solutions & Integrated Advertising Manager, at vdebellis@marvel.com. For Marvel subscription inquiries, please call 888-511-5480. **Manufactured between 3/22/2019 and 4/23/2019 by SOLISCO PRINTERS, SCOTT, QC, CANADA.**

0987654321

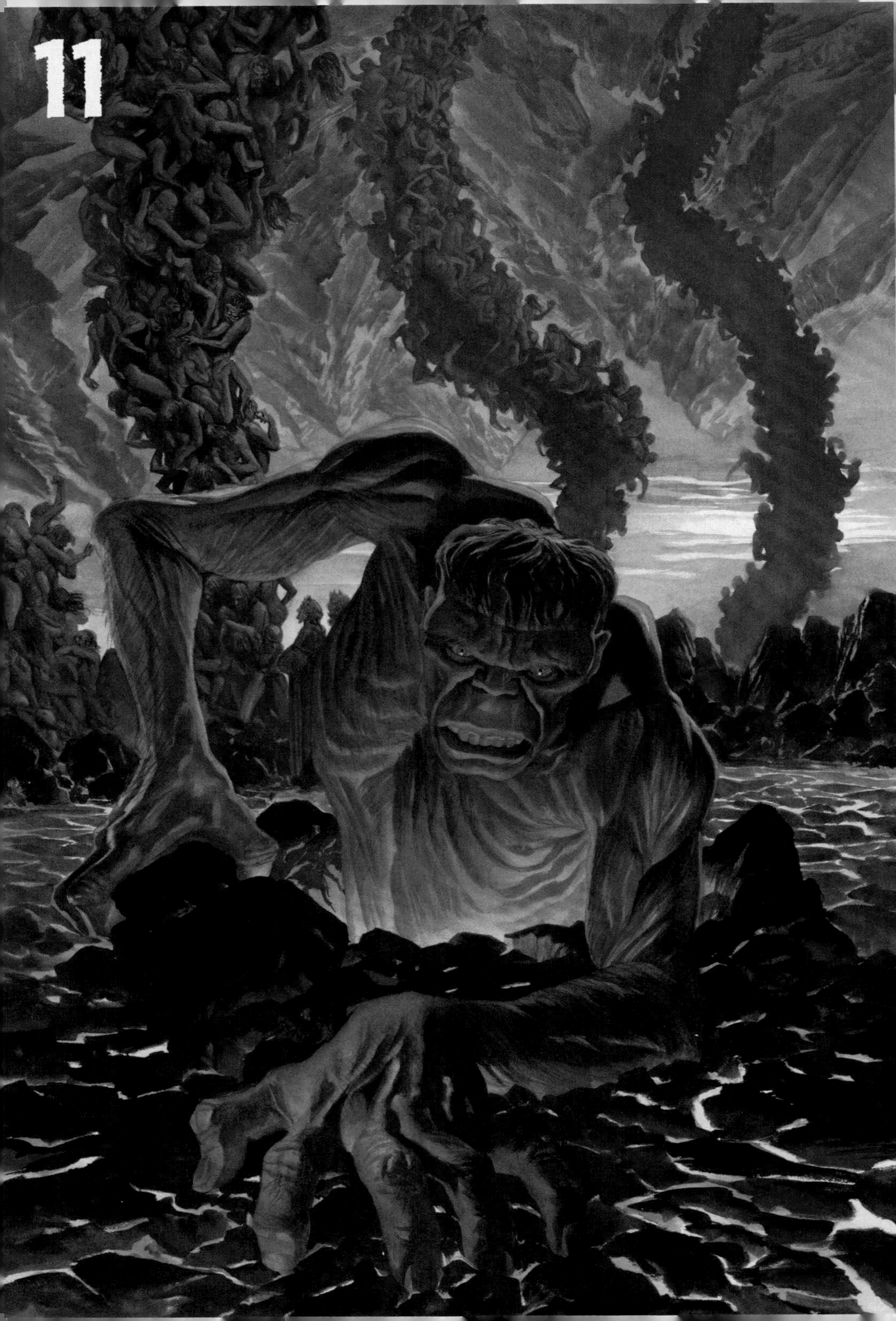
11

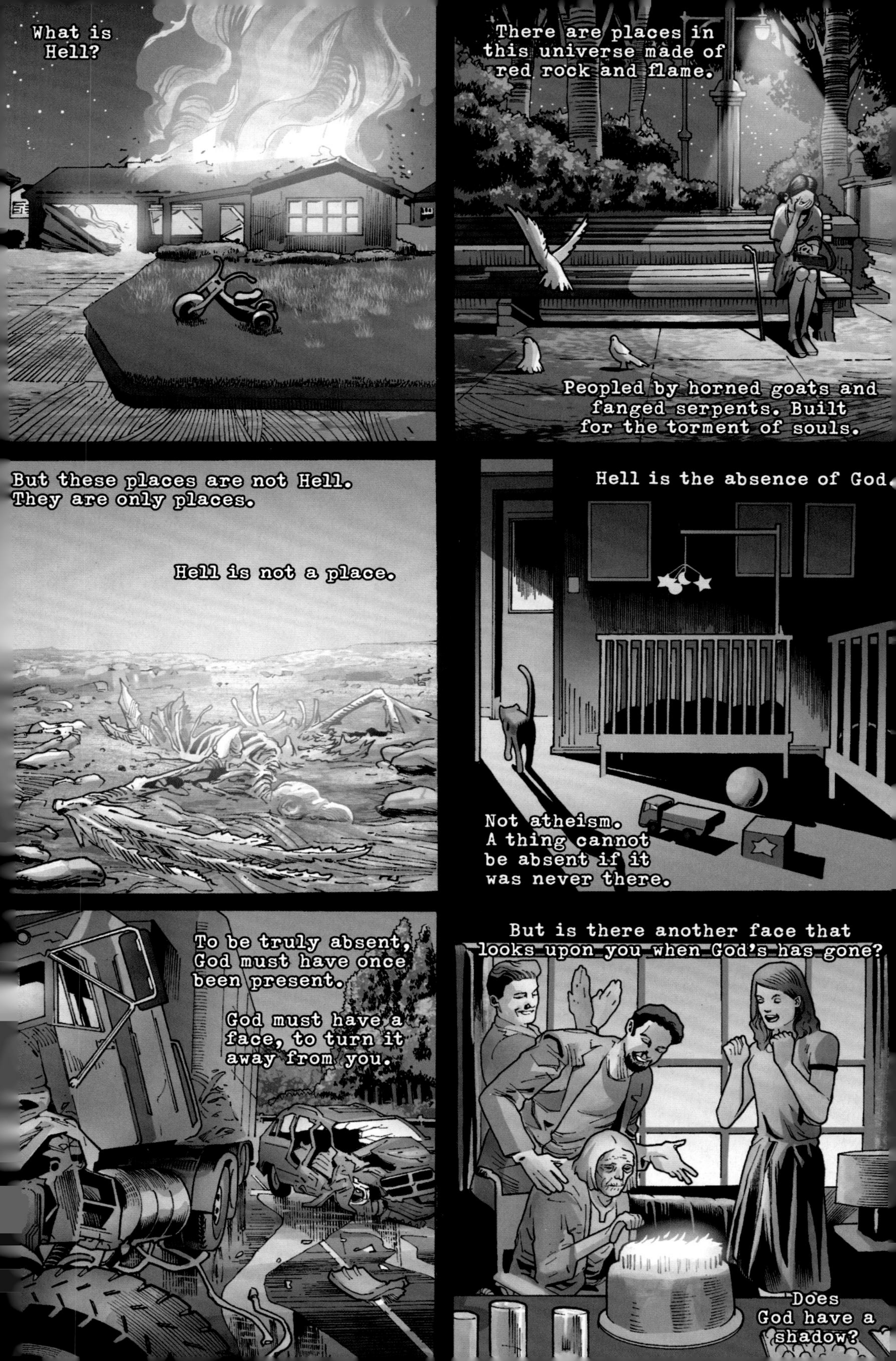
What is Hell?
There are places in this universe made of red rock and flame.
Peopled by horned goats and fanged serpents. Built for the torment of souls.
But these places are not Hell. They are only places.
Hell is not a place.
Hell is the absence of God.
Not atheism. A thing cannot be absent if it was never there.
To be truly absent, God must have once been present.
God must have a face, to turn it away from you.
But is there another face that looks upon you when God's has gone?
Does God have a shadow?

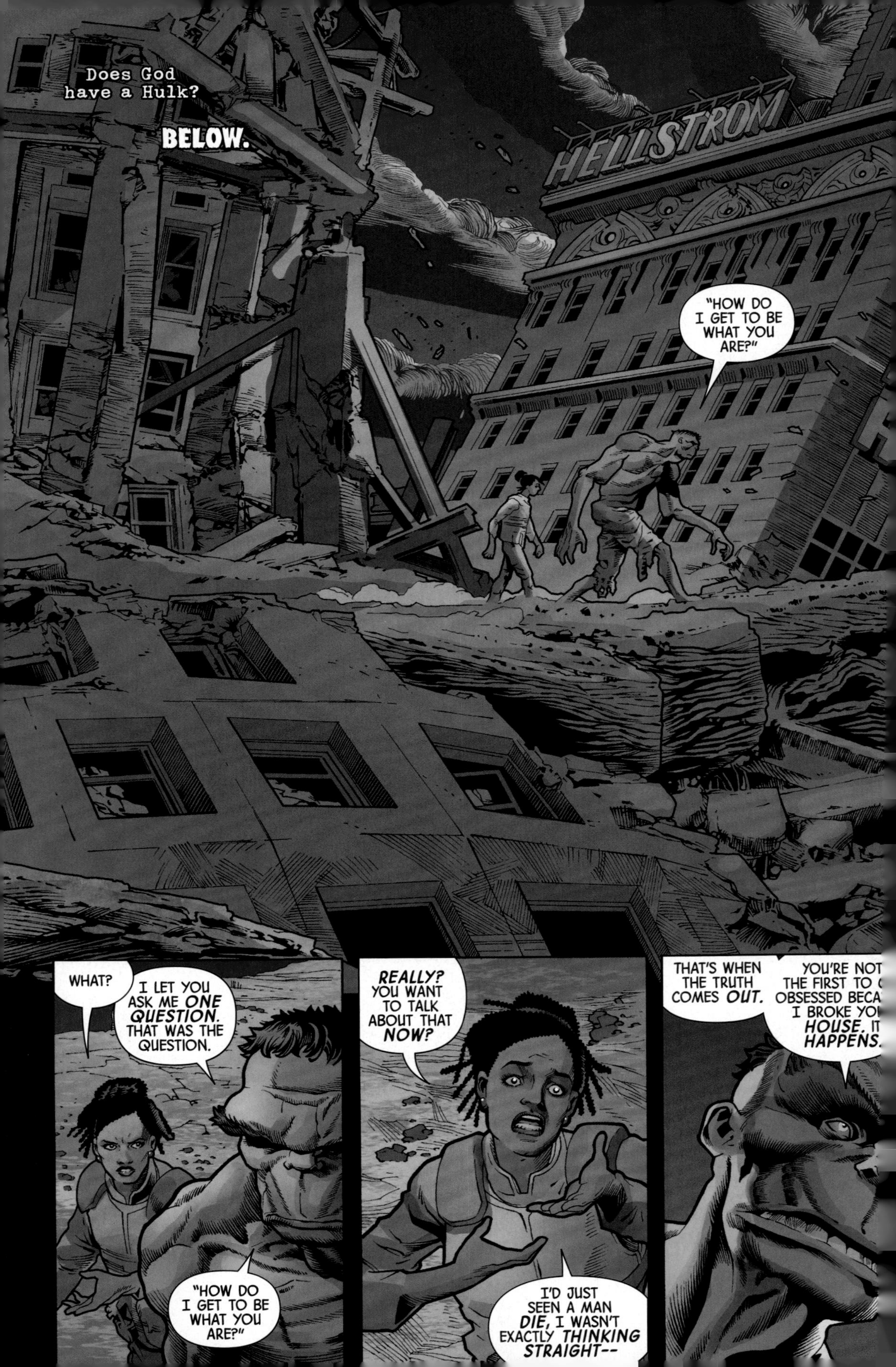
Does God have a Hulk?
BELOW.
HELLSTROM
"HOW DO I GET TO BE WHAT YOU ARE?"
WHAT?
I LET YOU ASK ME ONE QUESTION. THAT WAS THE QUESTION.
"HOW DO I GET TO BE WHAT YOU ARE?"
REALLY? YOU WANT TO TALK ABOUT THAT NOW?
I'D JUST SEEN A MAN DIE, I WASN'T EXACTLY THINKING STRAIGHT--
THAT'S WHEN THE TRUTH COMES OUT.

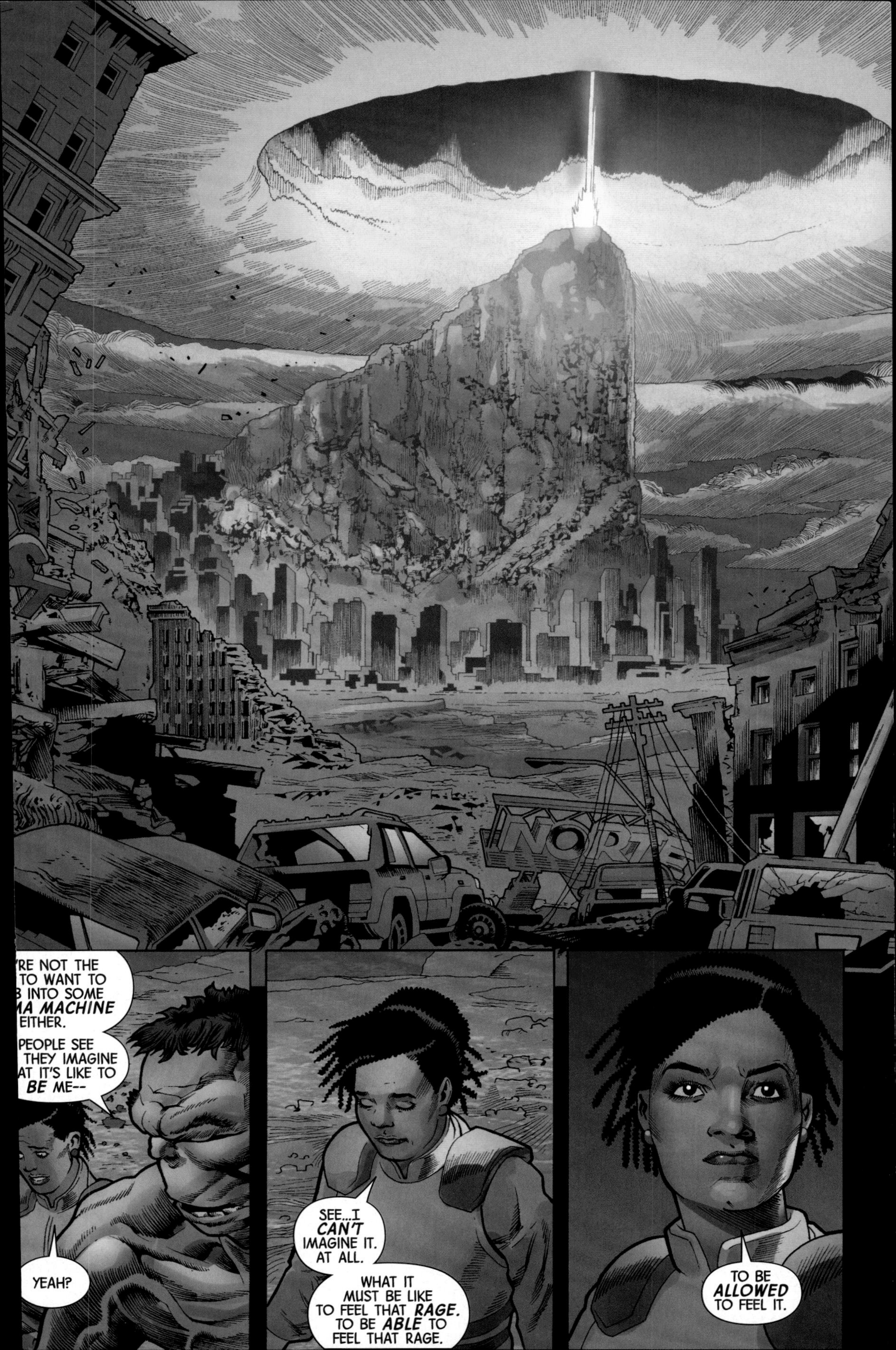
NORTE
'RE NOT THE TO WANT TO B INTO SOME MA MACHINE EITHER.
PEOPLE SEE THEY IMAGINE AT IT'S LIKE TO BE ME--
YEAH?
SEE...I CAN'T IMAGINE IT. AT ALL.
WHAT IT MUST BE LIKE TO FEEL THAT RAGE. TO BE ABLE TO FEEL THAT RAGE.
TO BE ALLOWED TO FEEL IT.

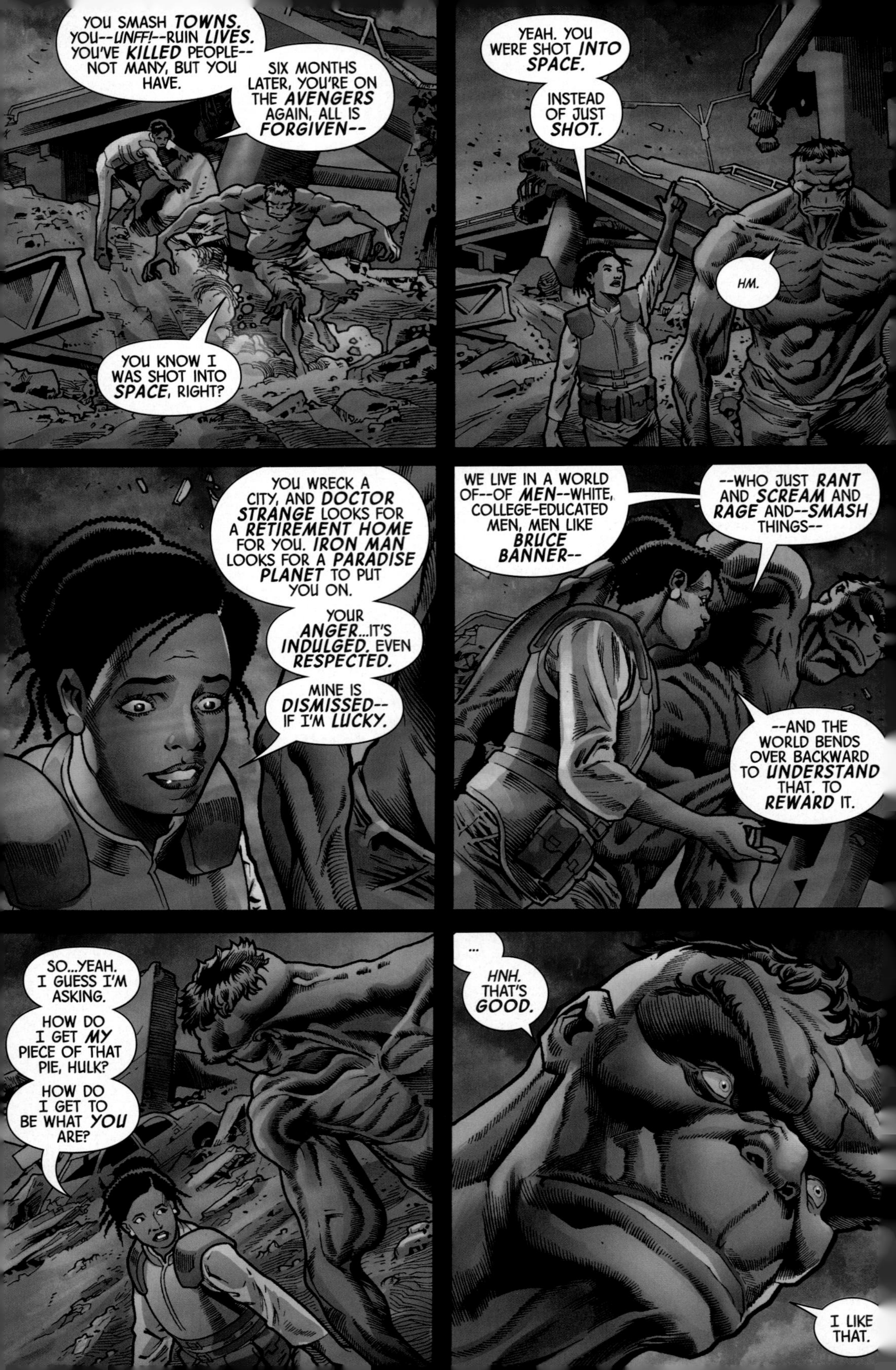
YOU SMASH TOWNS. YOU--UNFF!--RUIN LIVES. YOU'VE KILLED PEOPLE--NOT MANY, BUT YOU HAVE.
SIX MONTHS LATER, YOU'RE ON THE AVENGERS AGAIN, ALL IS FORGIVEN--
YOU KNOW I WAS SHOT INTO SPACE, RIGHT?
YEAH. YOU WERE SHOT INTO SPACE.
INSTEAD OF JUST SHOT.
HM.
YOU WRECK A CITY, AND DOCTOR STRANGE LOOKS FOR A RETIREMENT HOME FOR YOU. IRON MAN LOOKS FOR A PARADISE PLANET TO PUT YOU ON.
YOUR ANGER...IT'S INDULGED. EVEN RESPECTED.
MINE IS DISMISSED--IF I'M LUCKY.
WE LIVE IN A WORLD OF--OF MEN--WHITE, COLLEGE-EDUCATED MEN, MEN LIKE BRUCE BANNER--
--WHO JUST RANT AND SCREAM AND RAGE AND--SMASH THINGS--
--AND THE WORLD BENDS OVER BACKWARD TO UNDERSTAND THAT. TO REWARD IT.
SO...YEAH. I GUESS I'M ASKING.
HOW DO I GET MY PIECE OF THAT PIE, HULK?
HOW DO I GET TO BE WHAT YOU ARE?
...
HNH. THAT'S GOOD.
I LIKE THAT.

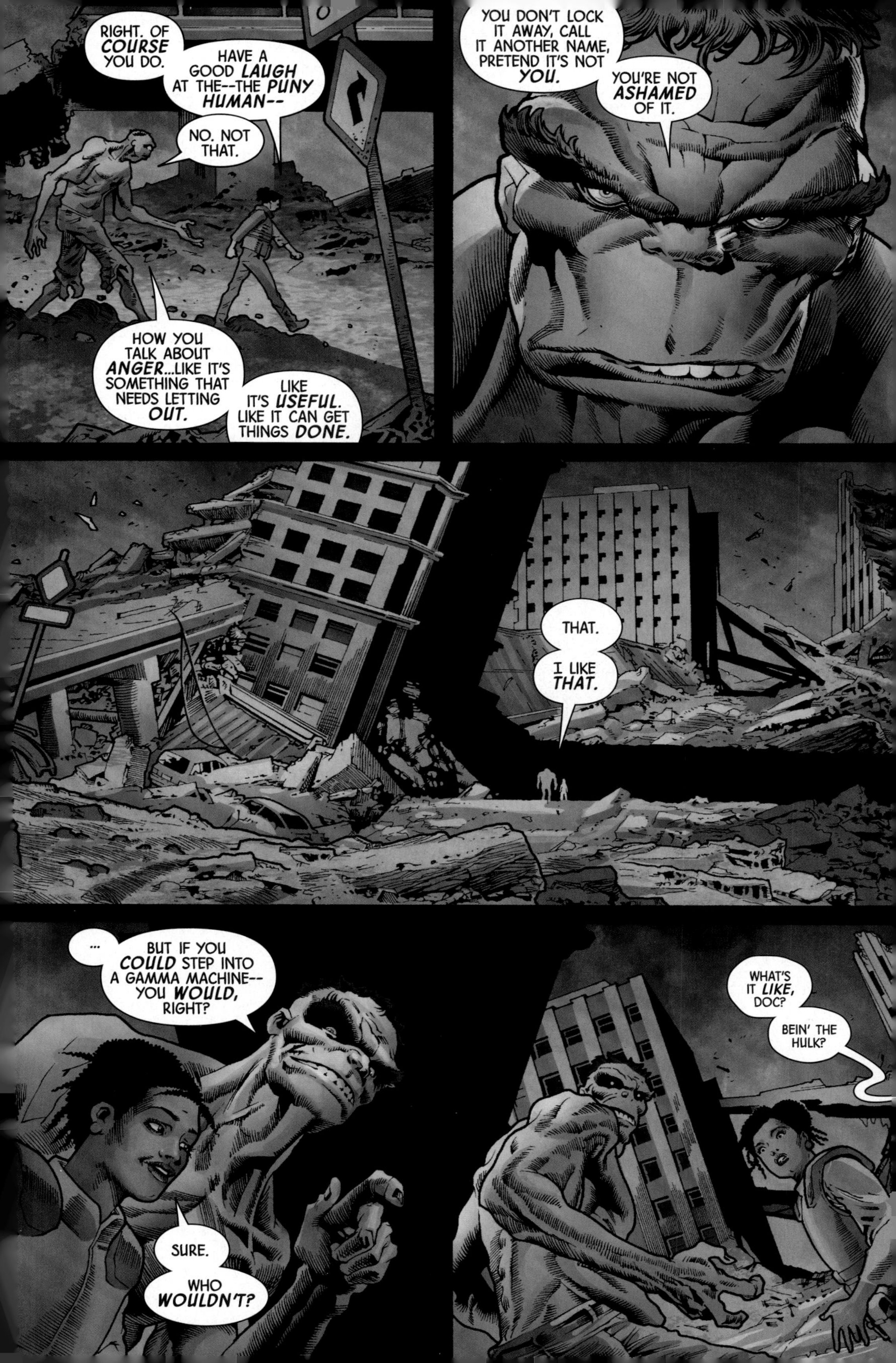
RIGHT. OF COURSE YOU DO.
HAVE A GOOD LAUGH AT THE--THE PUNY HUMAN--
NO. NOT THAT.
HOW YOU TALK ABOUT ANGER...LIKE IT'S SOMETHING THAT NEEDS LETTING OUT.
LIKE IT'S USEFUL. LIKE IT CAN GET THINGS DONE.
YOU DON'T LOCK IT AWAY, CALL IT ANOTHER NAME, PRETEND IT'S NOT YOU.
YOU'RE NOT ASHAMED OF IT.
THAT.
I LIKE THAT.
...
BUT IF YOU COULD STEP INTO A GAMMA MACHINE--YOU WOULD, RIGHT?
SURE.
WHO WOULDN'T?
WHAT'S IT LIKE, DOC?
BEIN' THE HULK?

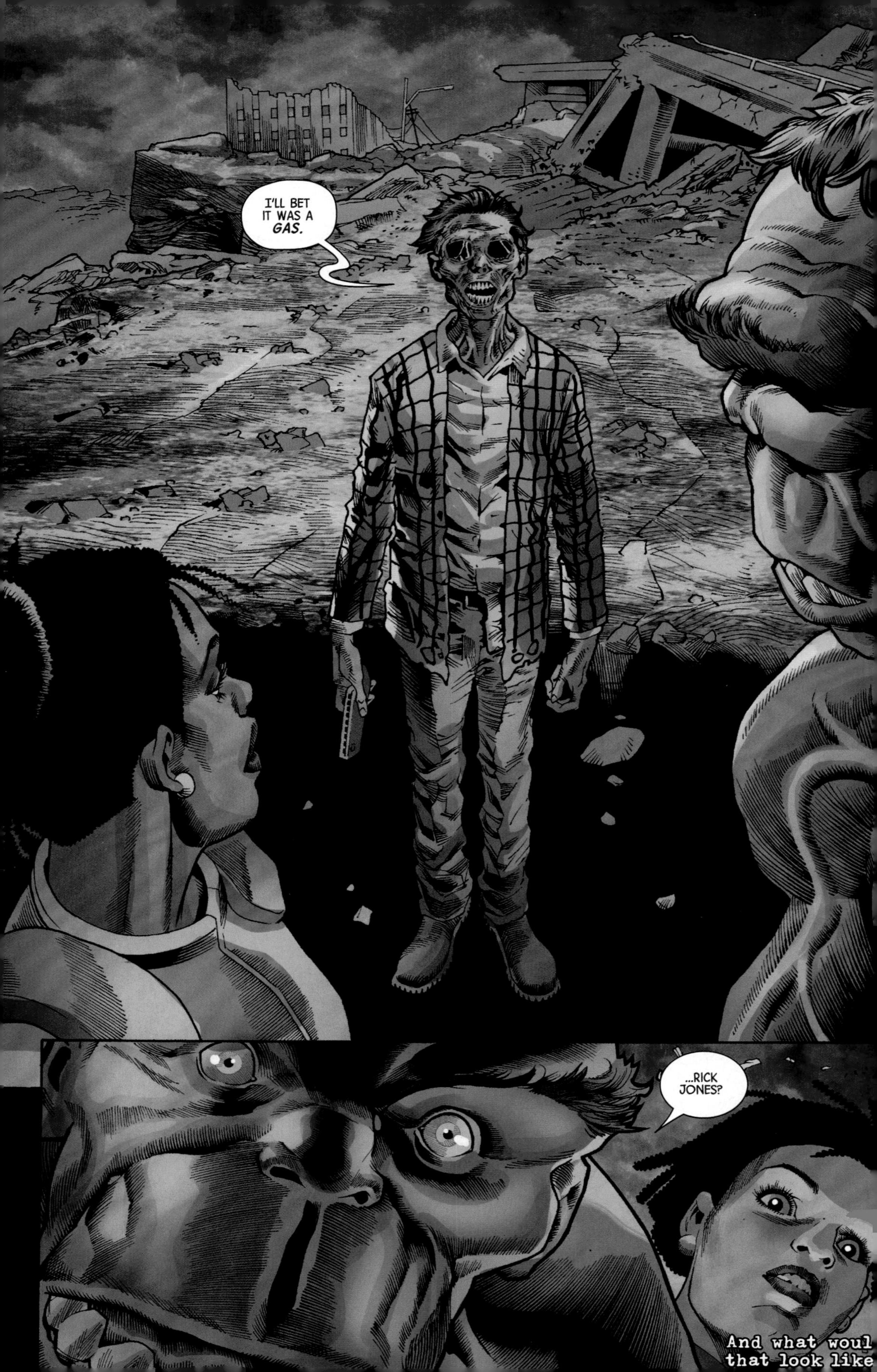
I'LL BET IT WAS A *GAS.*
...RICK JONES?
And what woul
that look like

What is the anger of God?

We are told it is in the flood, or the storm.

Insurance men say that these are God's acts, against which we are unprotected.

But that is the irrational side speaking.

The rational side - science - says it was our doing after all.

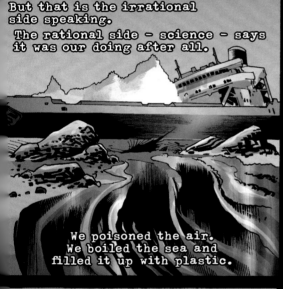

We poisoned the air. We boiled the sea and filled it up with plastic.

We decided hating each other was more vital than saving each other.

We were given a miracle world, and we broke it. Perhaps we thought God would give us another.

It won't work that way.

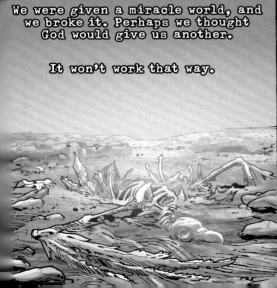

What is God's anger?

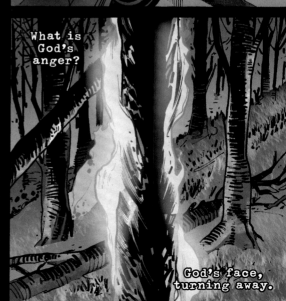

God's face, turning away.

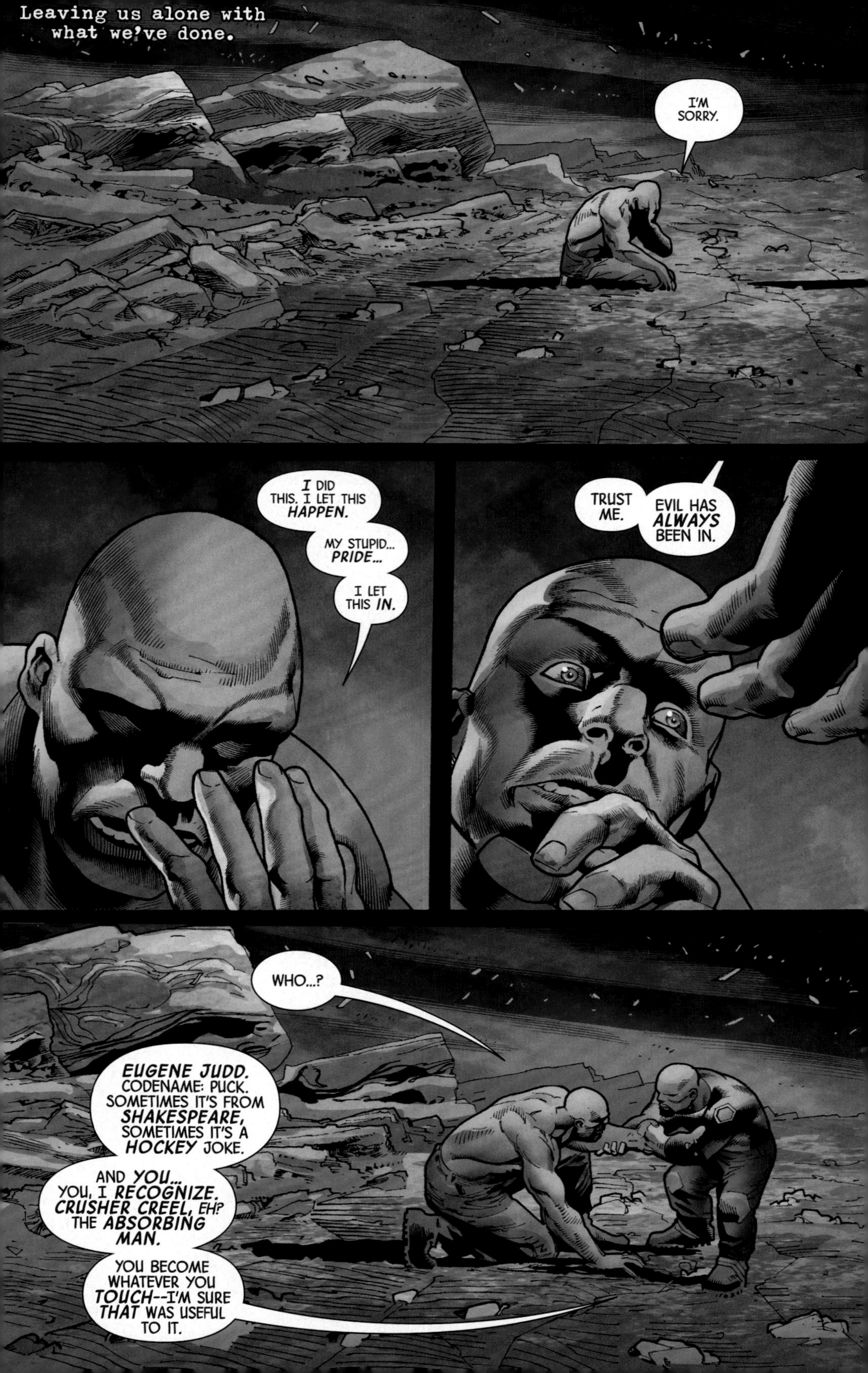
Leaving us alone with what we've done.
I'M SORRY.
I DID THIS. I LET THIS HAPPEN.
MY STUPID... PRIDE...
I LET THIS IN.
TRUST ME.
EVIL HAS ALWAYS BEEN IN.
WHO...?
EUGENE JUDD. CODENAME: PUCK. SOMETIMES IT'S FROM SHAKESPEARE, SOMETIMES IT'S A HOCKEY JOKE.
AND YOU... YOU, I RECOGNIZE. CRUSHER CREEL, EH? THE ABSORBING MAN.
YOU BECOME WHATEVER YOU TOUCH--I'M SURE THAT WAS USEFUL TO IT.

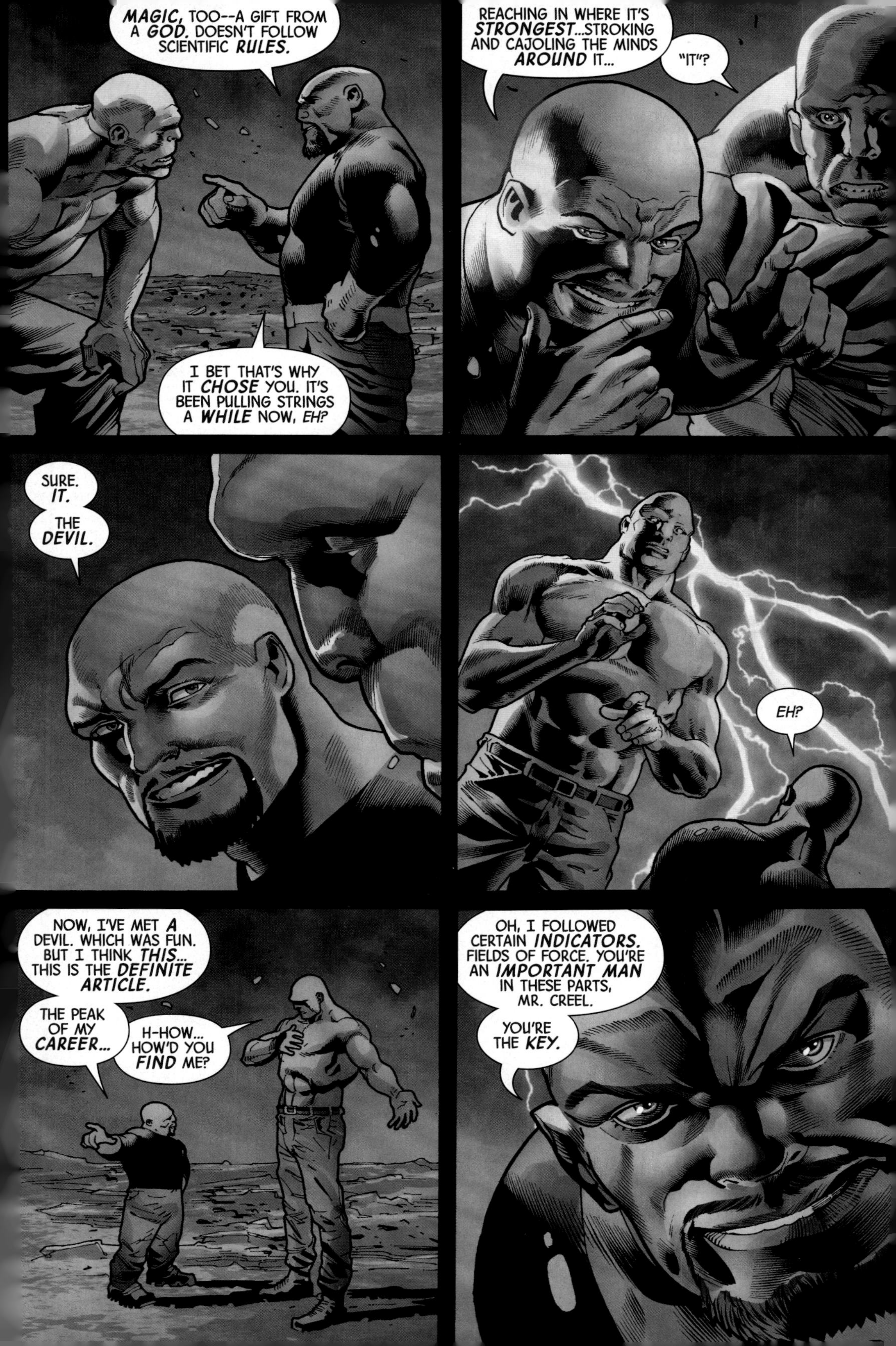
MAGIC, TOO--A GIFT FROM A GOD. DOESN'T FOLLOW SCIENTIFIC RULES.
I BET THAT'S WHY IT CHOSE YOU. IT'S BEEN PULLING STRINGS A WHILE NOW, EH?
REACHING IN WHERE IT'S STRONGEST...STROKING AND CAJOLING THE MINDS AROUND IT...
"IT"?
SURE. IT.
THE DEVIL.
EH?
NOW, I'VE MET A DEVIL. WHICH WAS FUN. BUT I THINK THIS... THIS IS THE DEFINITE ARTICLE.
THE PEAK OF MY CAREER...
H-HOW... HOW'D YOU FIND ME?
OH, I FOLLOWED CERTAIN INDICATORS. FIELDS OF FORCE. YOU'RE AN IMPORTANT MAN IN THESE PARTS, MR. CREEL.
YOU'RE THE KEY.

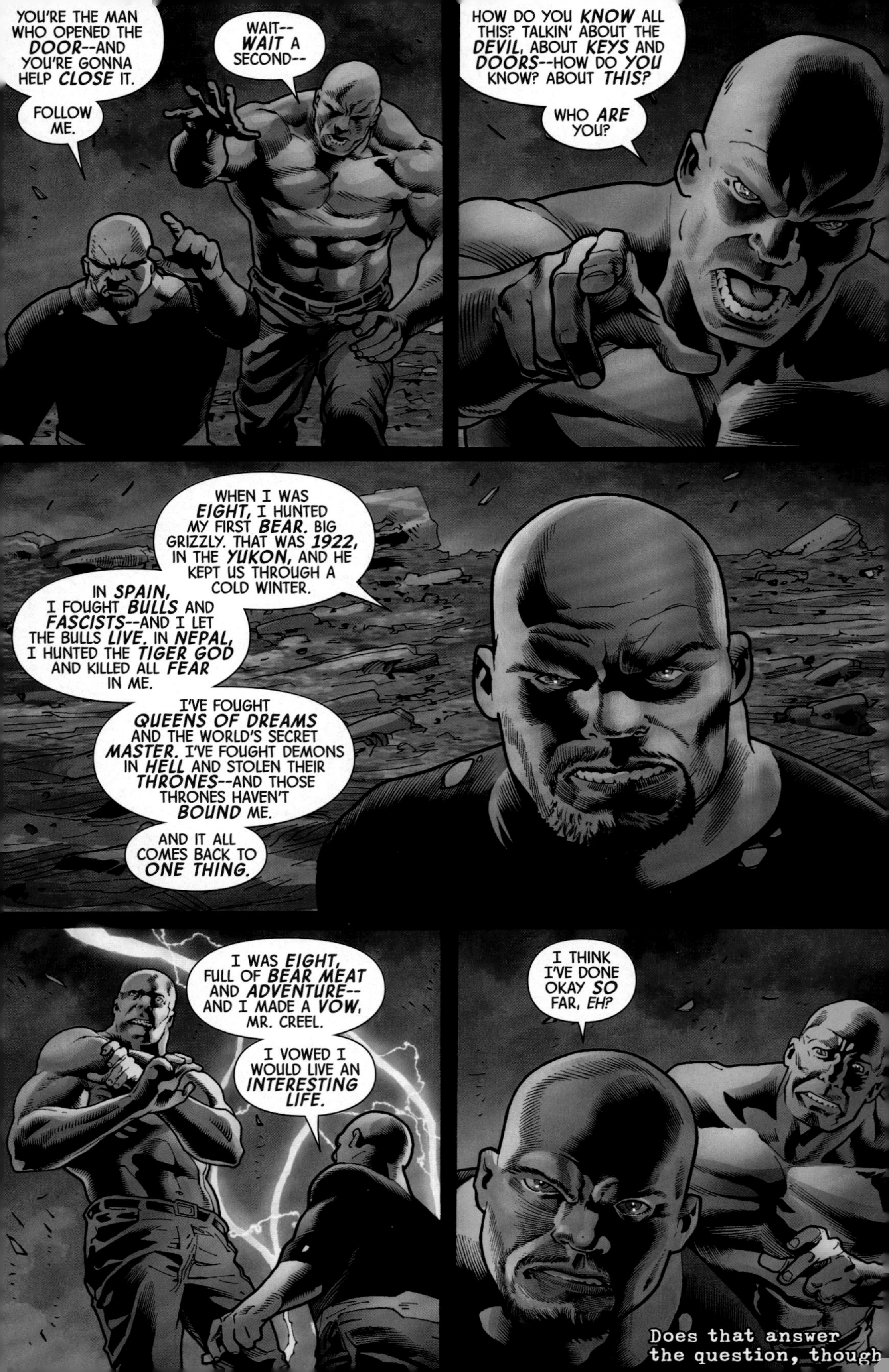
YOU'RE THE MAN WHO OPENED THE DOOR--AND YOU'RE GONNA HELP CLOSE IT.
FOLLOW ME.
WAIT-- WAIT A SECOND--
HOW DO YOU KNOW ALL THIS? TALKIN' ABOUT THE DEVIL, ABOUT KEYS AND DOORS--HOW DO YOU KNOW? ABOUT THIS?
WHO ARE YOU?
WHEN I WAS EIGHT, I HUNTED MY FIRST BEAR. BIG GRIZZLY. THAT WAS 1922, IN THE YUKON, AND HE KEPT US THROUGH A COLD WINTER.
IN SPAIN, I FOUGHT BULLS AND FASCISTS--AND I LET THE BULLS LIVE. IN NEPAL, I HUNTED THE TIGER GOD AND KILLED ALL FEAR IN ME.
I'VE FOUGHT QUEENS OF DREAMS AND THE WORLD'S SECRET MASTER. I'VE FOUGHT DEMONS IN HELL AND STOLEN THEIR THRONES--AND THOSE THRONES HAVEN'T BOUND ME.
AND IT ALL COMES BACK TO ONE THING.
I WAS EIGHT, FULL OF BEAR MEAT AND ADVENTURE--AND I MADE A VOW, MR. CREEL.
I VOWED I WOULD LIVE AN INTERESTING LIFE.
I THINK I'VE DONE OKAY SO FAR, EH?
Does that answer the question, though

We can speak of the anger of God.

But does God have a Hulk?

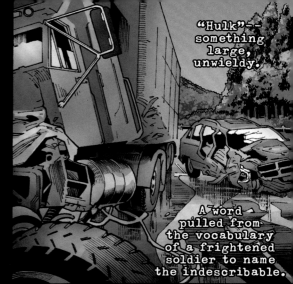

"Hulk"-- something large, unwieldy.

A word pulled from the vocabulary of a frightened soldier to name the indescribable.

The primary definition is a rotted ship.
Vast and strong, but gutted. Empty of treasure.

A shell.

There is a concept in the *Qabalah* called the Tree of Life.

A map of ten spheres or emanations describing both creation and mankind's spiritual path.

But the tree has an opposite side. A shadow side.

This is known as the *Qlippoth*.

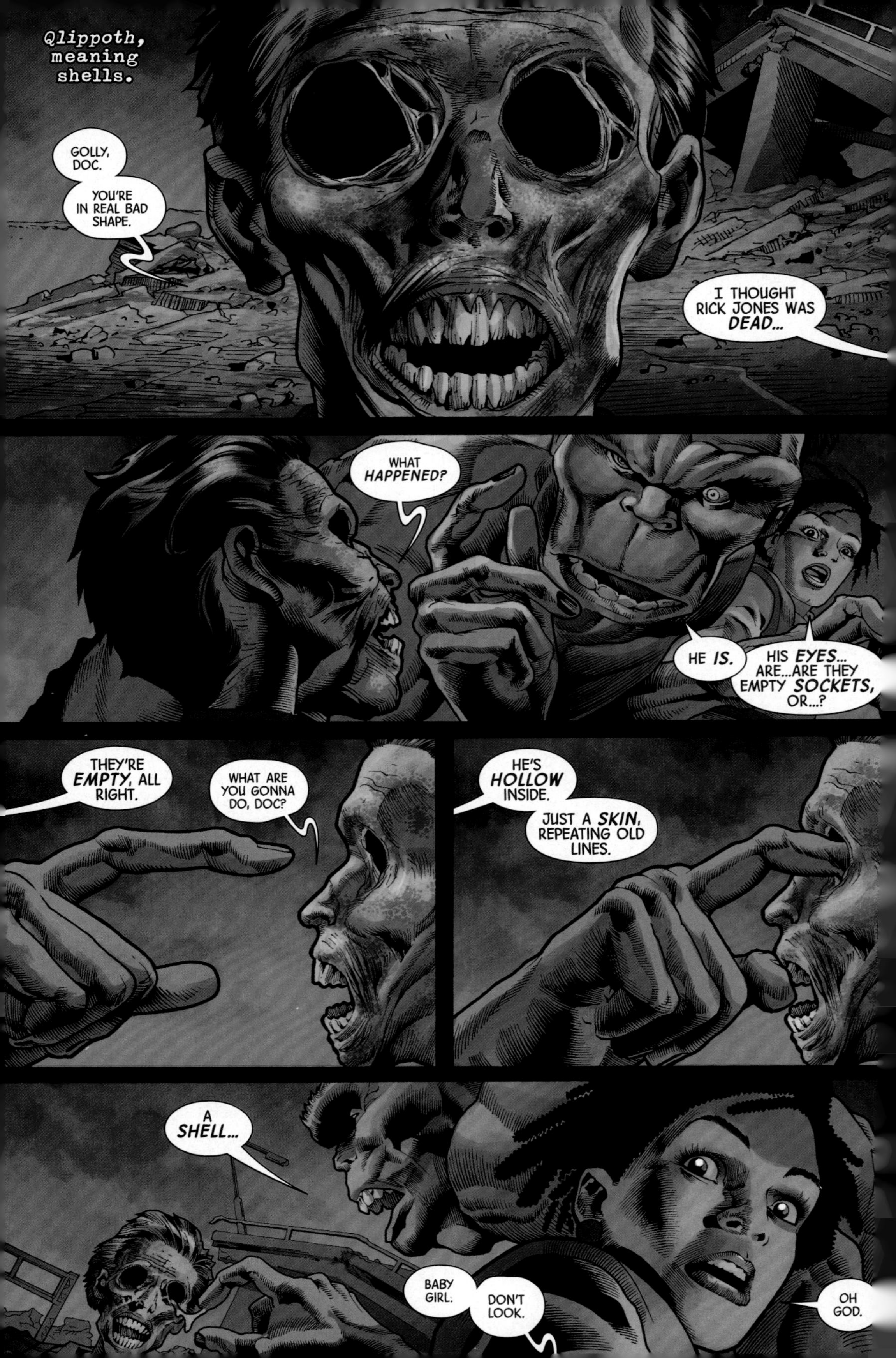
Qlippoth, meaning shells.
GOLLY, DOC.
YOU'RE IN REAL BAD SHAPE.
I THOUGHT RICK JONES WAS DEAD...
WHAT HAPPENED?
HE IS.
HIS EYES... ARE...ARE THEY EMPTY SOCKETS, OR...?
THEY'RE EMPTY, ALL RIGHT.
WHAT ARE YOU GONNA DO, DOC?
HE'S HOLLOW INSIDE.
JUST A SKIN, REPEATING OLD LINES.
A SHELL...
BABY GIRL.
DON'T LOOK.
OH GOD.

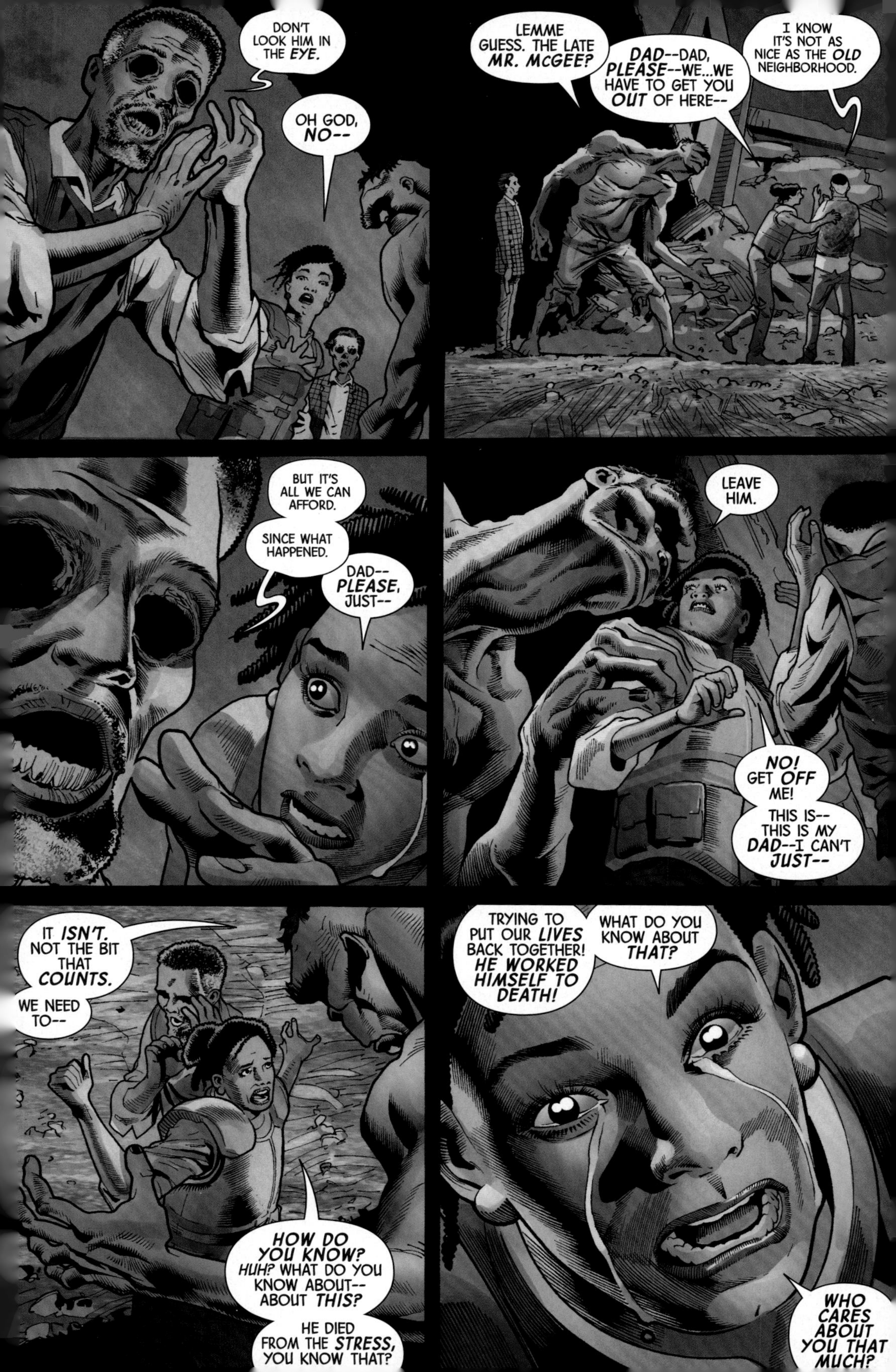

DON'T LOOK HIM IN THE *EYE.*
OH GOD, *NO--*
LEMME GUESS. THE LATE *MR. McGEE?*
DAD--DAD, *PLEASE*--WE...WE HAVE TO GET YOU *OUT* OF HERE--
I KNOW IT'S NOT AS NICE AS THE *OLD* NEIGHBORHOOD.
BUT IT'S ALL WE CAN AFFORD.
SINCE WHAT HAPPENED.
DAD-- *PLEASE,* JUST--
LEAVE HIM.
NO! GET *OFF* ME!
THIS IS-- THIS IS MY *DAD*--I CAN'T *JUST--*
IT *ISN'T.* NOT THE BIT THAT *COUNTS.*
WE NEED TO--
HOW DO YOU KNOW? HUH? WHAT DO YOU KNOW ABOUT-- ABOUT *THIS?*
HE DIED FROM THE *STRESS,* YOU KNOW THAT?
TRYING TO PUT OUR *LIVES* BACK TOGETHER! *HE WORKED HIMSELF TO DEATH!*
WHAT DO YOU KNOW ABOUT *THAT?*
WHO CARES ABOUT YOU THAT MUCH?

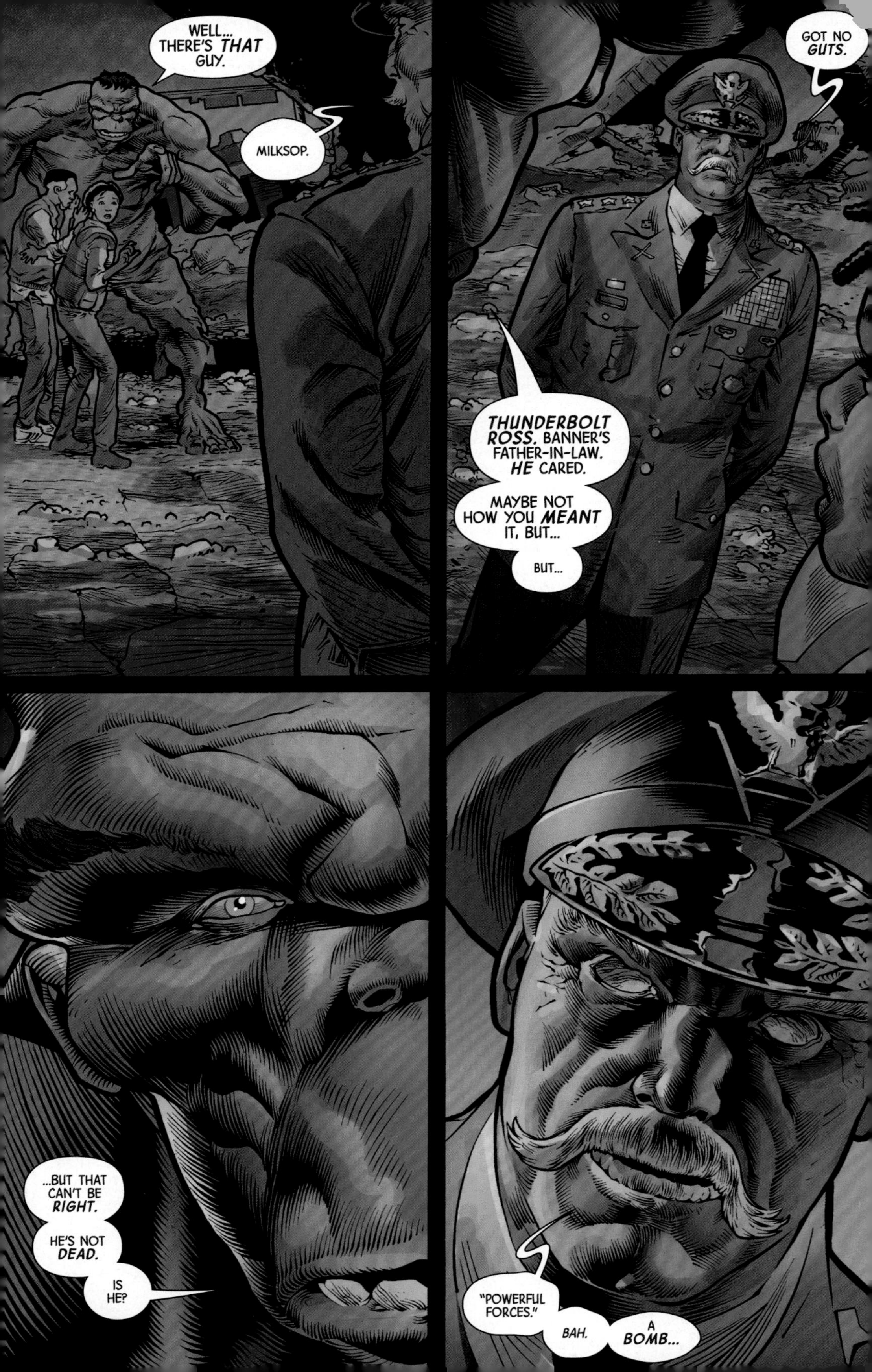
WELL... THERE'S THAT GUY.
MILKSOP.
GOT NO GUTS.
THUNDERBOLT ROSS. BANNER'S FATHER-IN-LAW. HE CARED.
MAYBE NOT HOW YOU MEANT IT, BUT...
BUT...
...BUT THAT CAN'T BE RIGHT.
HE'S NOT DEAD.
IS HE?
"POWERFUL FORCES."
BAH.
A BOMB...

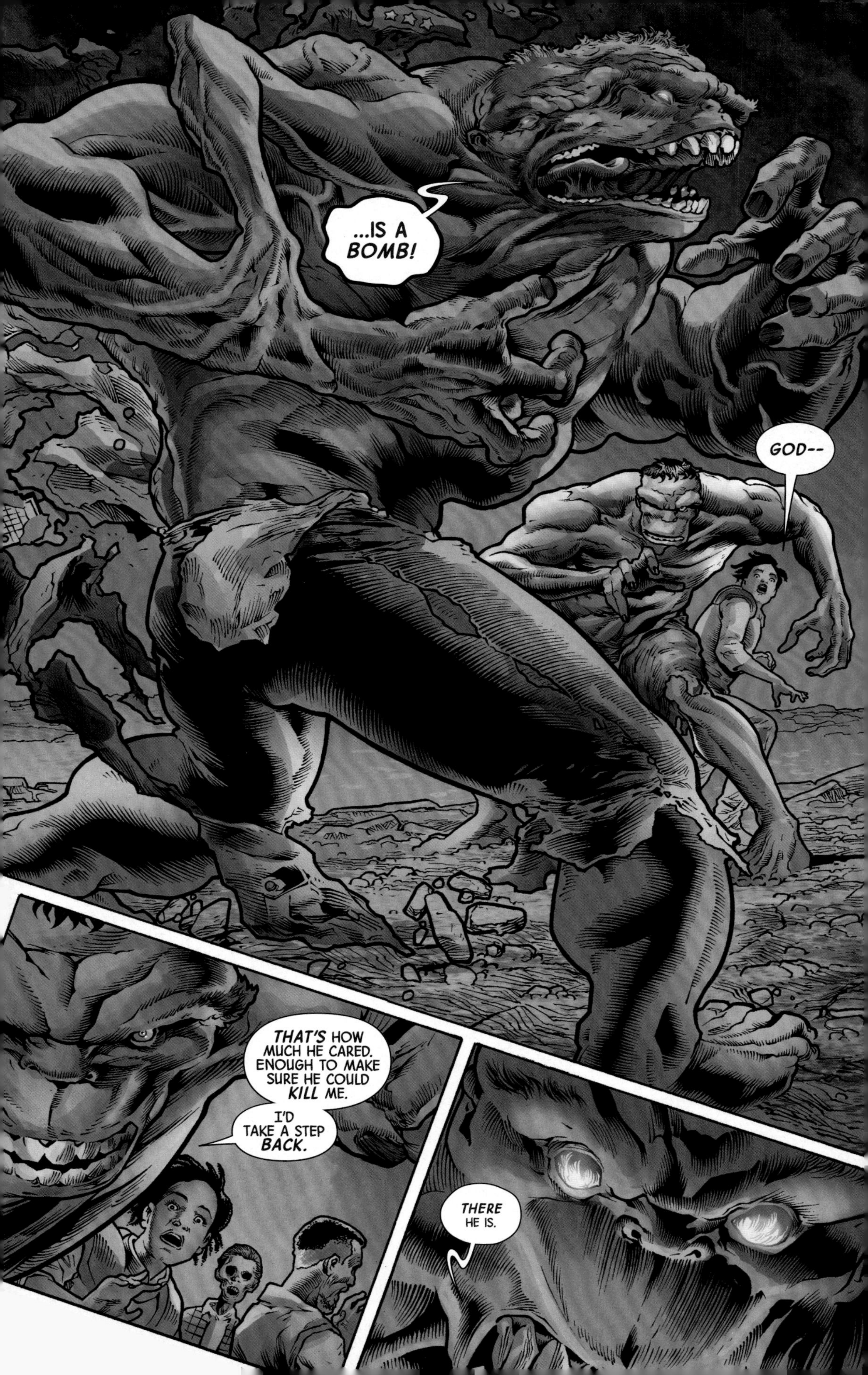
...IS A BOMB!
GOD--
THAT'S HOW MUCH HE CARED. ENOUGH TO MAKE SURE HE COULD KILL ME.
I'D TAKE A STEP BACK.
THERE HE IS.

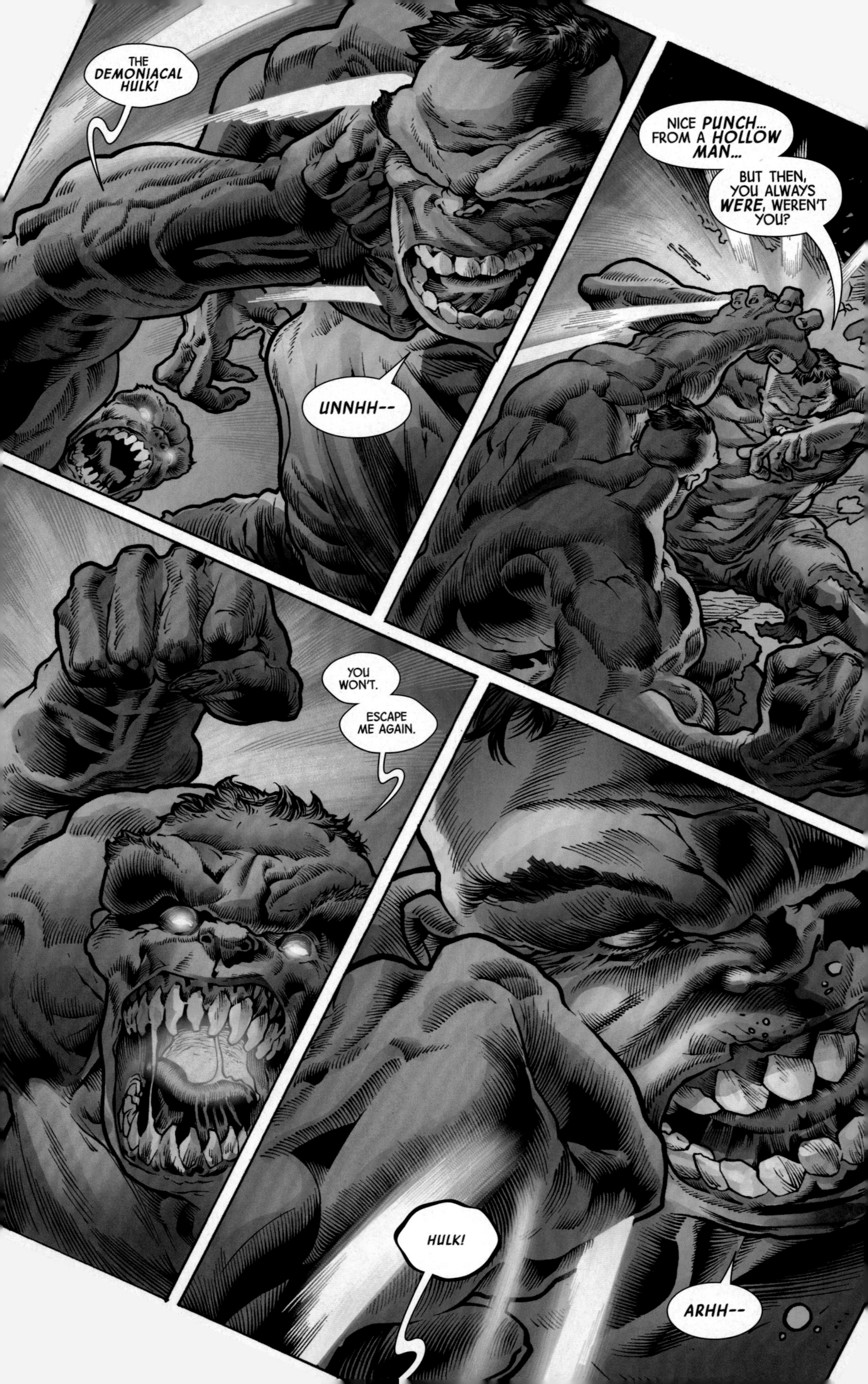

THE DEMONIACAL HULK!
UNNHH--
NICE PUNCH... FROM A HOLLOW MAN...
BUT THEN, YOU ALWAYS WERE, WEREN'T YOU?
YOU WON'T.
ESCAPE ME AGAIN.
HULK!
ARHH--

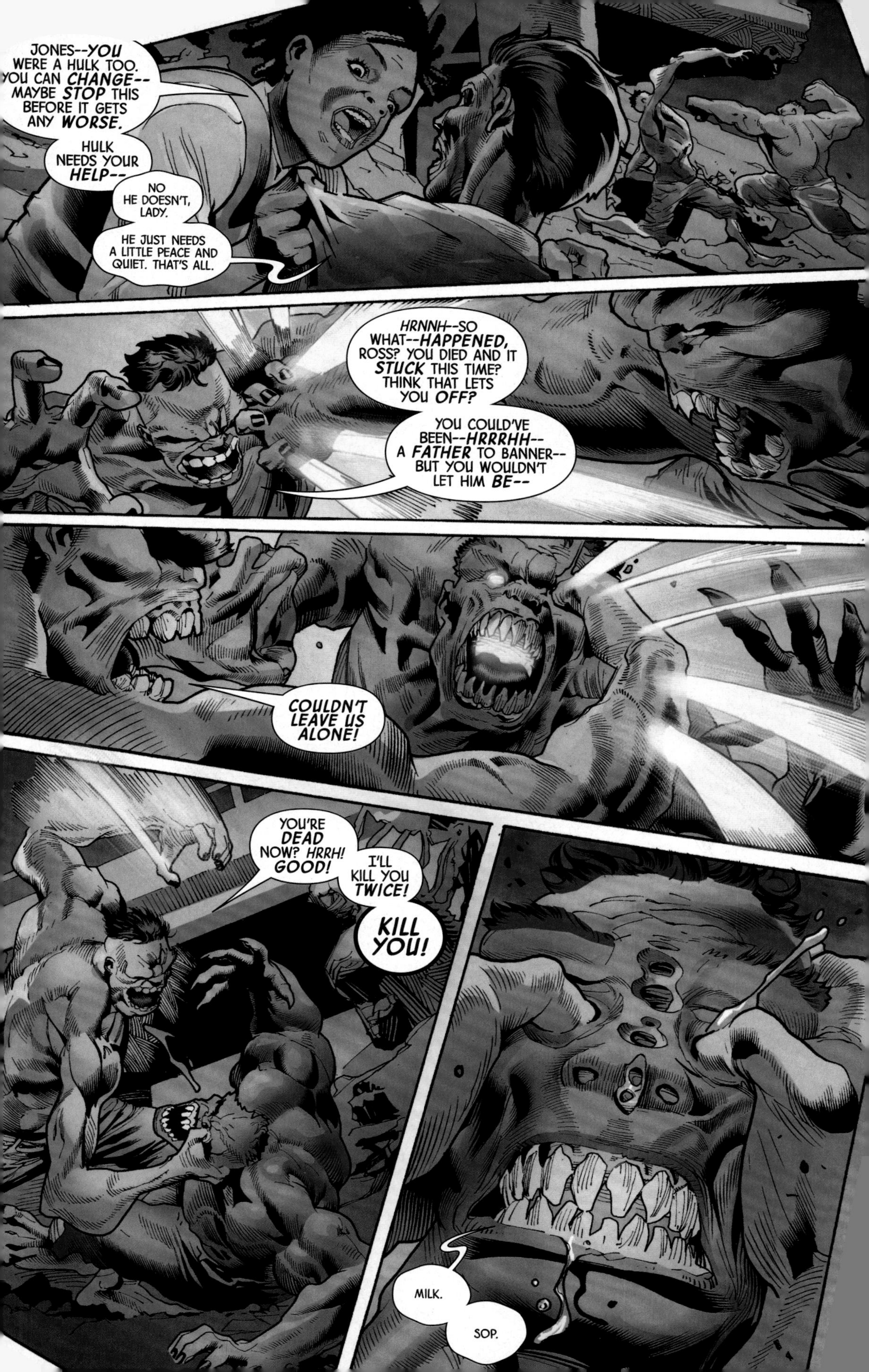
JONES--YOU WERE A HULK TOO. YOU CAN CHANGE-- MAYBE STOP THIS BEFORE IT GETS ANY WORSE.
HULK NEEDS YOUR HELP--
NO HE DOESN'T, LADY.
HE JUST NEEDS A LITTLE PEACE AND QUIET. THAT'S ALL.
HRNNH--SO WHAT--HAPPENED, ROSS? YOU DIED AND IT STUCK THIS TIME? THINK THAT LETS YOU OFF?
YOU COULD'VE BEEN--HRRRHH-- A FATHER TO BANNER-- BUT YOU WOULDN'T LET HIM BE--
COULDN'T LEAVE US ALONE!
YOU'RE DEAD NOW? HRRH! GOOD!
I'LL KILL YOU TWICE!
KILL YOU!
MILK.
SOP.

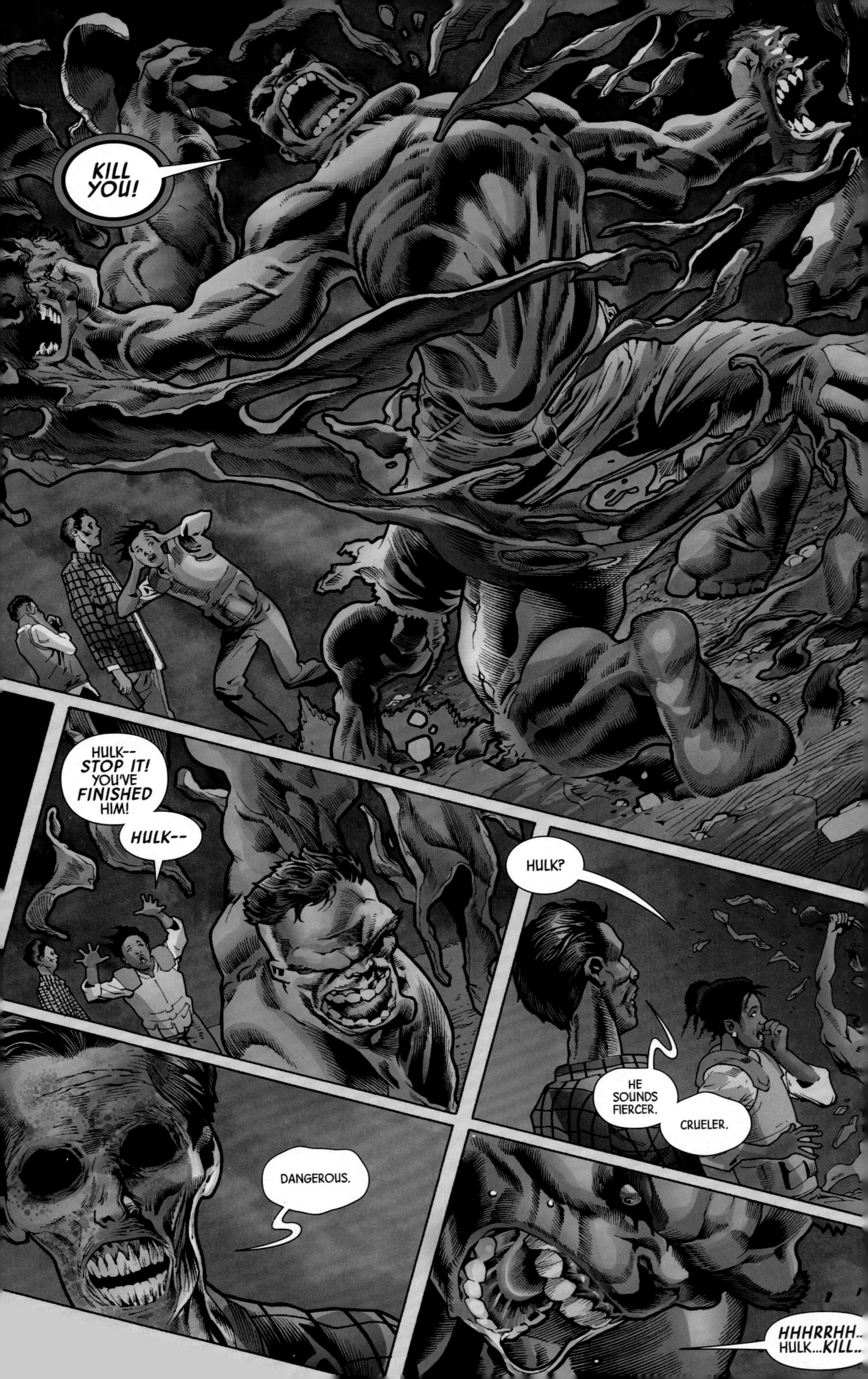

KILL YOU!
HULK-- STOP IT! YOU'VE FINISHED HIM!
HULK--
HULK?
HE SOUNDS FIERCER.
CRUELER.
DANGEROUS.
HHHRRHH... HULK...KILL...

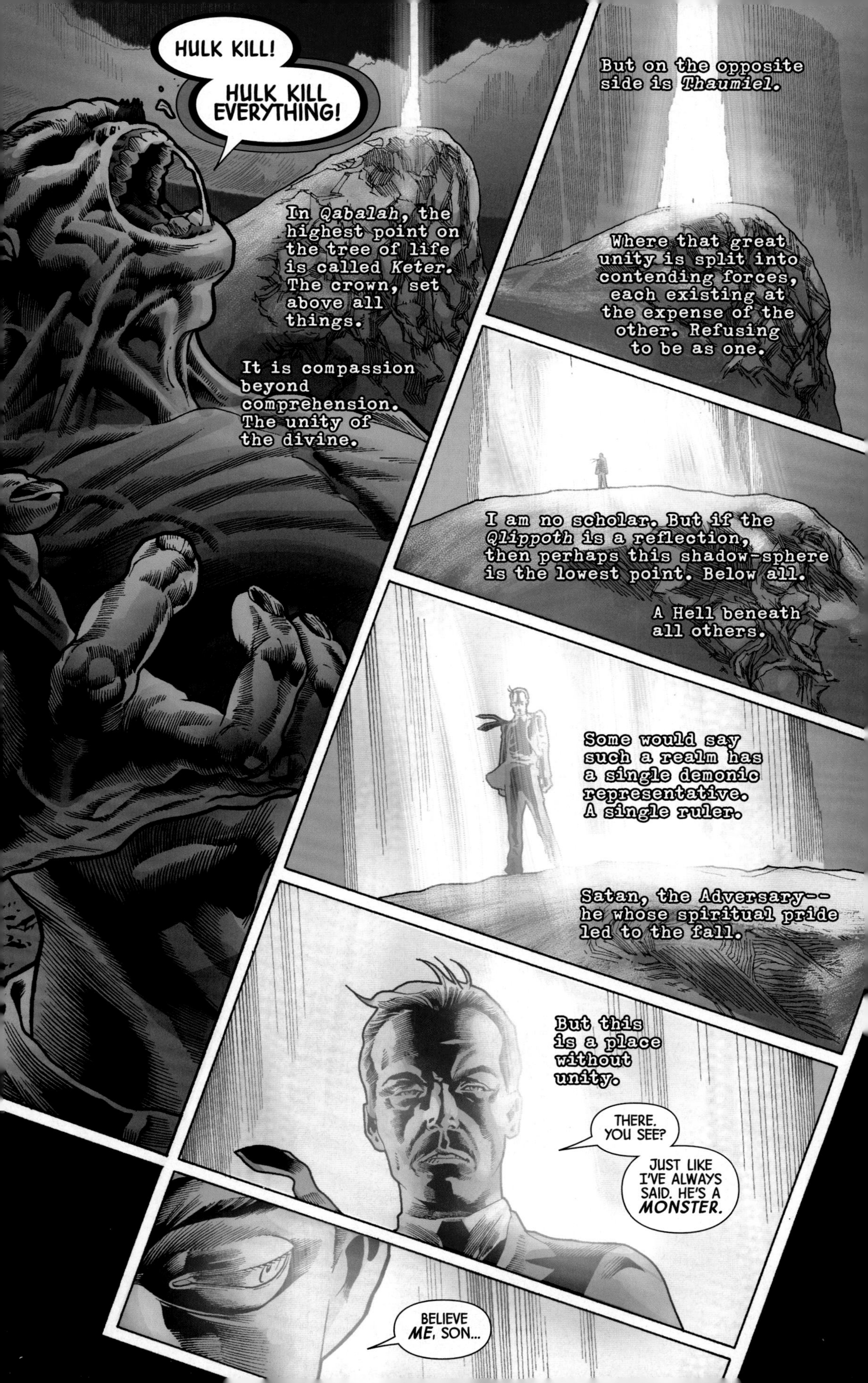
HULK KILL!
HULK KILL EVERYTHING!
In *Qabalah*, the highest point on the tree of life is called *Keter*. The crown, set above all things.
It is compassion beyond comprehension. The unity of the divine.
But on the opposite side is *Thaumiel*.
Where that great unity is split into contending forces, each existing at the expense of the other. Refusing to be as one.
I am no scholar. But if the *Qlippoth* is a reflection, then perhaps this shadow-sphere is the lowest point. Below all.
A Hell beneath all others.
Some would say such a realm has a single demonic representative. A single ruler.
Satan, the Adversary-- he whose spiritual pride led to the fall.
But this is a place without unity.
THERE. YOU SEE?
JUST LIKE I'VE ALWAYS SAID. HE'S A *MONSTER*.
BELIEVE *ME*, SON...

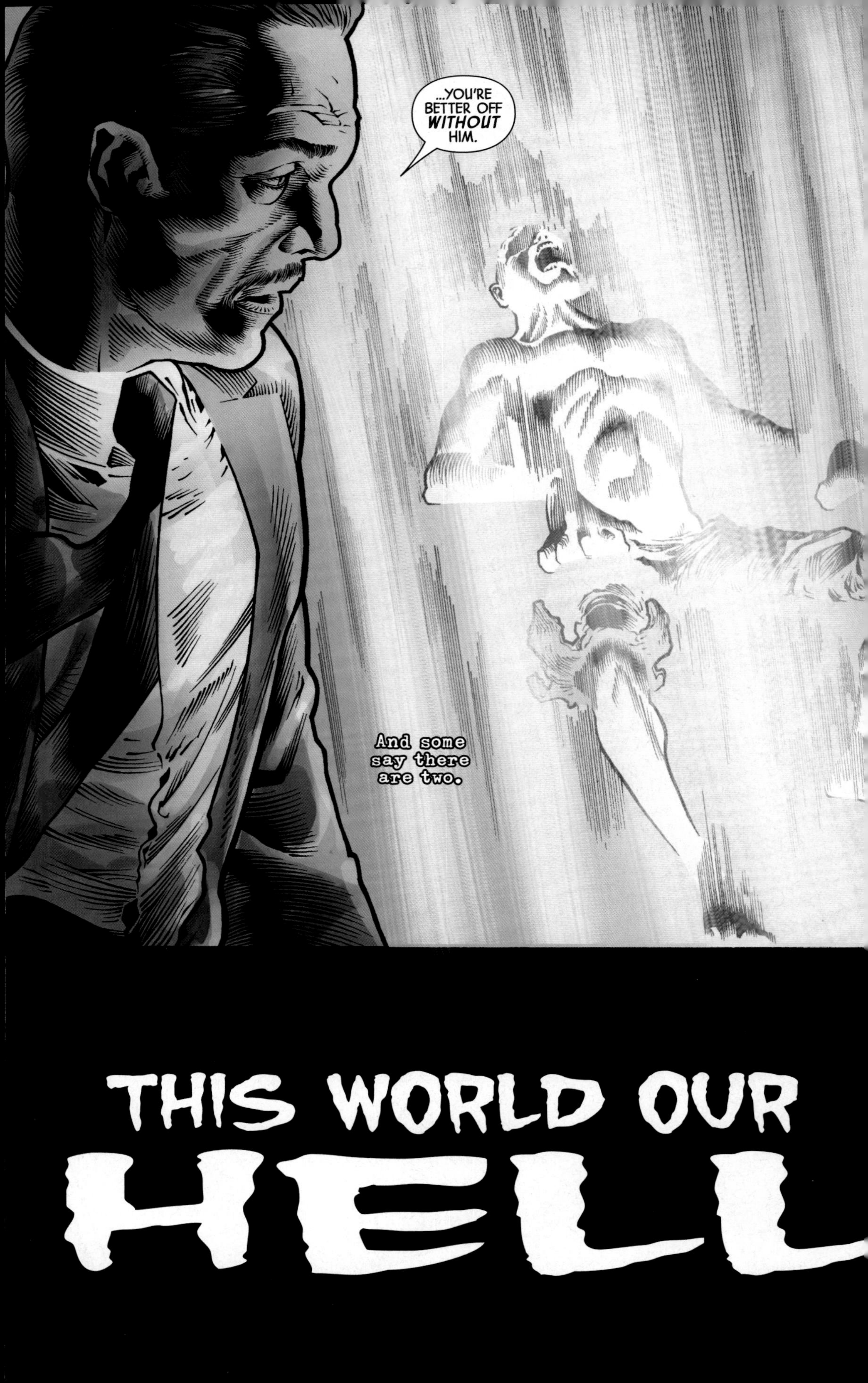

...YOU'RE BETTER OFF *WITHOUT* HIM.
And some say there are two.

THIS WORLD OUR HELL

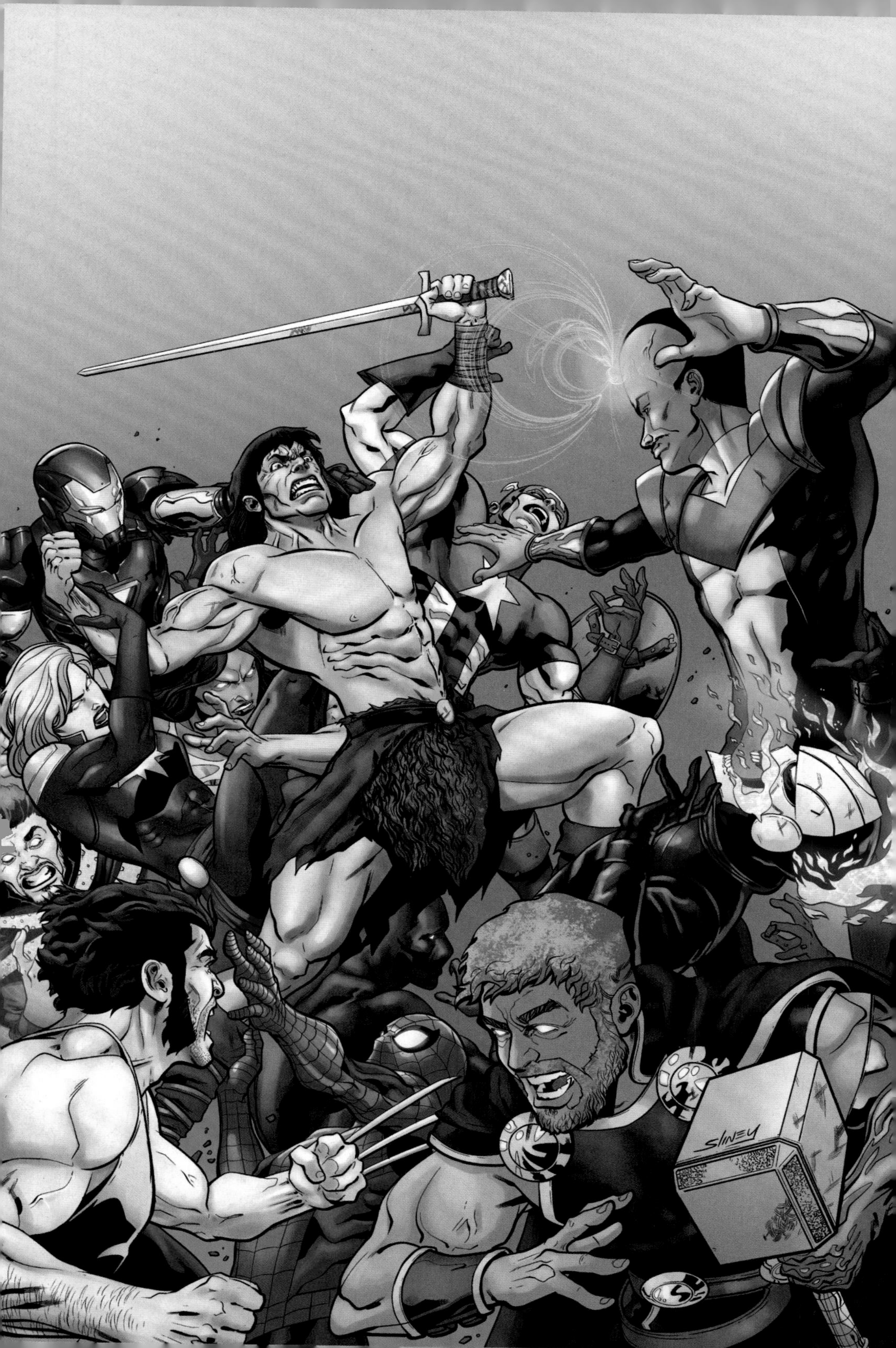
SLINEY

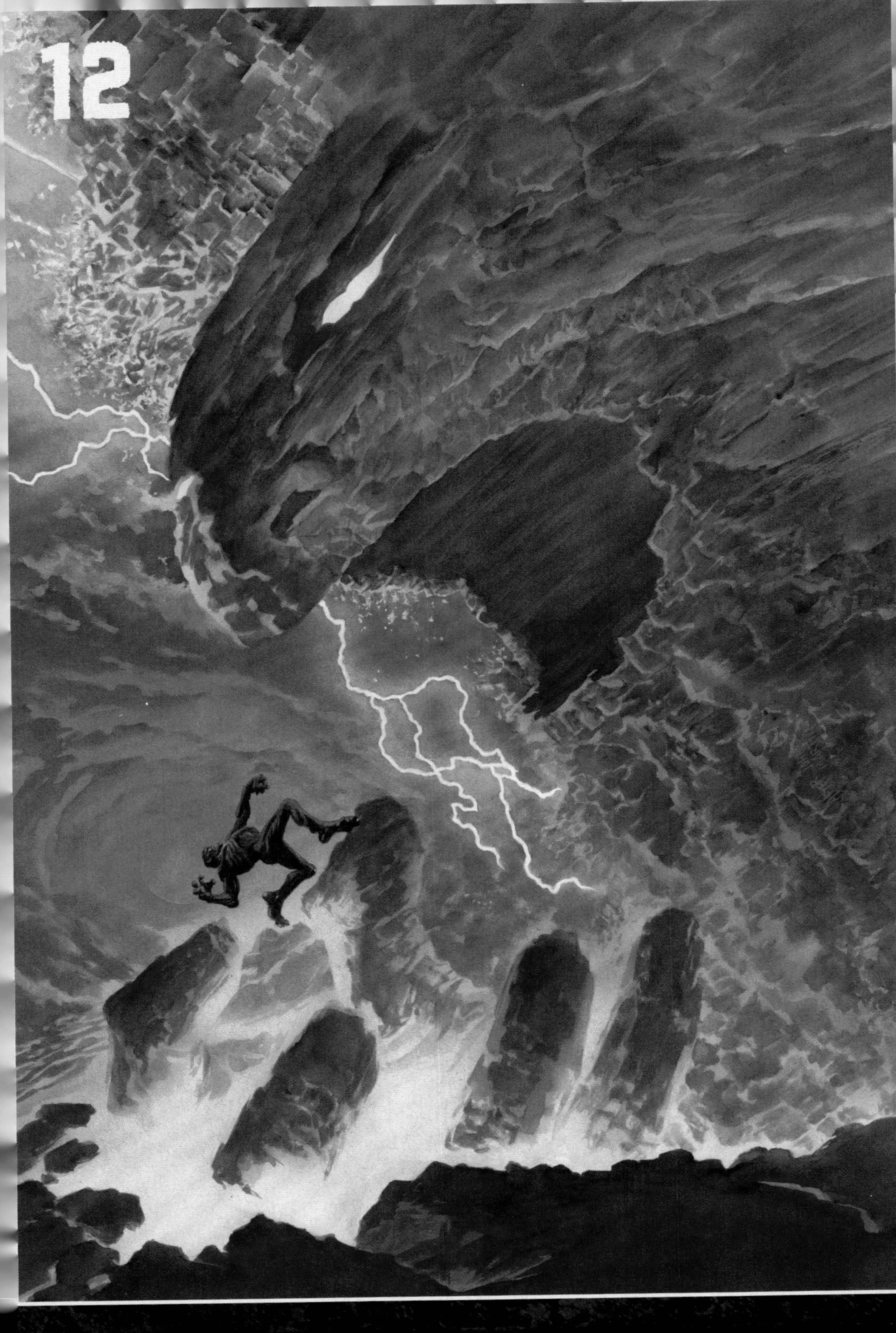
12

"YE ARE OF YOUR FATHER THE DEVIL, AND THE LUSTS OF YOUR FATHER YE WILL DO."

What is the Devil?

In modern culture, the Devil is clearly defined.

He is the slanderer, the whisperer in mankind's ear. Tempting us to sin against God.

To break the rules by which our betters define good and evil.

All evil, then, springs from him.

We are told.

From an early age, we learn dichotomy. Day and night. The rational and the irrational.

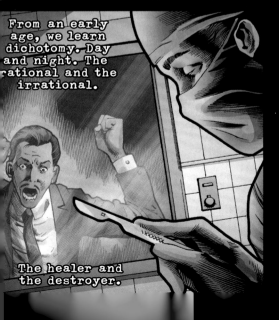

The healer and the destroyer.

On one side, then, we have the creator.

The maker of ineffable plans, who works only for our good.

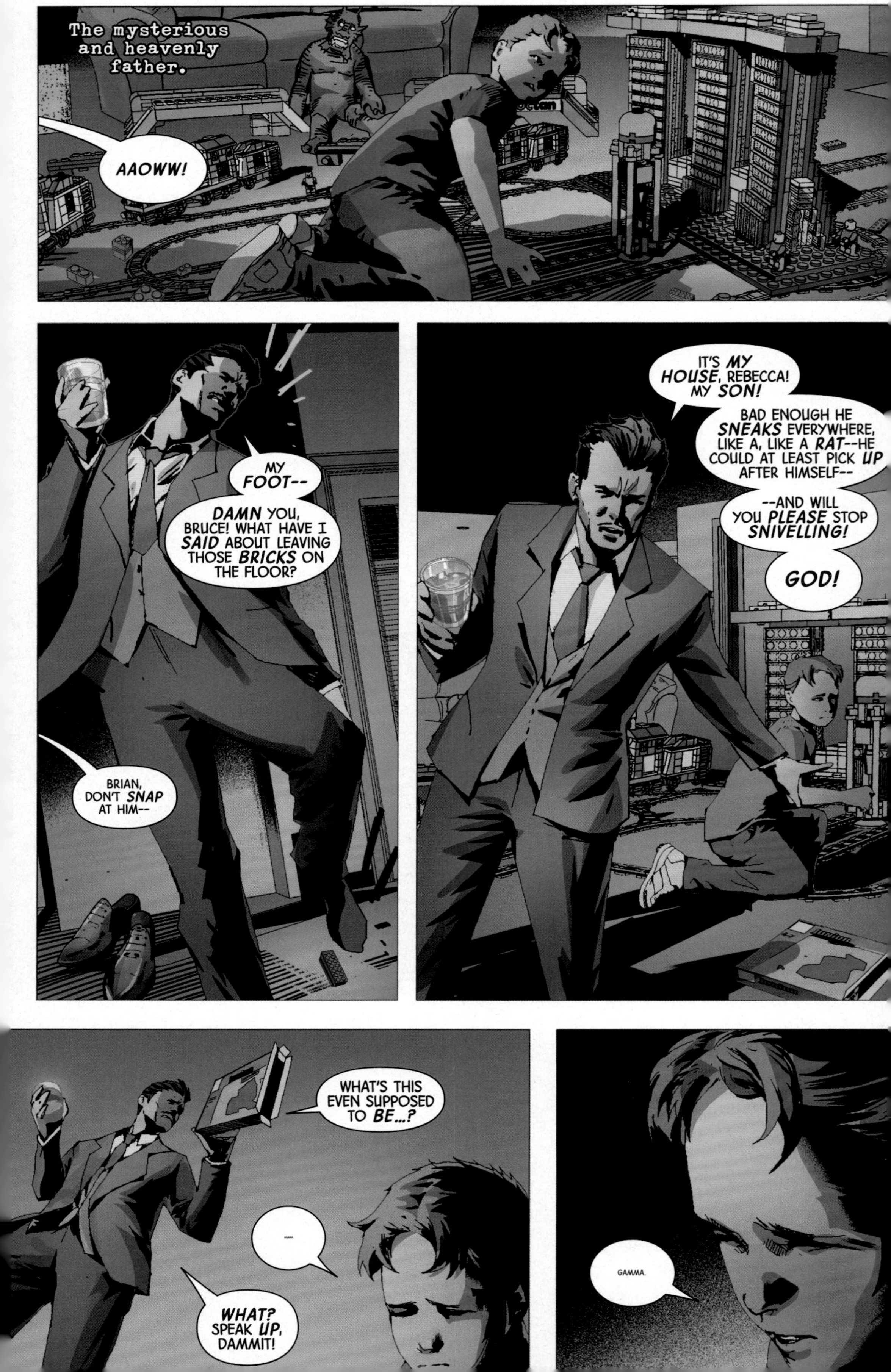
The mysterious and heavenly father.
AAOWW!
MY FOOT--
DAMN YOU, BRUCE! WHAT HAVE I SAID ABOUT LEAVING THOSE BRICKS ON THE FLOOR?
BRIAN, DON'T SNAP AT HIM--
IT'S MY HOUSE, REBECCA! MY SON!
BAD ENOUGH HE SNEAKS EVERYWHERE, LIKE A, LIKE A RAT--HE COULD AT LEAST PICK UP AFTER HIMSELF--
--AND WILL YOU PLEASE STOP SNIVELLING!
GOD!
WHAT'S THIS EVEN SUPPOSED TO BE...?
WHAT? SPEAK UP, DAMMIT!
GAMMA.

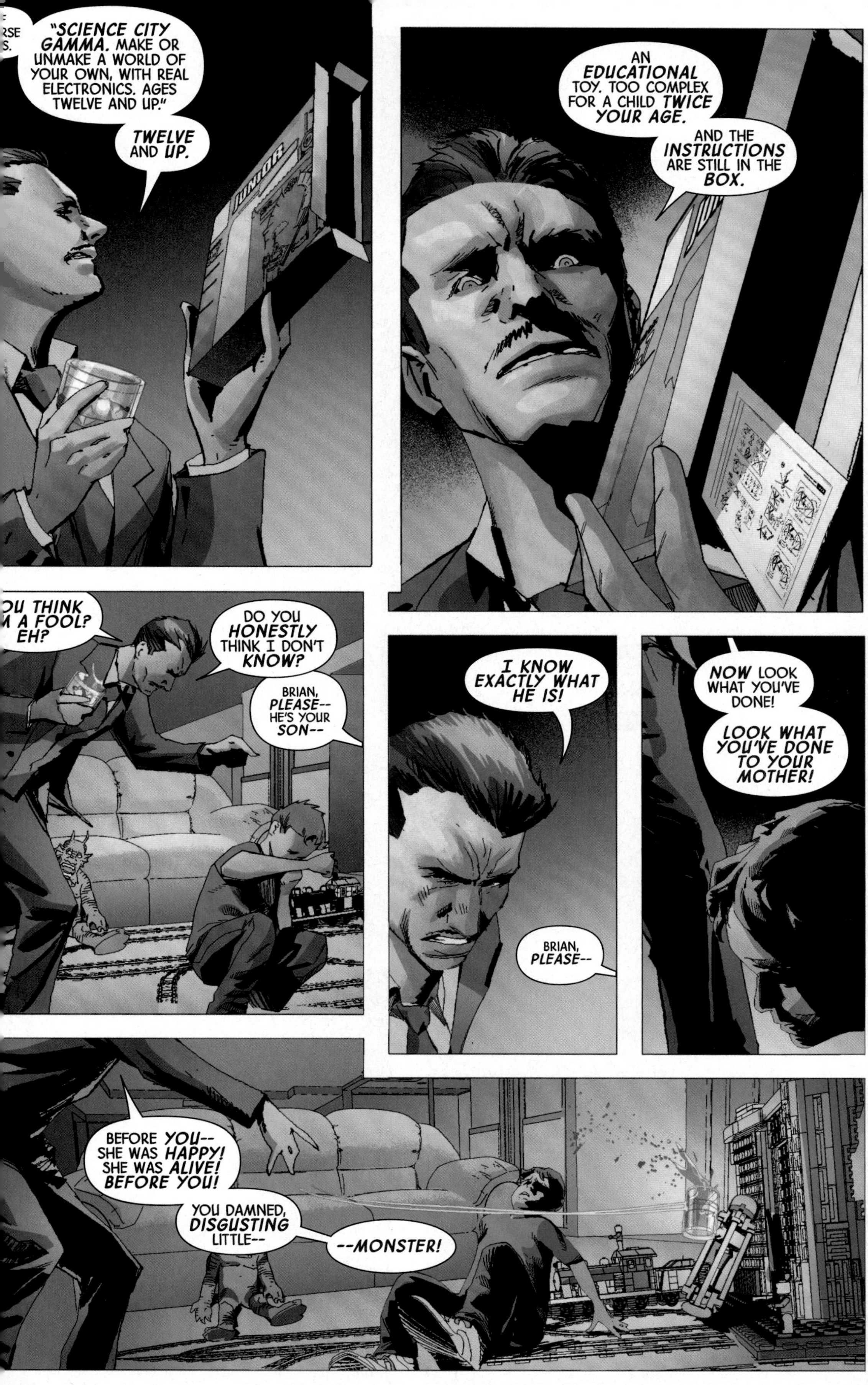
"SCIENCE CITY GAMMA. MAKE OR UNMAKE A WORLD OF YOUR OWN, WITH REAL ELECTRONICS. AGES TWELVE AND UP."
TWELVE AND UP.
AN EDUCATIONAL TOY. TOO COMPLEX FOR A CHILD TWICE YOUR AGE.
AND THE INSTRUCTIONS ARE STILL IN THE BOX.
DO YOU HONESTLY THINK I DON'T KNOW?
BRIAN, PLEASE-- HE'S YOUR SON--
I KNOW EXACTLY WHAT HE IS!
BRIAN, PLEASE--
NOW LOOK WHAT YOU'VE DONE!
LOOK WHAT YOU'VE DONE TO YOUR MOTHER!
BEFORE YOU-- SHE WAS HAPPY! SHE WAS ALIVE! BEFORE YOU!
YOU DAMNED, DISGUSTING LITTLE--
--MONSTER!

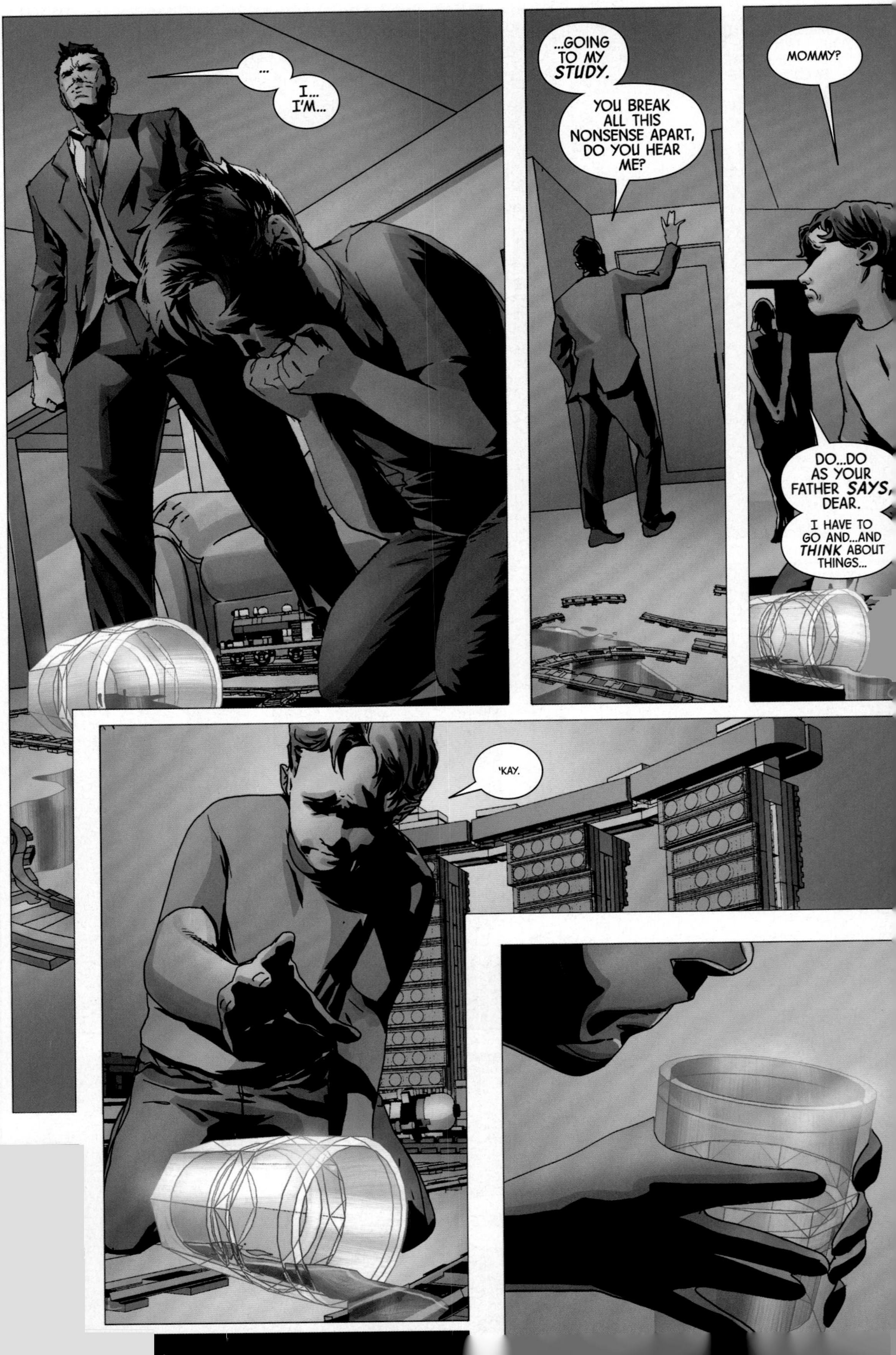
...
I... I'M...
...GOING TO MY STUDY.
YOU BREAK ALL THIS NONSENSE APART, DO YOU HEAR ME?
MOMMY?
DO...DO AS YOUR FATHER SAYS, DEAR.
I HAVE TO GO AND...AND THINK ABOUT THINGS...
'KAY.

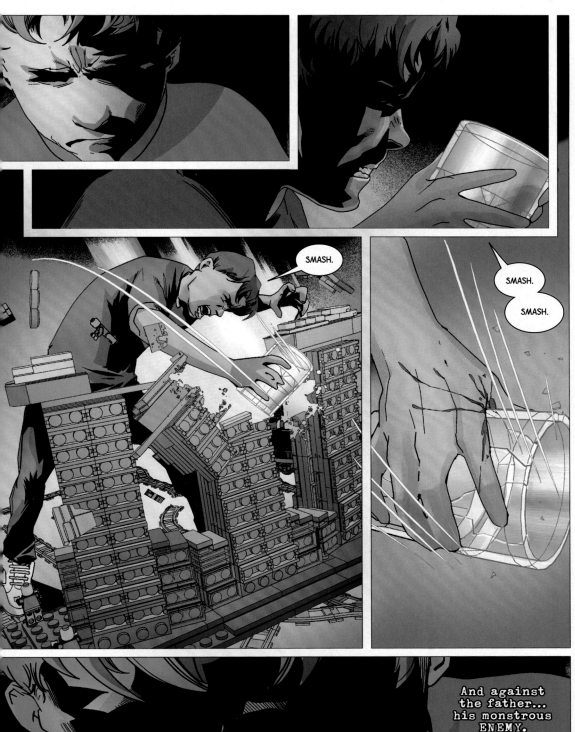

SMASH.

SMASH.

SMASH.

And against the father... his monstrous ENEMY.

SMASH.

The breaker-apart.

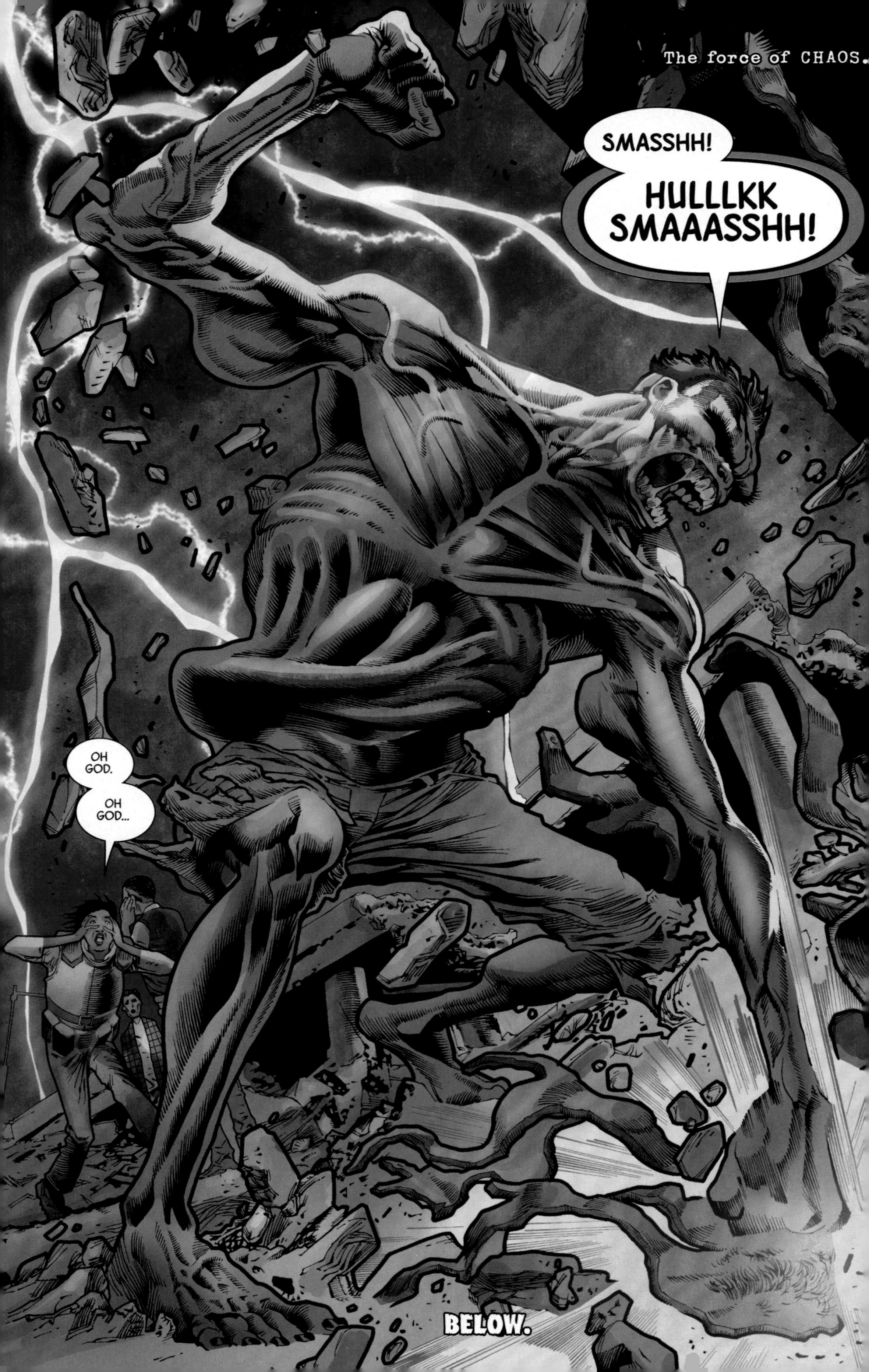
The force of CHAOS.
SMASSHH!
HULLLKK SMAAASSHH!
OH GOD.
OH GOD...
BELOW.

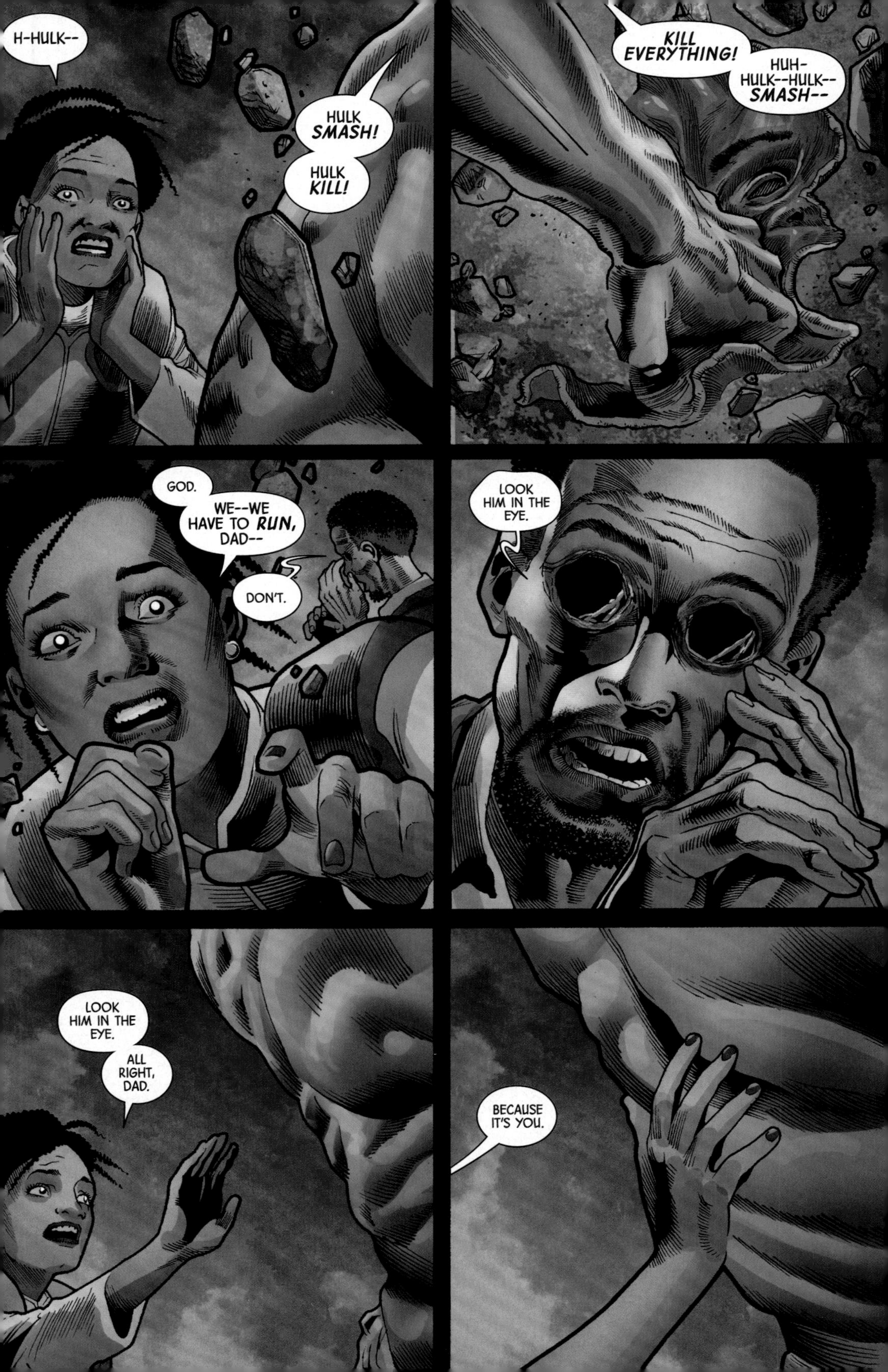

H-HULK--
HULK SMASH!
HULK KILL!
KILL EVERYTHING!
HUH-HULK--HULK--SMASH--
GOD.
WE--WE HAVE TO RUN, DAD--
DON'T.
LOOK HIM IN THE EYE.
LOOK HIM IN THE EYE.
ALL RIGHT, DAD.
BECAUSE IT'S YOU.

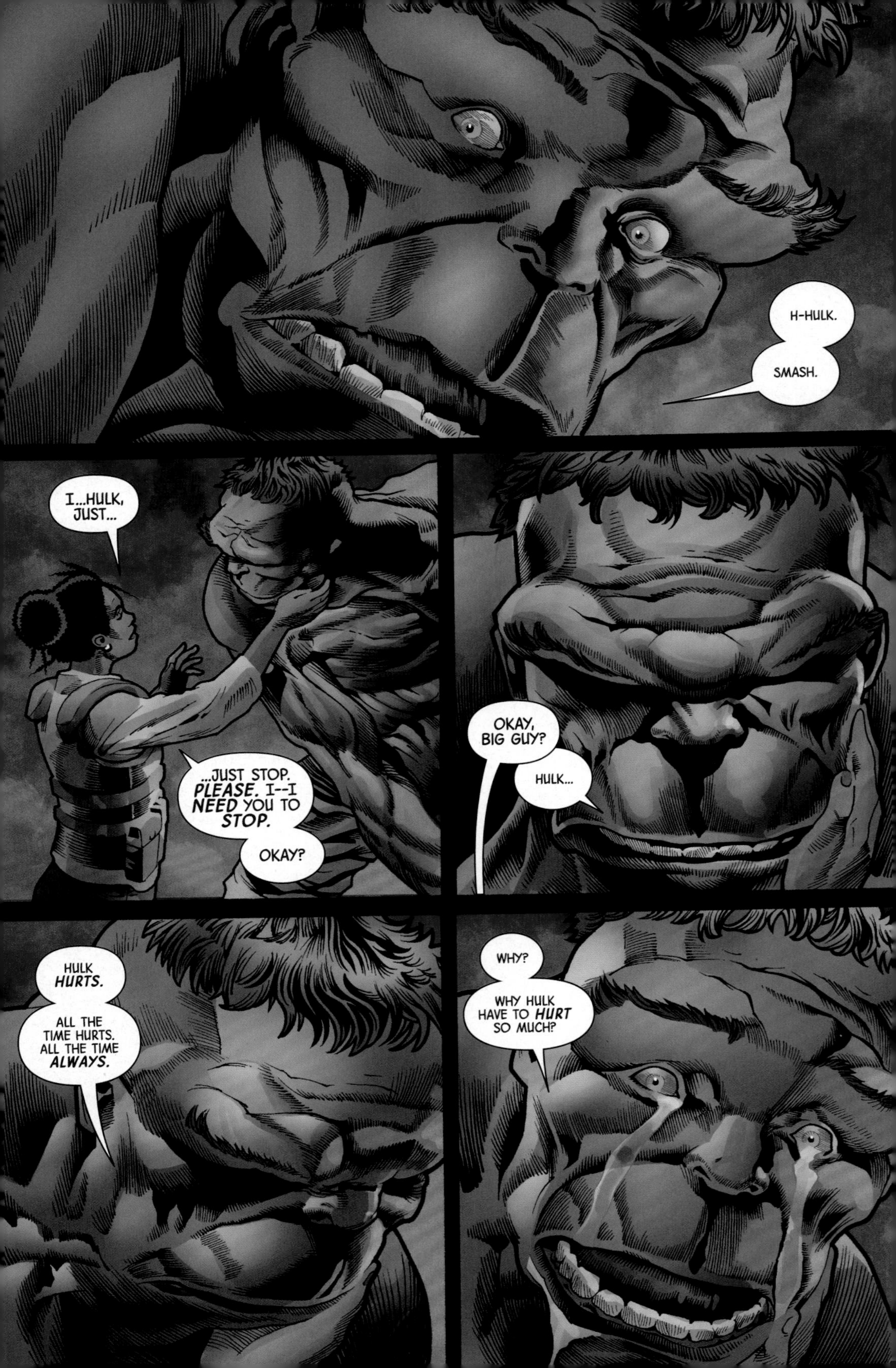
H-HULK.
SMASH.
I...HULK, JUST...
...JUST STOP. PLEASE. I--I NEED YOU TO STOP.
OKAY?
OKAY, BIG GUY?
HULK...
HULK HURTS.
ALL THE TIME HURTS. ALL THE TIME ALWAYS.
WHY?
WHY HULK HAVE TO HURT SO MUCH?

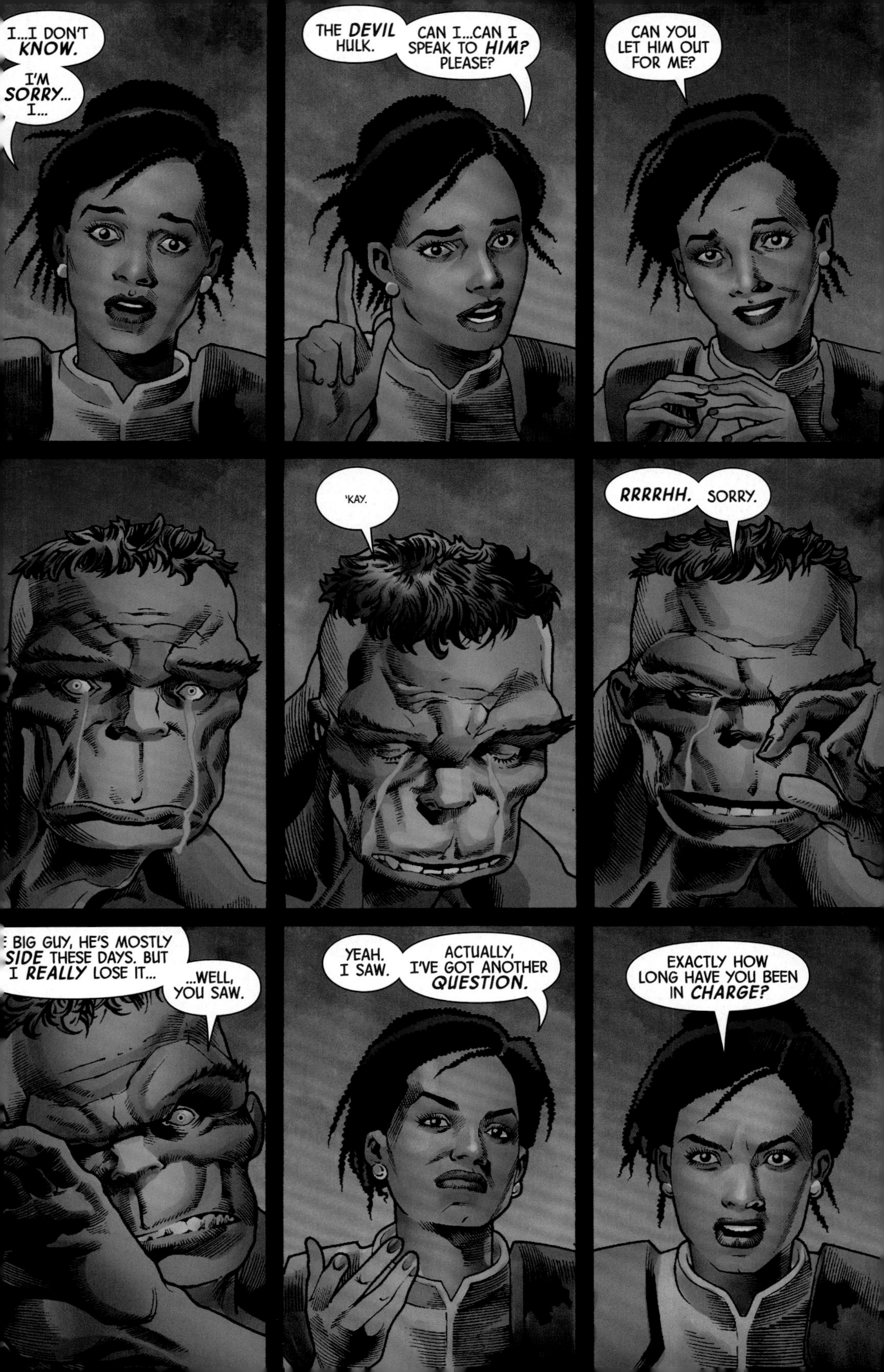
I...I DON'T KNOW.
I'M SORRY... I...
THE DEVIL HULK.
CAN I...CAN I SPEAK TO HIM? PLEASE?
CAN YOU LET HIM OUT FOR ME?
'KAY.
RRRRHH.
SORRY.
BIG GUY, HE'S MOSTLY
SIDE THESE DAYS. BUT
I REALLY LOSE IT...
...WELL, YOU SAW.
YEAH. I SAW.
ACTUALLY, I'VE GOT ANOTHER QUESTION.
EXACTLY HOW LONG HAVE YOU BEEN IN CHARGE?

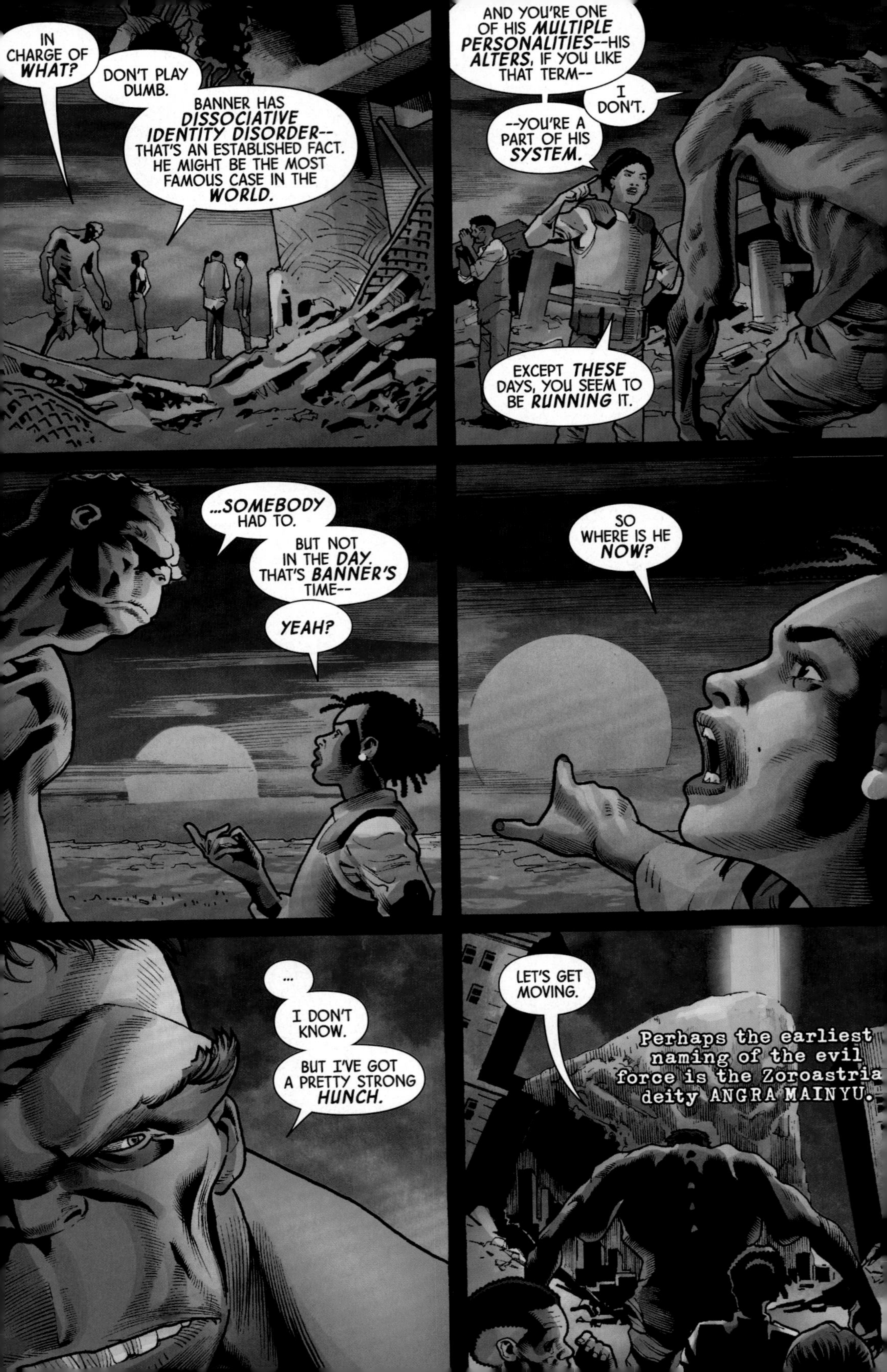
IN CHARGE OF WHAT?
DON'T PLAY DUMB.
BANNER HAS DISSOCIATIVE IDENTITY DISORDER-- THAT'S AN ESTABLISHED FACT. HE MIGHT BE THE MOST FAMOUS CASE IN THE WORLD.
AND YOU'RE ONE OF HIS MULTIPLE PERSONALITIES--HIS ALTERS, IF YOU LIKE THAT TERM--
I DON'T.
--YOU'RE A PART OF HIS SYSTEM.
EXCEPT THESE DAYS, YOU SEEM TO BE RUNNING IT.
...SOMEBODY HAD TO.
BUT NOT IN THE DAY. THAT'S BANNER'S TIME--
YEAH?
SO WHERE IS HE NOW?
...
I DON'T KNOW.
BUT I'VE GOT A PRETTY STRONG HUNCH.
LET'S GET MOVING.
Perhaps the earliest naming of the evil force is the Zoroastria deity ANGRA MAINYU.

literally the "chaotic spirit," or "destructive mind."

That which is defined by opposition to good.

In the Zurvanite tradition, Angra Mainyu and Ahura Mazda, the lord of creation, are the twin sons of Zurvan, who is Time itself.

Angra Mainyu tore free of Time's womb and thus, as first-born, inherited creation for 9,000 years.

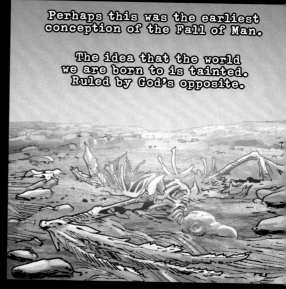

Perhaps this was the earliest conception of the Fall of Man.

The idea that the world we are born to is tainted. Ruled by God's opposite.

Interestingly, Angra Mainyu has it in his power to create good works.

He simply refuses to.

Evil is actively chosen.

Perhaps that is what defines the Devil, in the end.

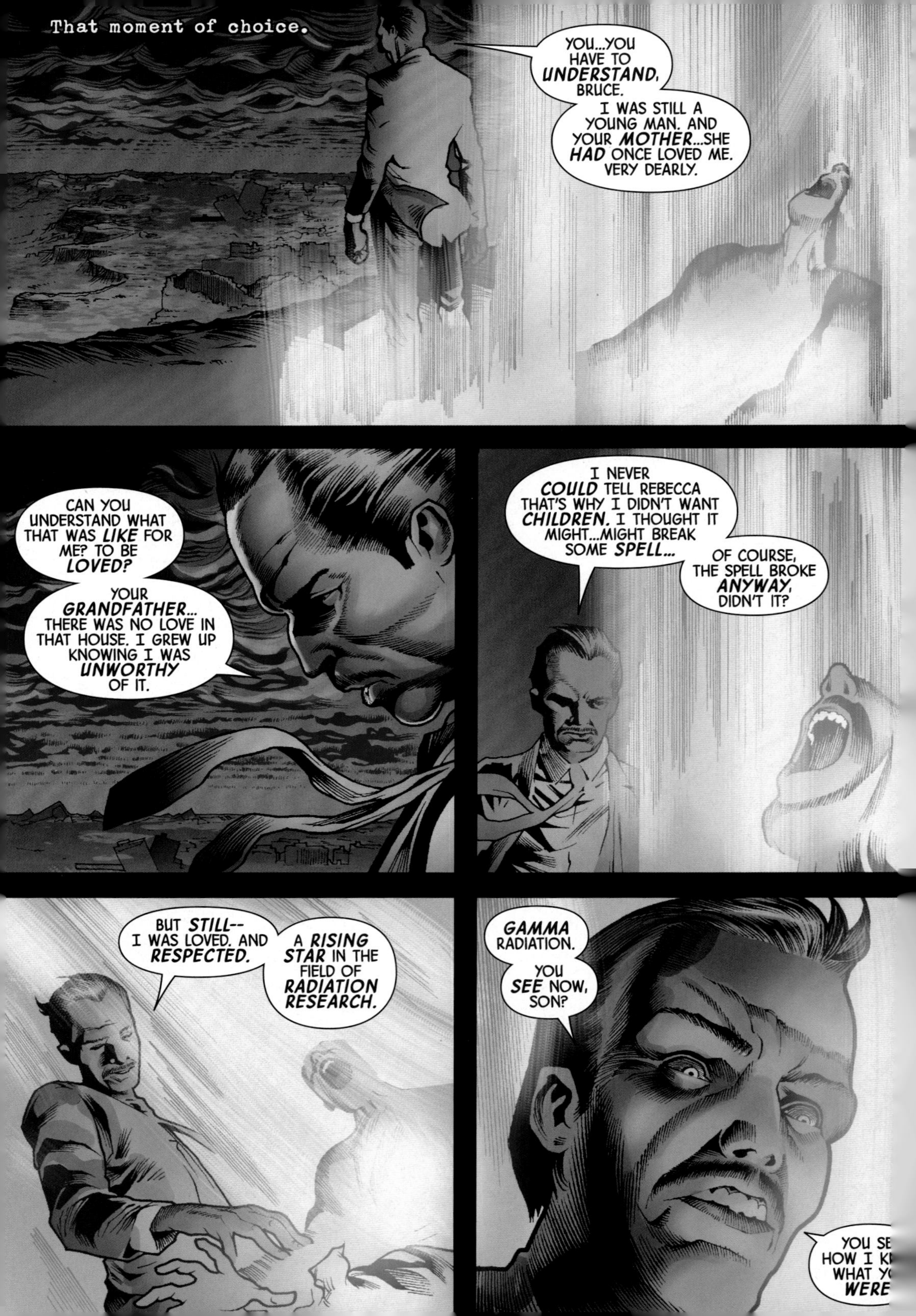

That moment of choice.
YOU...YOU HAVE TO UNDERSTAND, BRUCE.
I WAS STILL A YOUNG MAN. AND YOUR MOTHER...SHE HAD ONCE LOVED ME. VERY DEARLY.
CAN YOU UNDERSTAND WHAT THAT WAS LIKE FOR ME? TO BE LOVED?
YOUR GRANDFATHER... THERE WAS NO LOVE IN THAT HOUSE. I GREW UP KNOWING I WAS UNWORTHY OF IT.
I NEVER COULD TELL REBECCA THAT'S WHY I DIDN'T WANT CHILDREN. I THOUGHT IT MIGHT...MIGHT BREAK SOME SPELL...
OF COURSE, THE SPELL BROKE ANYWAY, DIDN'T IT?
BUT STILL-- I WAS LOVED. AND RESPECTED.
A RISING STAR IN THE FIELD OF RADIATION RESEARCH.
GAMMA RADIATION.
YOU SEE NOW, SON?

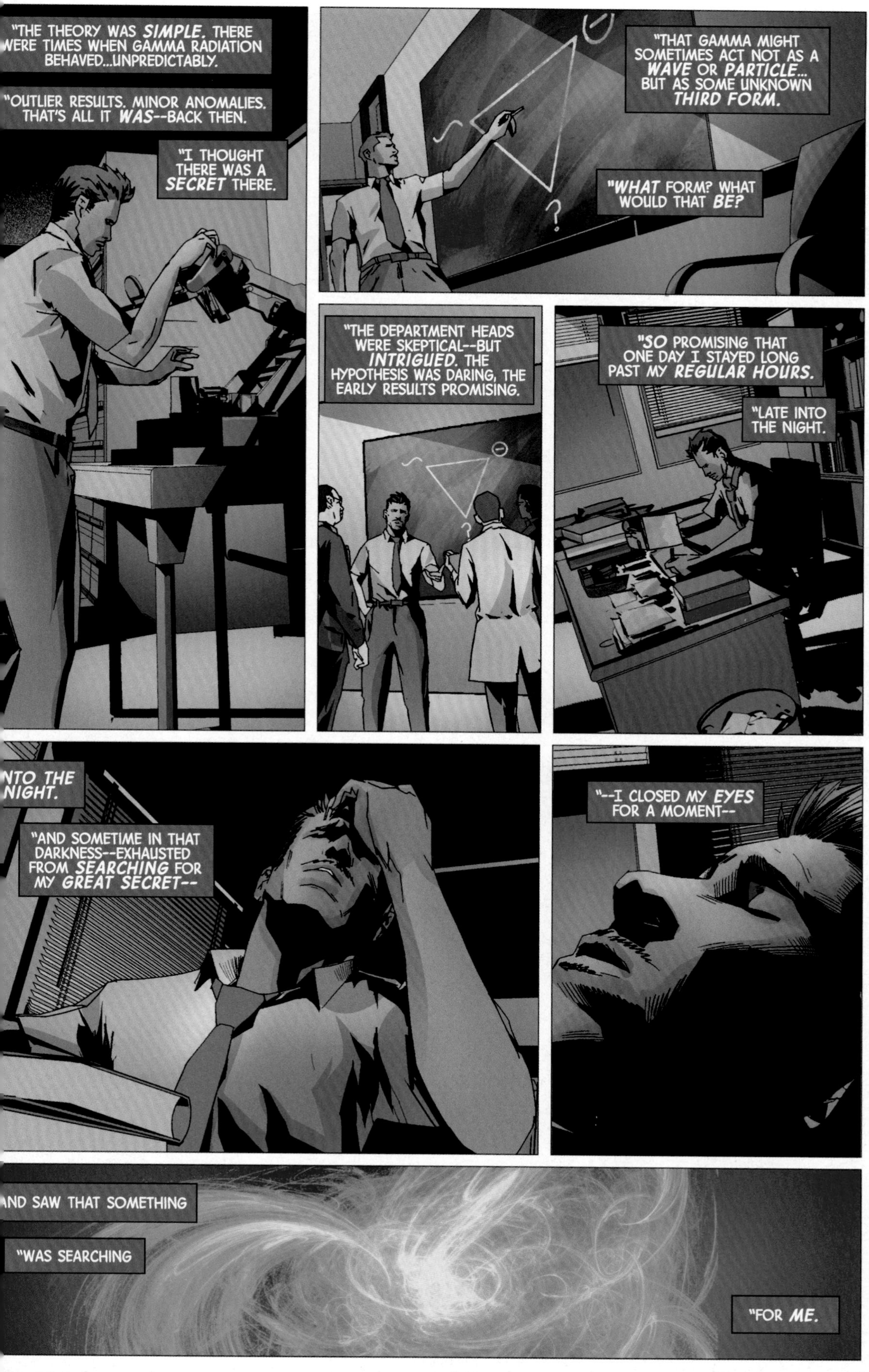
"THE THEORY WAS SIMPLE. THERE WERE TIMES WHEN GAMMA RADIATION BEHAVED...UNPREDICTABLY.
"OUTLIER RESULTS. MINOR ANOMALIES. THAT'S ALL IT WAS--BACK THEN.
"I THOUGHT THERE WAS A SECRET THERE.
"THAT GAMMA MIGHT SOMETIMES ACT NOT AS A WAVE OR PARTICLE... BUT AS SOME UNKNOWN THIRD FORM.
"WHAT FORM? WHAT WOULD THAT BE?
"THE DEPARTMENT HEADS WERE SKEPTICAL--BUT INTRIGUED. THE HYPOTHESIS WAS DARING, THE EARLY RESULTS PROMISING.
"SO PROMISING THAT ONE DAY I STAYED LONG PAST MY REGULAR HOURS.
"LATE INTO THE NIGHT.
NTO THE NIGHT.
"AND SOMETIME IN THAT DARKNESS--EXHAUSTED FROM SEARCHING FOR MY GREAT SECRET--
"--I CLOSED MY EYES FOR A MOMENT--
ND SAW THAT SOMETHING
"WAS SEARCHING
"FOR ME.

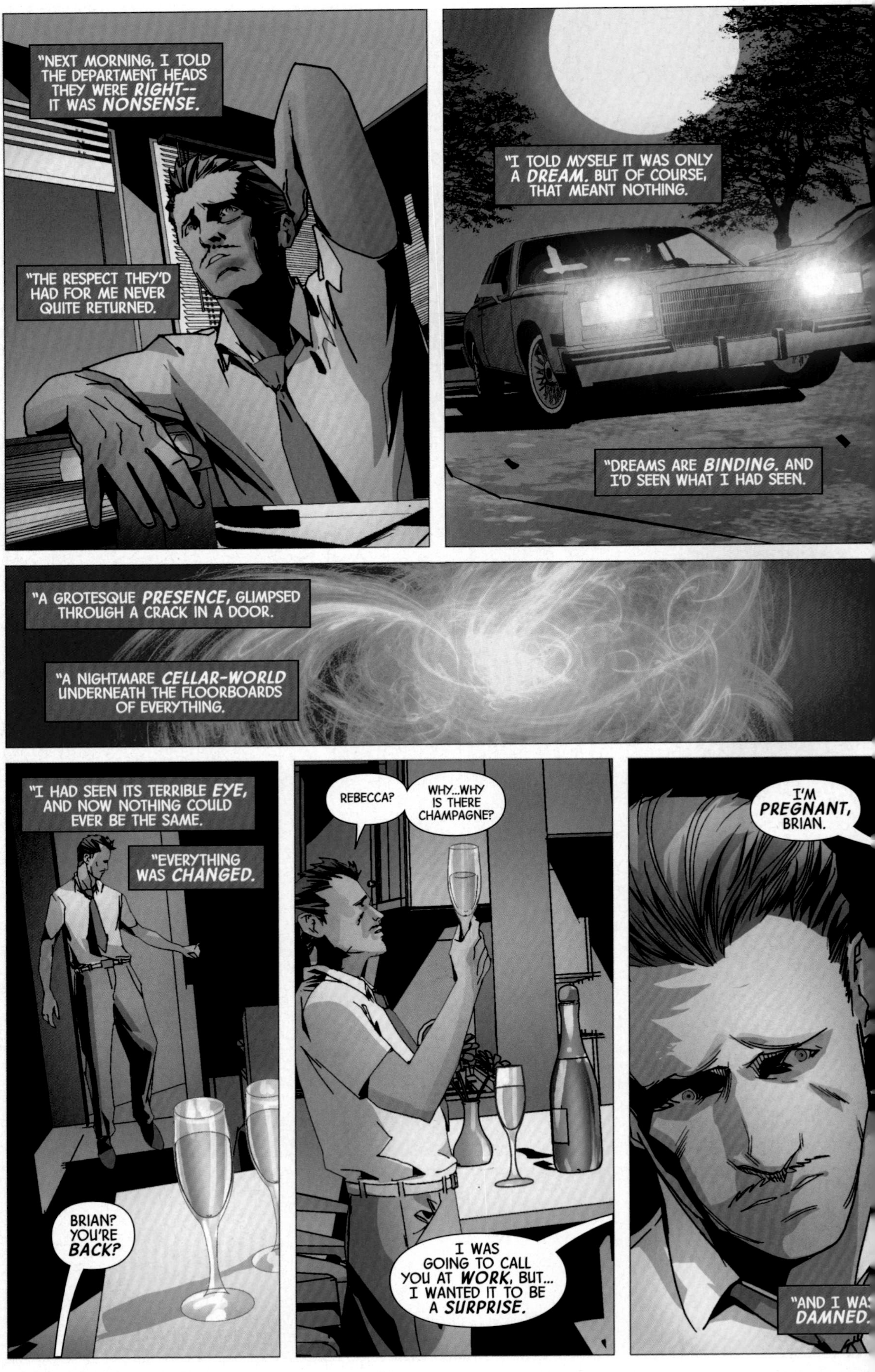
"NEXT MORNING, I TOLD THE DEPARTMENT HEADS THEY WERE RIGHT-- IT WAS NONSENSE.
"THE RESPECT THEY'D HAD FOR ME NEVER QUITE RETURNED.
"I TOLD MYSELF IT WAS ONLY A DREAM. BUT OF COURSE, THAT MEANT NOTHING.
"DREAMS ARE BINDING. AND I'D SEEN WHAT I HAD SEEN.
"A GROTESQUE PRESENCE, GLIMPSED THROUGH A CRACK IN A DOOR.
"A NIGHTMARE CELLAR-WORLD UNDERNEATH THE FLOORBOARDS OF EVERYTHING.
"I HAD SEEN ITS TERRIBLE EYE, AND NOW NOTHING COULD EVER BE THE SAME.
"EVERYTHING WAS CHANGED.
BRIAN? YOU'RE BACK?
REBECCA?
WHY...WHY IS THERE CHAMPAGNE?
I WAS GOING TO CALL YOU AT WORK, BUT... I WANTED IT TO BE A SURPRISE.
I'M PREGNANT, BRIAN.
"AND I WAS DAMNED.

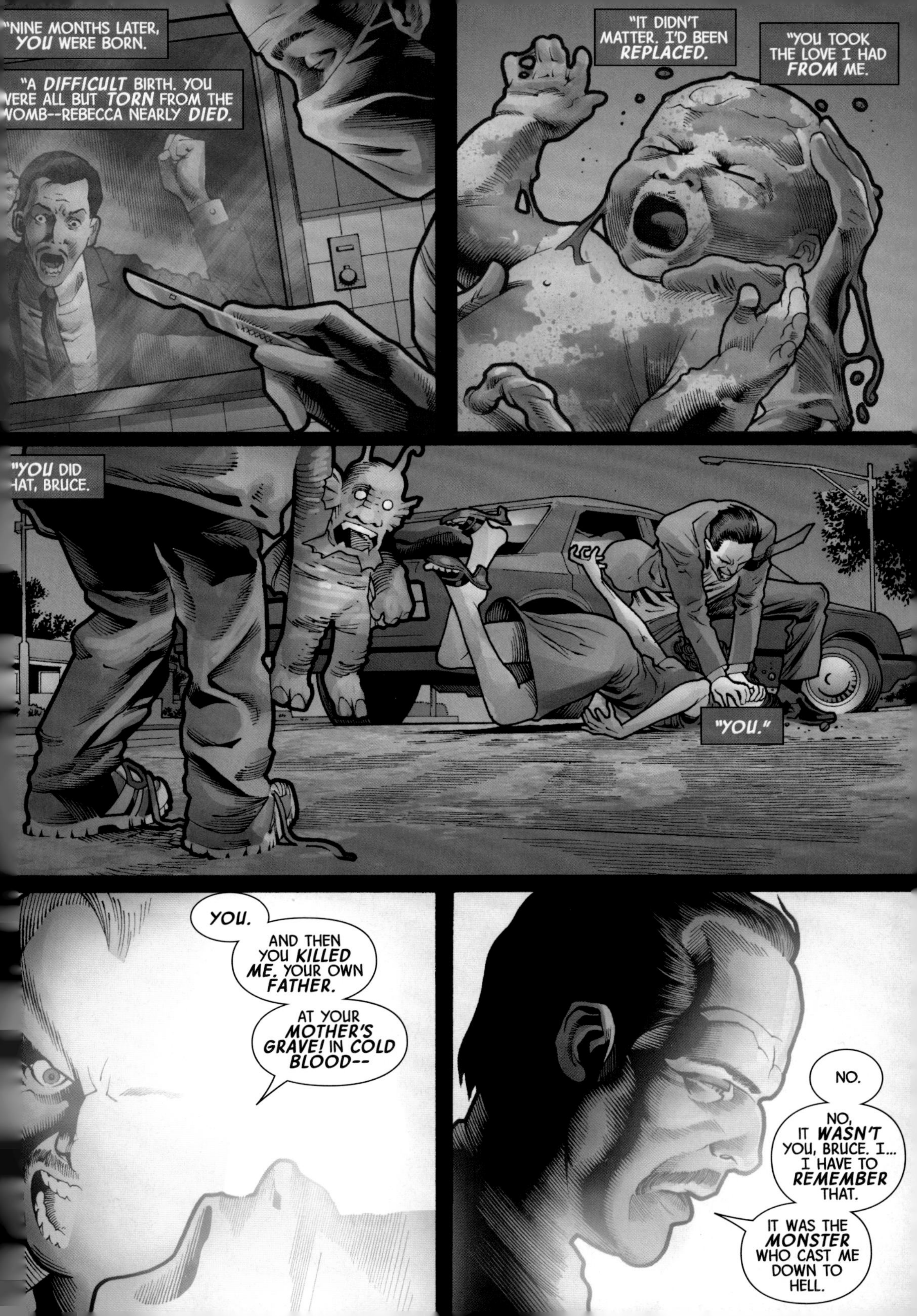
"NINE MONTHS LATER, YOU WERE BORN.
"A DIFFICULT BIRTH. YOU WERE ALL BUT TORN FROM THE WOMB--REBECCA NEARLY DIED.
"IT DIDN'T MATTER. I'D BEEN REPLACED.
"YOU TOOK THE LOVE I HAD FROM ME.
"YOU DID THAT, BRUCE.
"YOU."
YOU.
AND THEN YOU KILLED ME. YOUR OWN FATHER.
AT YOUR MOTHER'S GRAVE! IN COLD BLOOD--
NO.
NO, IT WASN'T YOU, BRUCE. I... I HAVE TO REMEMBER THAT.
IT WAS THE MONSTER WHO CAST ME DOWN TO HELL.

"AND THEN WHEN I TRIED TO--TO PROTEST THE *INJUSTICE* OF THAT--

"--THE MONSTER KILLED ME *AGAIN*. SENT ME TO A *FARTHER* HELL...A *LOWER* DEEP..."

...WHERE THE THING FROM MY DREAM WAS *WAITING* FOR ME. HERE, BELOW EVERYTHING.

CREATION'S SECRET *REFLECTION*, VASTER THAN WE CAN SEE OR KNOW.

IT CAN ONLY *INFLUENCE* OUR WORLD, YOU SEE. TO WORK *DIRECTLY*...IT NEEDS A *HOST PERSONALITY*. A *SOUL* IT CAN *SPEAK* AND *ACT* THROUGH.

IT HAD *ME* FOR THAT.

BUT NOW... NOW IT HAS *YOU*. MY IMMORTAL *SON*, HEAVY WITH THE SECRET THIRD FORM OF LIGHT.

YOU CAN BRING OUR WORLD *TO* IT. THROUGH THE *HOLE* YOU TORE WITH YOUR *BOMB*. THE *GREEN DOOR* YOU OPENED.

AND YOU CAN SET ME *FREE*.

But there i anothe Devil.

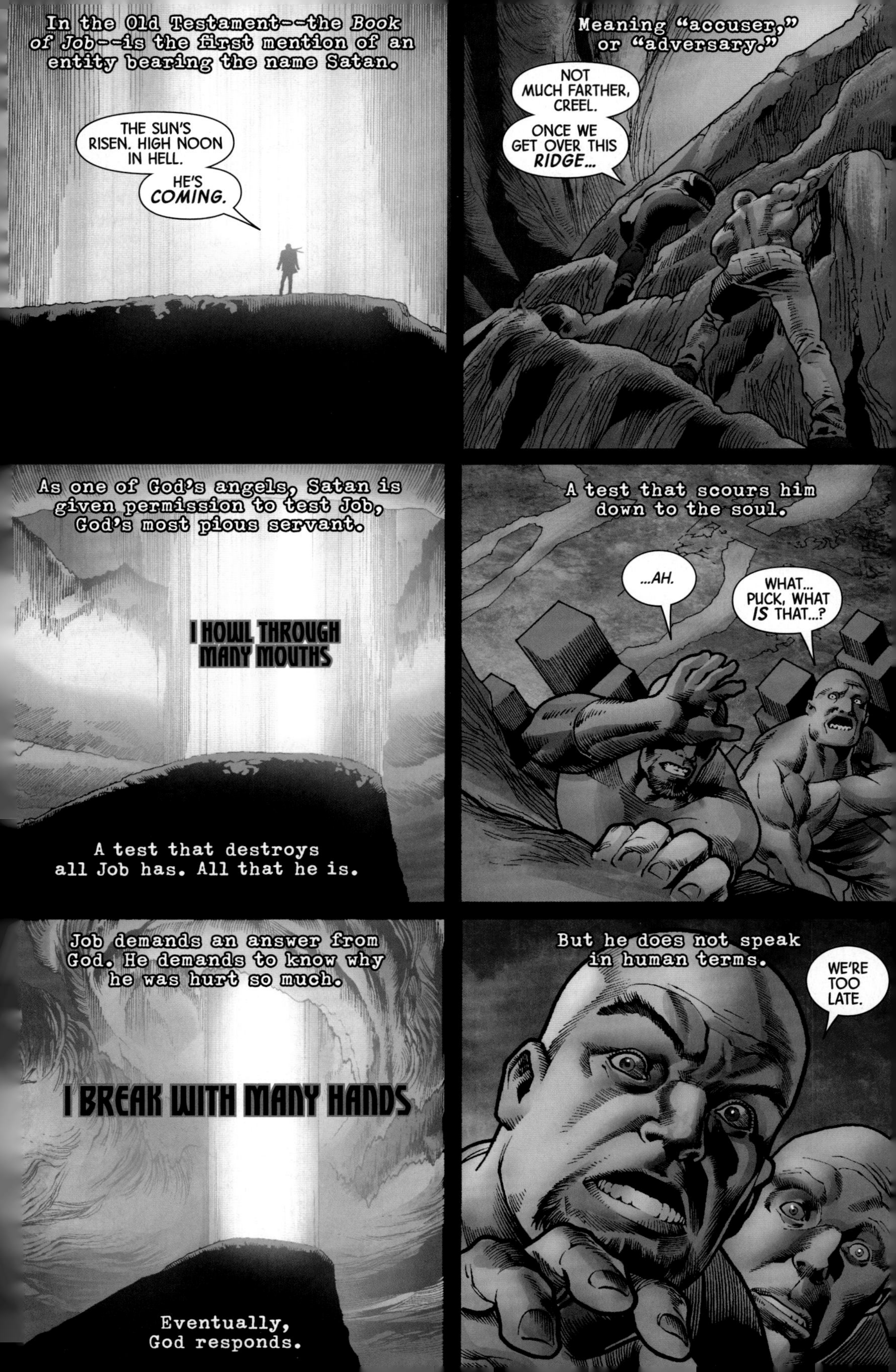

In the Old Testament--the *Book of Job*--is the first mention of an entity bearing the name Satan.
THE SUN'S RISEN. HIGH NOON IN HELL.
HE'S *COMING.*
Meaning "accuser," or "adversary."
NOT MUCH FARTHER, CREEL.
ONCE WE GET OVER THIS *RIDGE...*
As one of God's angels, Satan is given permission to test Job, God's most pious servant.
I HOWL THROUGH MANY MOUTHS
A test that destroys all Job has. All that he is.
A test that scours him down to the soul.
...AH.
WHAT... PUCK, WHAT *IS* THAT...?
Job demands an answer from God. He demands to know why he was hurt so much.
I BREAK WITH MANY HANDS
Eventually, God responds.
But he does not speak in human terms.
WE'RE TOO LATE.

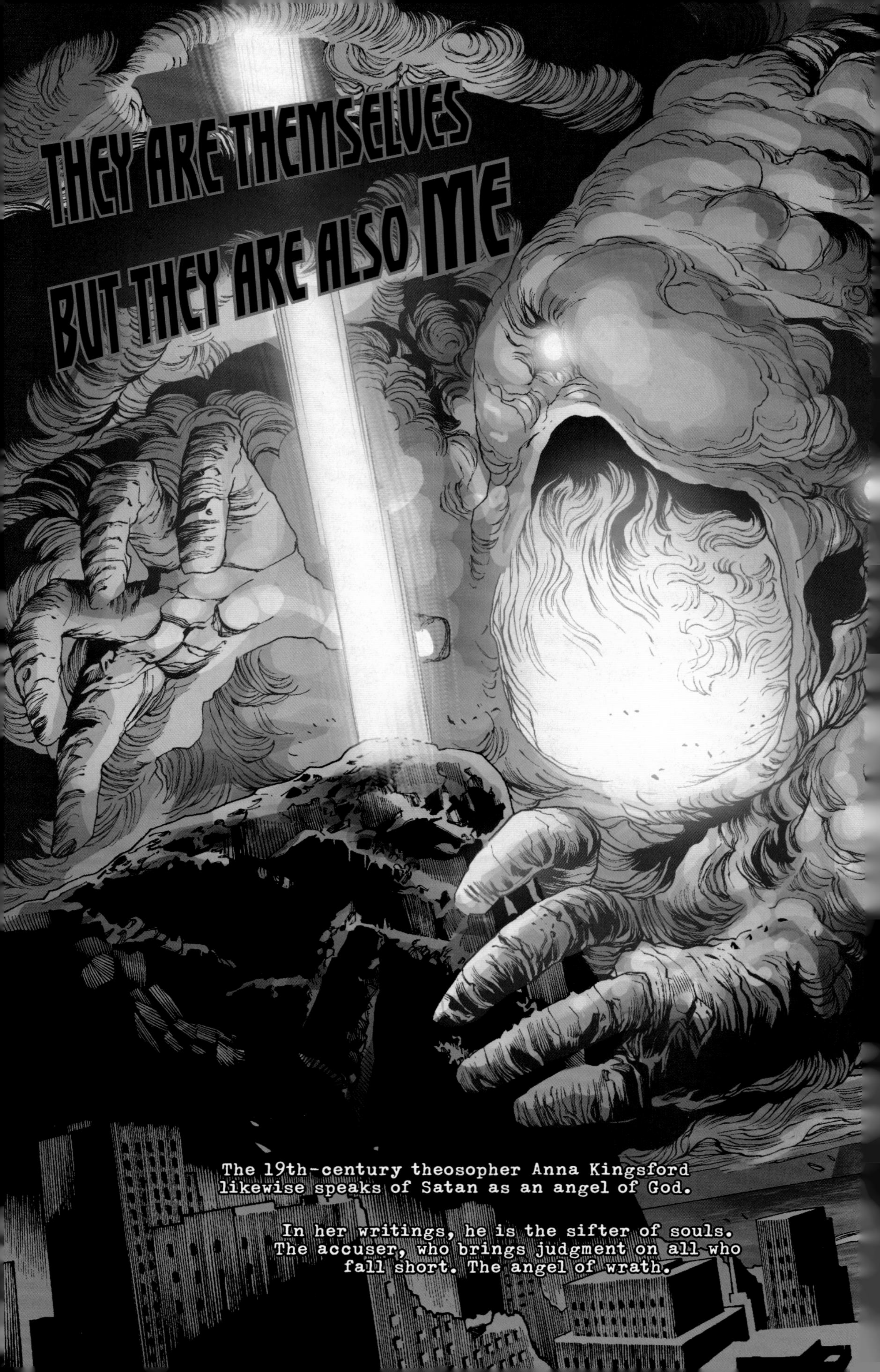
THEY ARE THEMSELVES
BUT THEY ARE ALSO ME
The 19th-century theosopher Anna Kingsford likewise speaks of Satan as an angel of God.
In her writings, he is the sifter of souls. The accuser, who brings judgment on all who fall short. The angel of wrath.

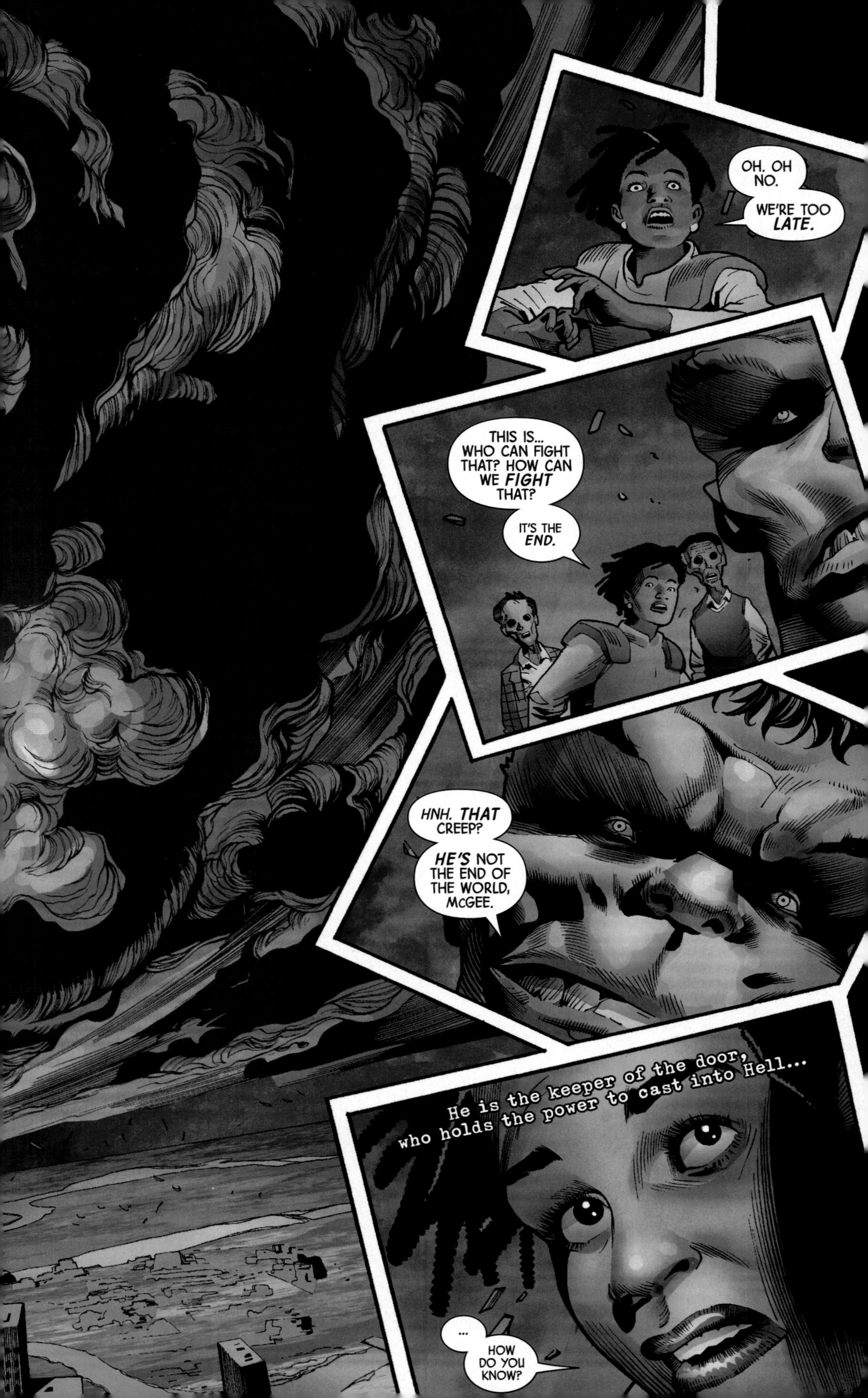
OH, OH NO.
WE'RE TOO LATE.
THIS IS... WHO CAN FIGHT THAT? HOW CAN WE FIGHT THAT?
IT'S THE END.
HNH. THAT CREEP?
HE'S NOT THE END OF THE WORLD, McGEE.
He is the keeper of the door, who holds the power to cast into Hell...
...
HOW DO YOU KNOW?

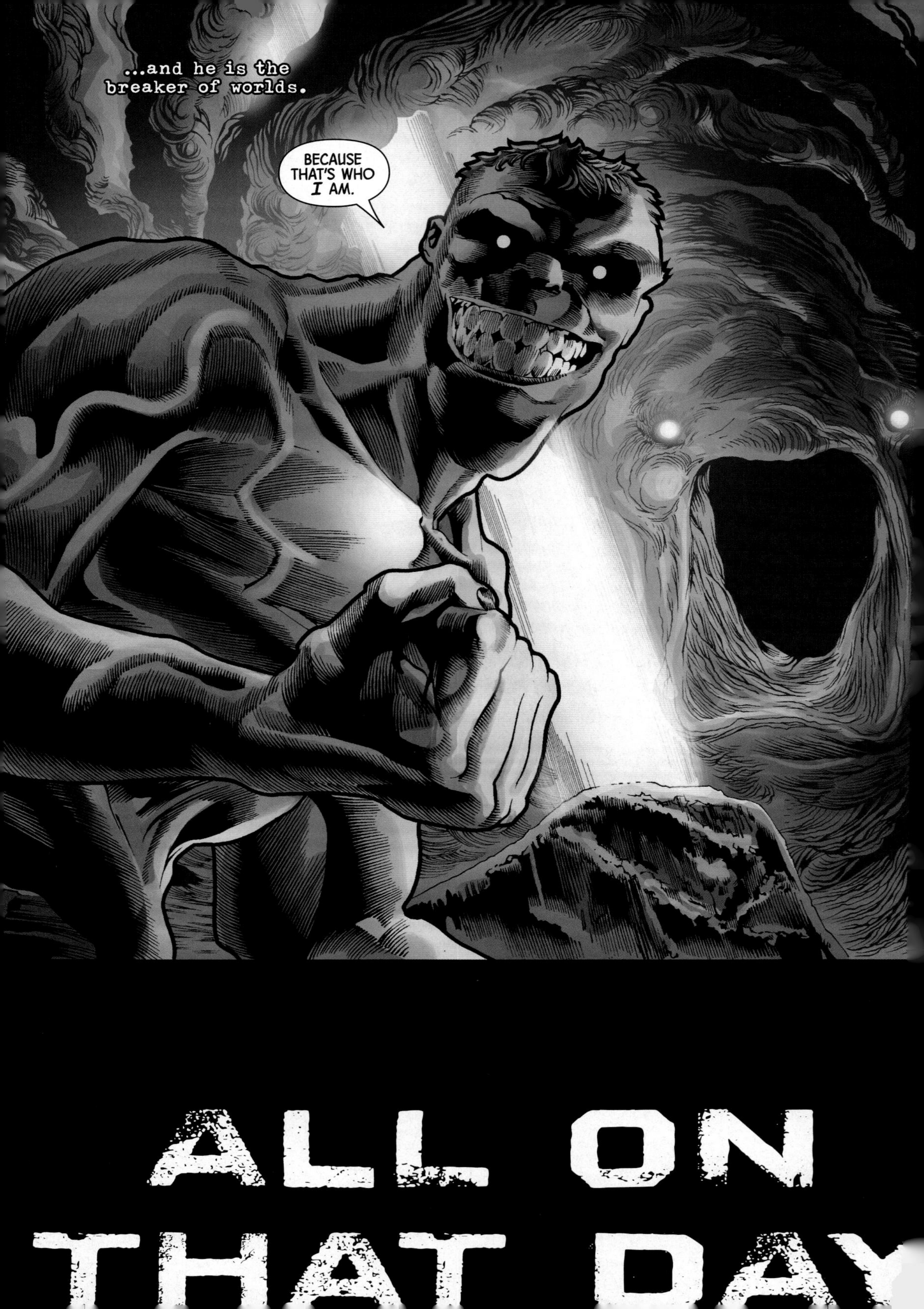
...and he is the breaker of worlds.
BECAUSE THAT'S WHO I AM.

ALL ON THAT DAY

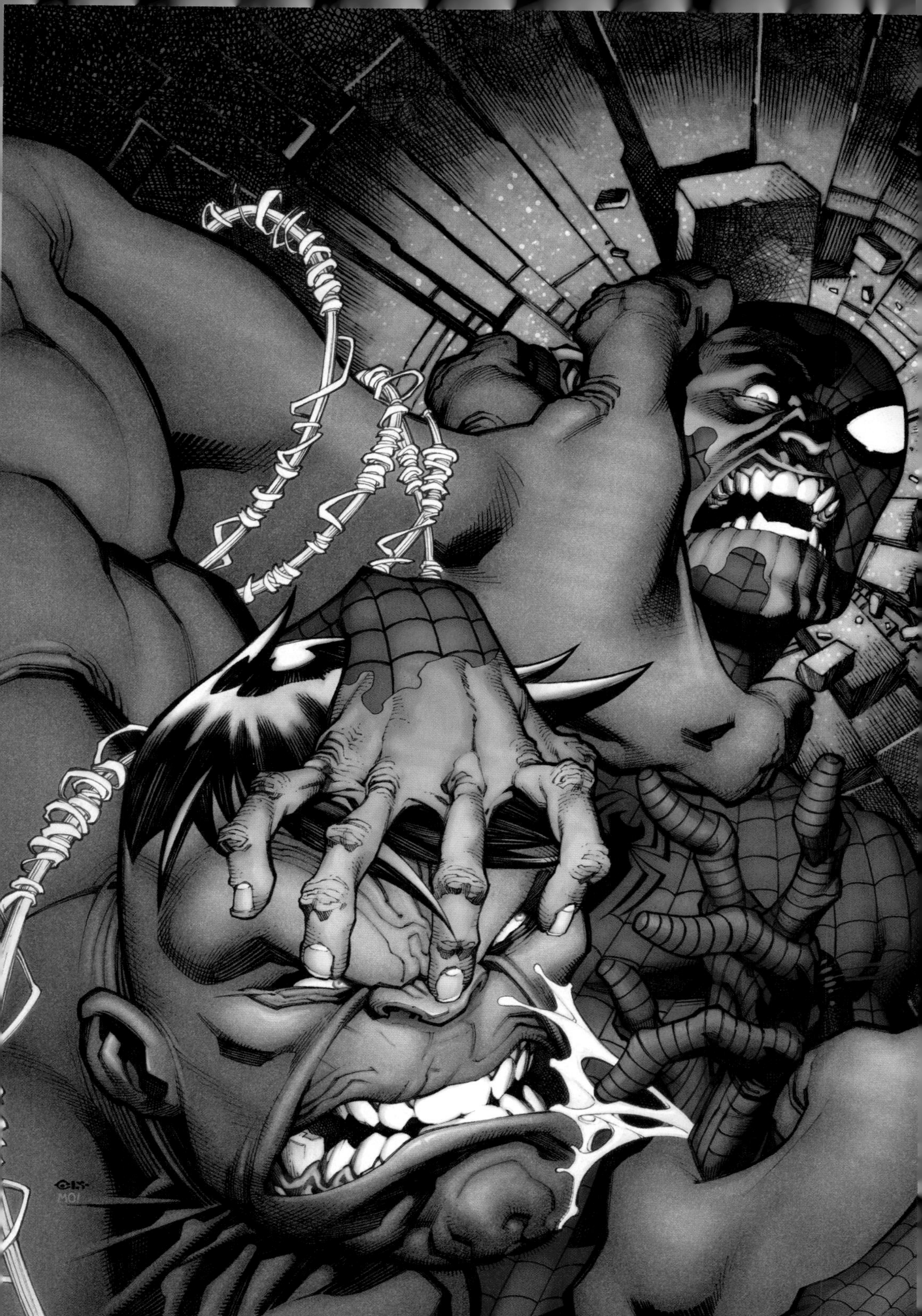

13

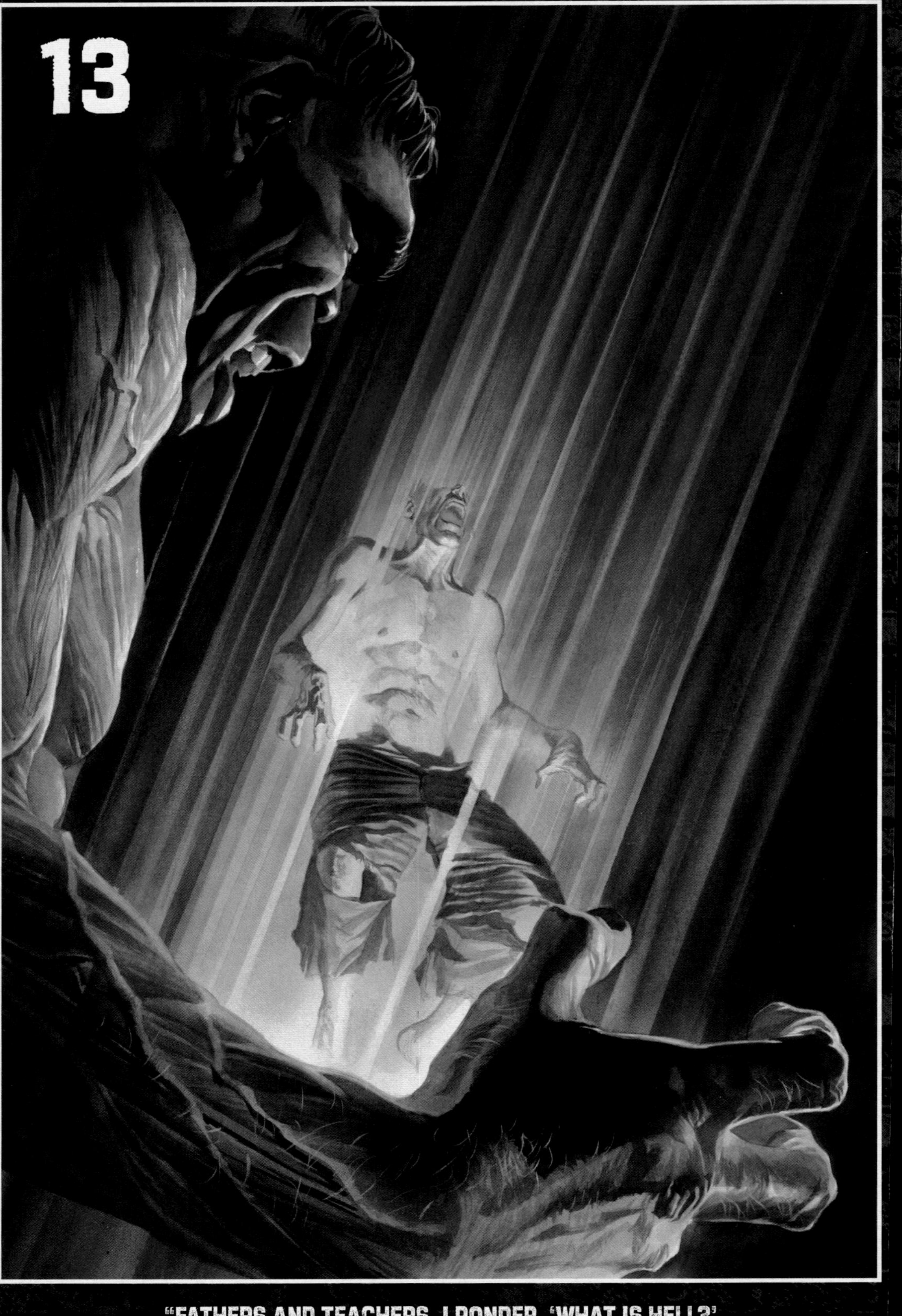

**"FATHERS AND TEACHERS, I PONDER, 'WHAT IS HELL?'
I MAINTAIN THAT IT IS THE SUFFERING OF BEING UNABLE TO LOVE."**

- FYODOR DOSTOYEVSKY, *THE BROTHERS KARAMAZOV*

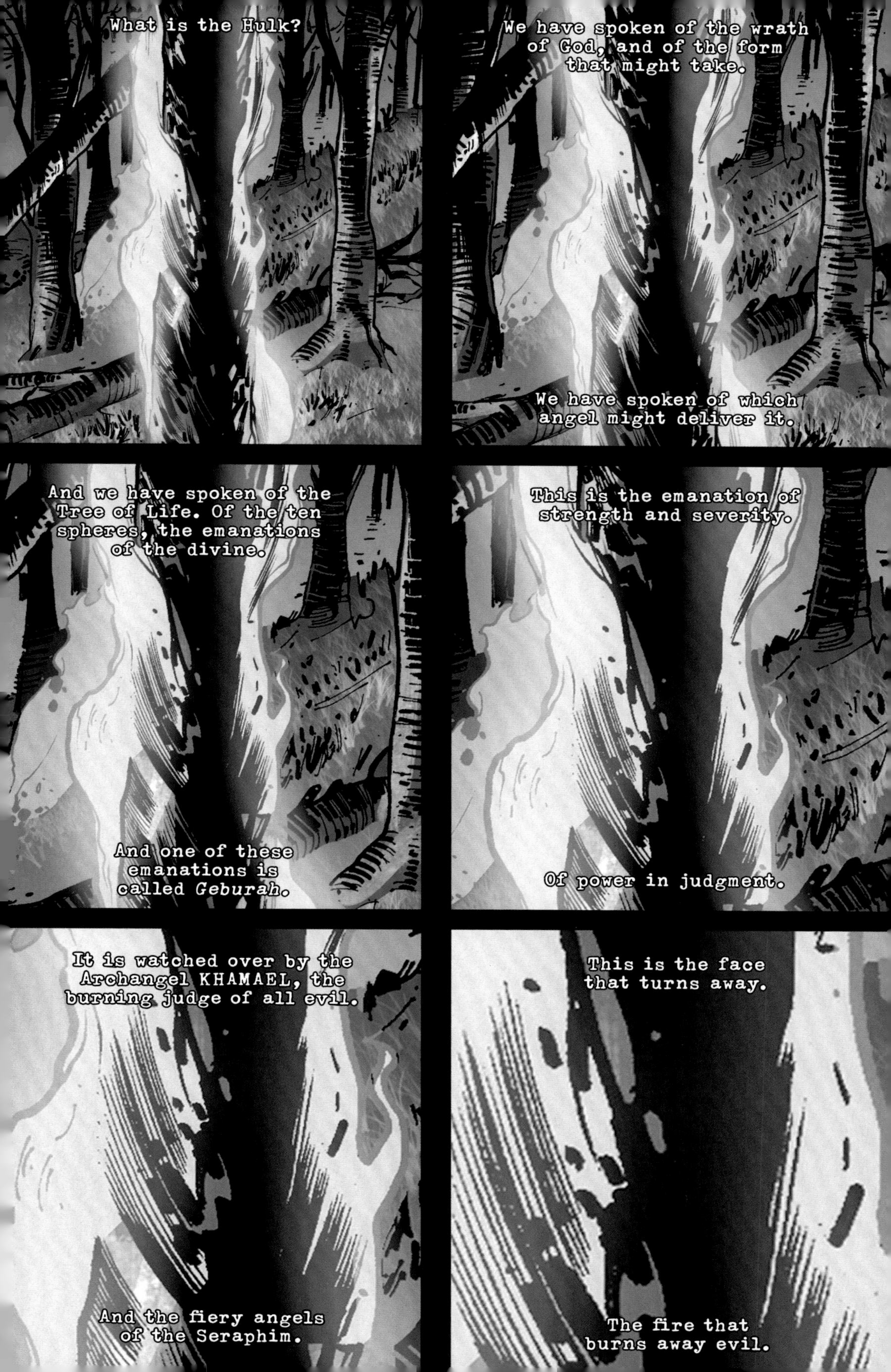
What is the Hulk?
We have spoken of the wrath of God, and of the form that might take.
We have spoken of which angel might deliver it.
And we have spoken of the Tree of Life. Of the ten spheres, the emanations of the divine.
And one of these emanations is called *Geburah*.
This is the emanation of strength and severity.
Of power in judgment.
It is watched over by the Archangel KHAMAEL, the burning judge of all evil.
And the fiery angels of the Seraphim.
This is the face that turns away.
The fire that burns away evil.

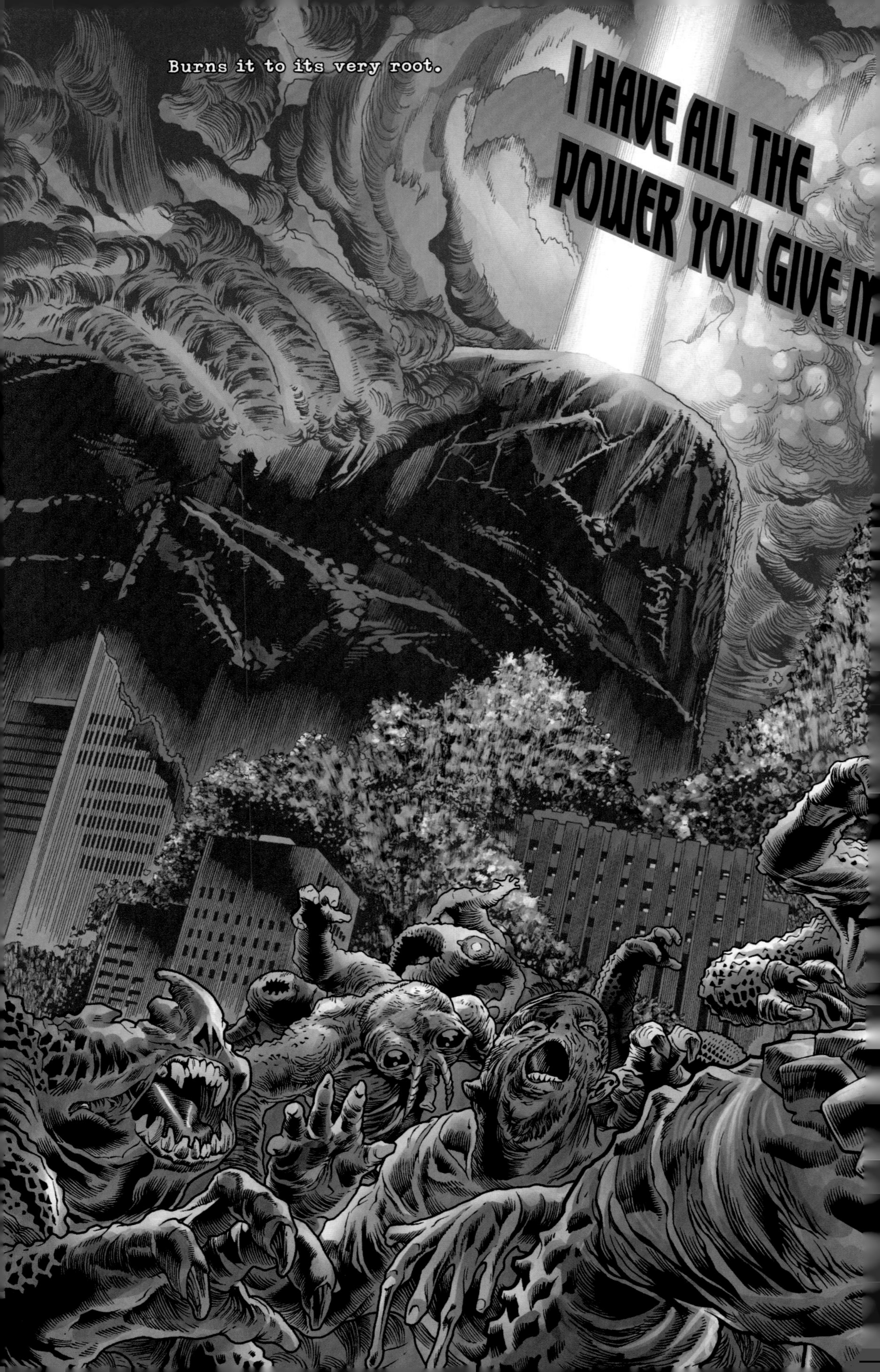
Burns it to its very root.
I HAVE ALL THE POWER YOU GIVE M

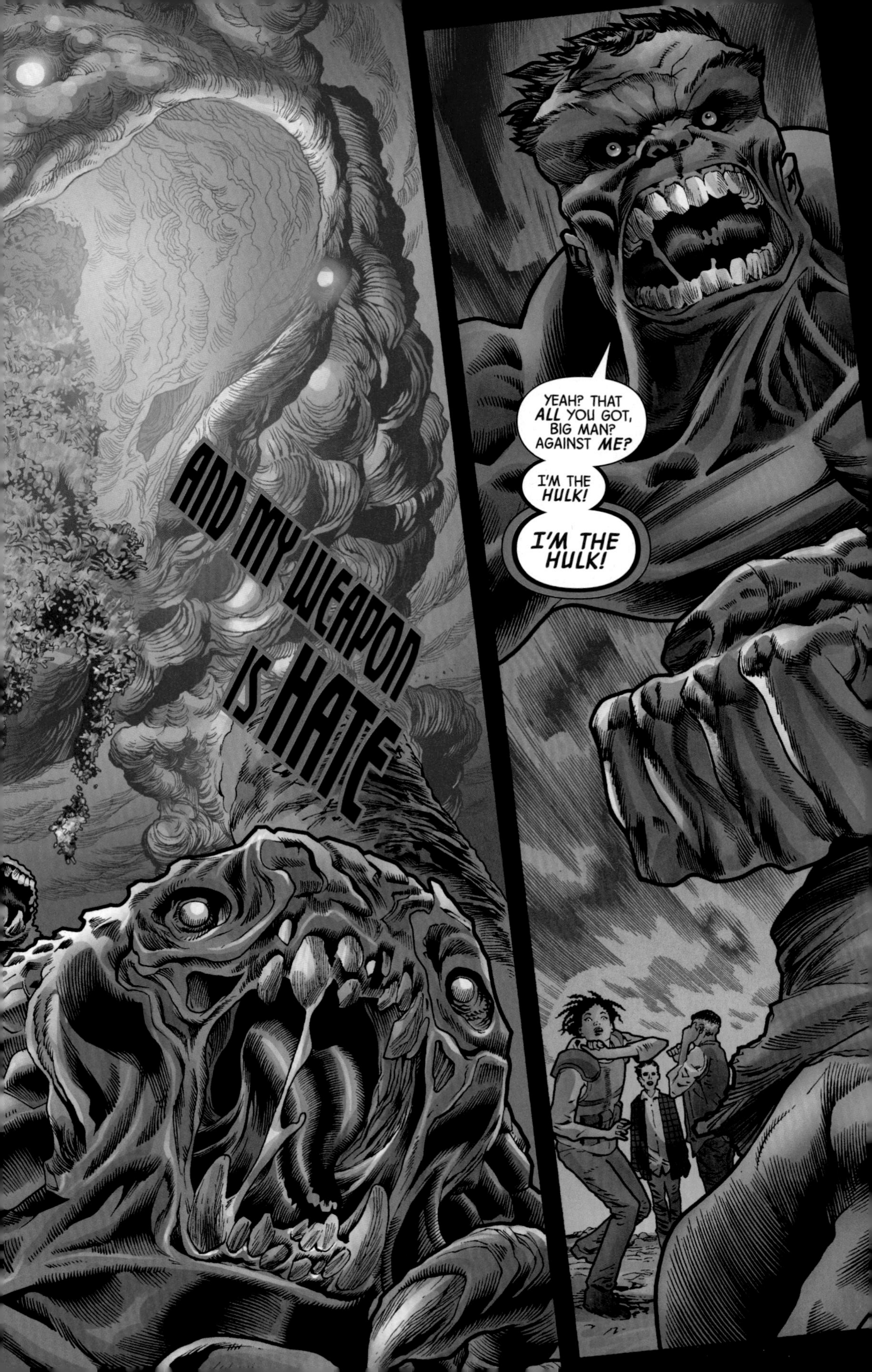
AND MY WEAPON IS HATE
YEAH? THAT ALL YOU GOT, BIG MAN? AGAINST ME?
I'M THE HULK!
I'M THE HULK!

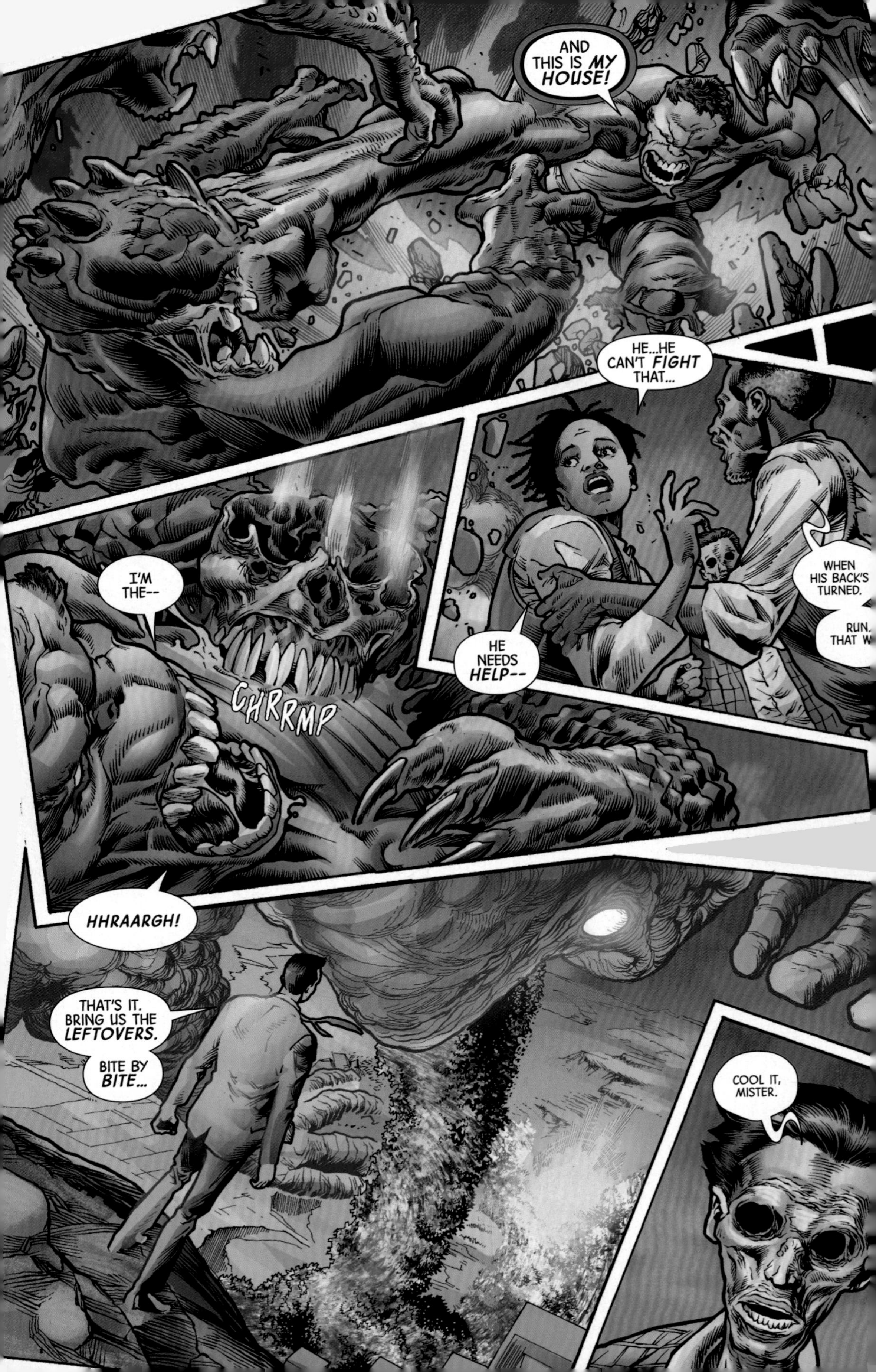
AND THIS IS MY HOUSE!
HE...HE CAN'T FIGHT THAT...
HE NEEDS HELP--
WHEN HIS BACK'S TURNED.
RUN. THAT W
I'M THE--
CHRRMP
HHRAARGH!
THAT'S IT. BRING US THE LEFTOVERS.
BITE BY BITE...
COOL IT, MISTER.

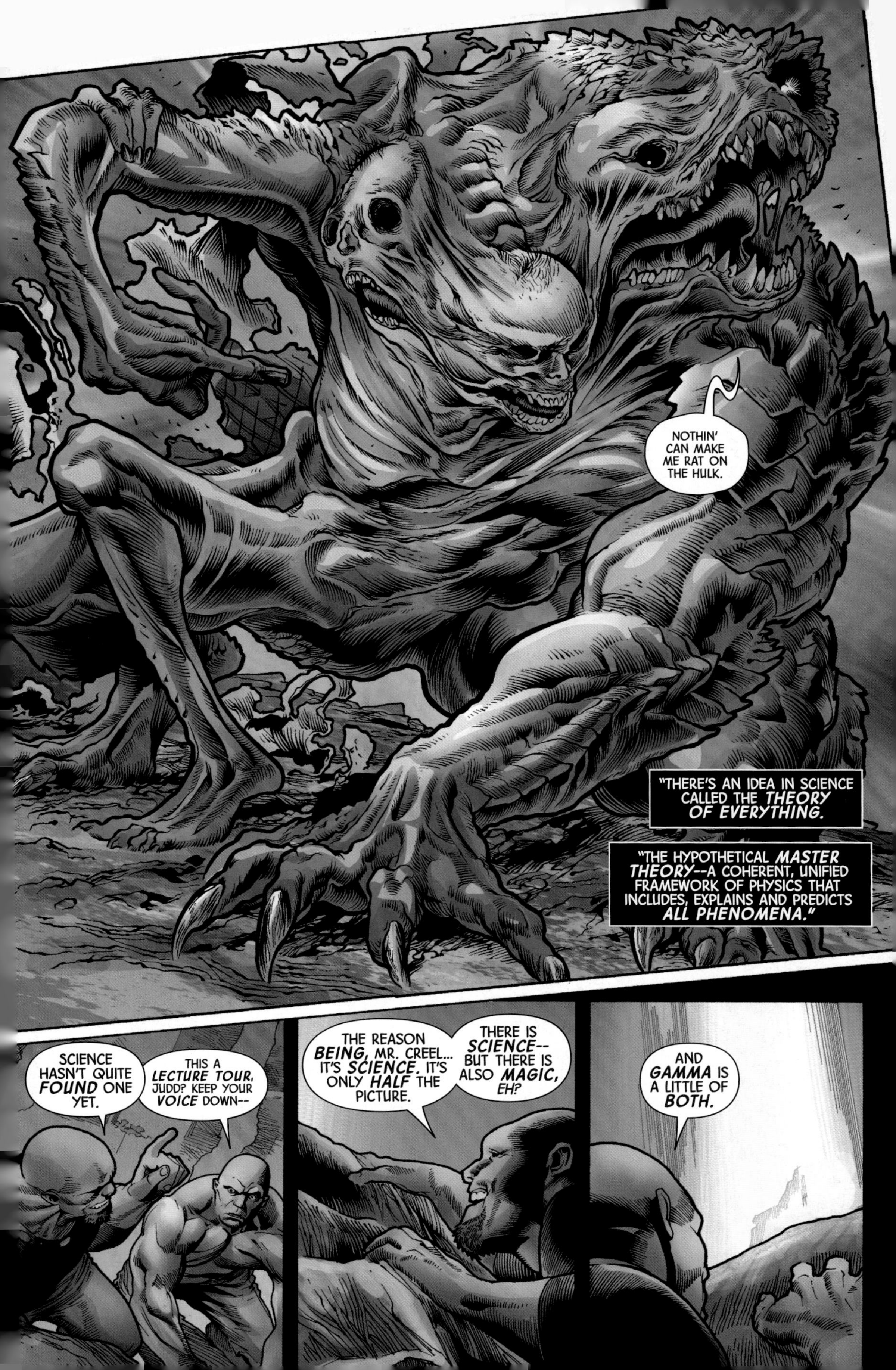
NOTHIN' CAN MAKE ME RAT ON THE HULK.
"THERE'S AN IDEA IN SCIENCE CALLED THE THEORY OF EVERYTHING.
"THE HYPOTHETICAL MASTER THEORY--A COHERENT, UNIFIED FRAMEWORK OF PHYSICS THAT INCLUDES, EXPLAINS AND PREDICTS ALL PHENOMENA."
SCIENCE HASN'T QUITE FOUND ONE YET.
THIS A LECTURE TOUR, JUDD? KEEP YOUR VOICE DOWN--
THE REASON BEING, MR. CREEL... IT'S SCIENCE. IT'S ONLY HALF THE PICTURE.
THERE IS SCIENCE-- BUT THERE IS ALSO MAGIC, EH?
AND GAMMA IS A LITTLE OF BOTH.

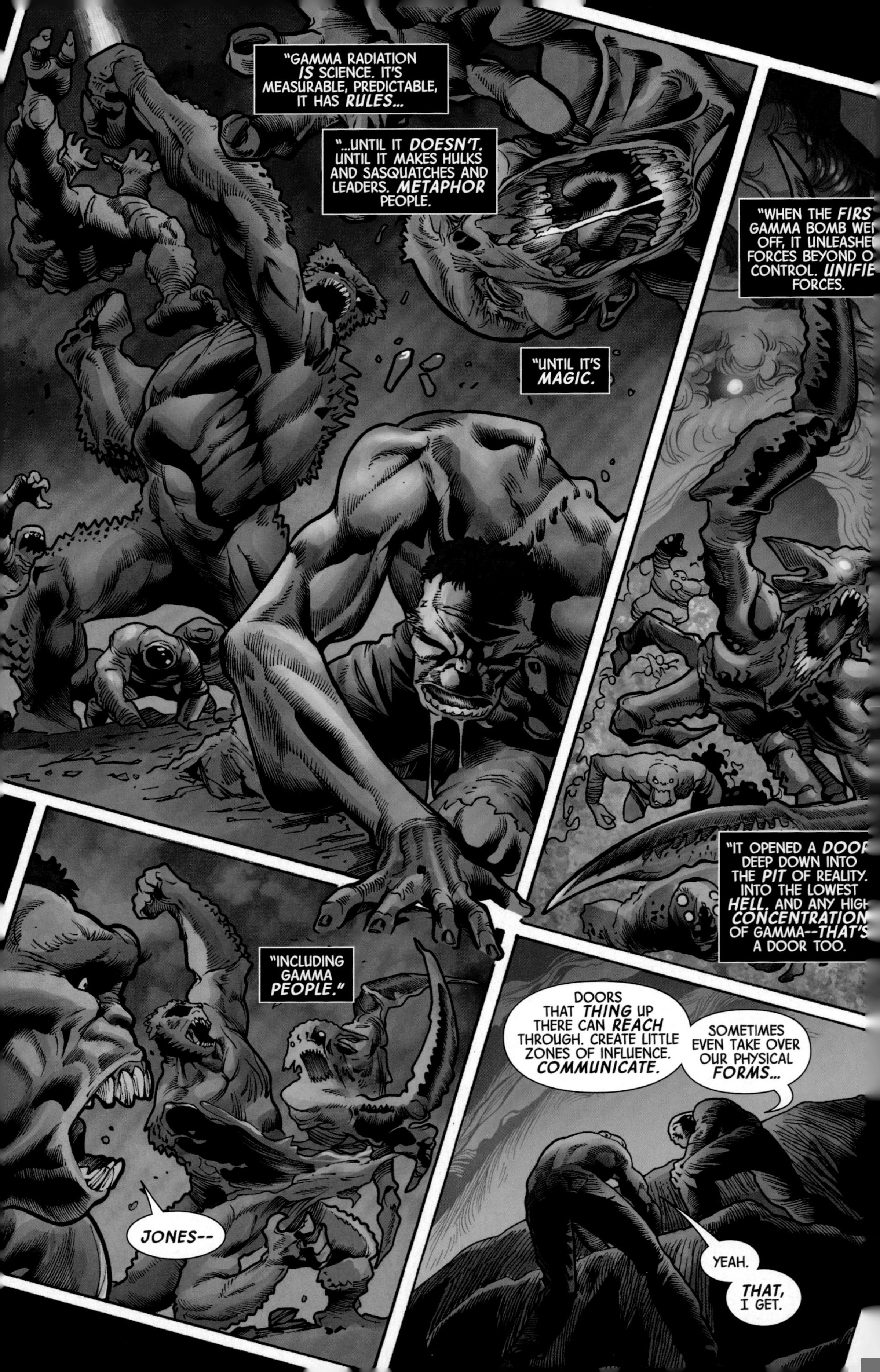
"GAMMA RADIATION IS SCIENCE. IT'S MEASURABLE, PREDICTABLE, IT HAS RULES...
"...UNTIL IT DOESN'T. UNTIL IT MAKES HULKS AND SASQUATCHES AND LEADERS. METAPHOR PEOPLE.
"UNTIL IT'S MAGIC.
"WHEN THE FIRS GAMMA BOMB WE OFF, IT UNLEASHE FORCES BEYOND O CONTROL. UNIFIE FORCES.
"IT OPENED A DOOR DEEP DOWN INTO THE PIT OF REALITY. INTO THE LOWEST HELL. AND ANY HIGH CONCENTRATION OF GAMMA--THAT'S A DOOR TOO.
"INCLUDING GAMMA PEOPLE."
JONES--
DOORS THAT THING UP THERE CAN REACH THROUGH. CREATE LITTLE ZONES OF INFLUENCE. COMMUNICATE.
SOMETIMES EVEN TAKE OVER OUR PHYSICAL FORMS...
YEAH.
THAT, I GET.

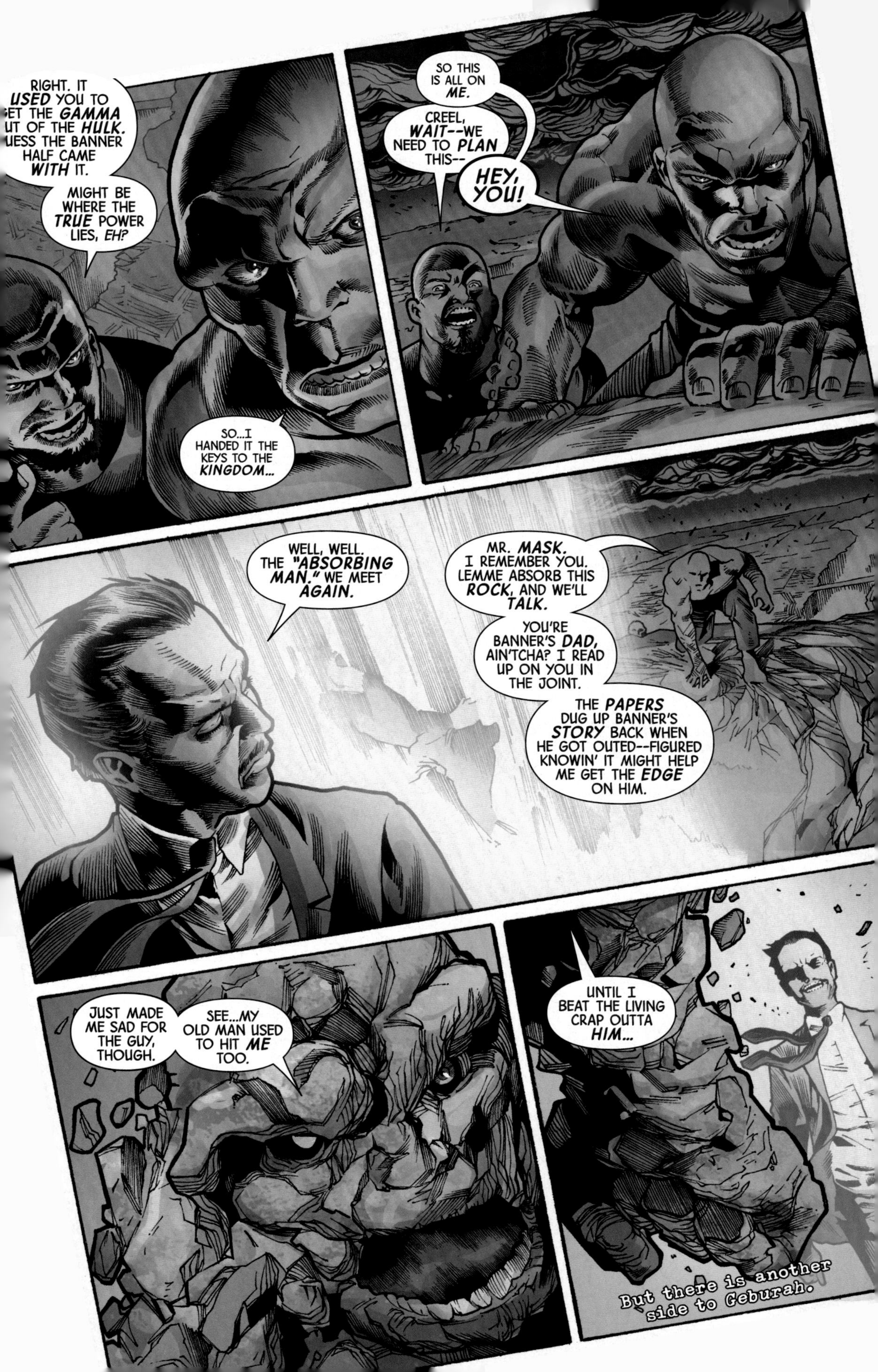
RIGHT. IT USED YOU TO GET THE GAMMA OUT OF THE HULK. GUESS THE BANNER HALF CAME WITH IT.
MIGHT BE WHERE THE TRUE POWER LIES, EH?
SO...I HANDED IT THE KEYS TO THE KINGDOM...
SO THIS IS ALL ON ME.
CREEL, WAIT--WE NEED TO PLAN THIS--
HEY, YOU!
WELL, WELL. THE "ABSORBING MAN." WE MEET AGAIN.
MR. MASK. I REMEMBER YOU. LEMME ABSORB THIS ROCK, AND WE'LL TALK.
YOU'RE BANNER'S DAD, AIN'TCHA? I READ UP ON YOU IN THE JOINT.
THE PAPERS DUG UP BANNER'S STORY BACK WHEN HE GOT OUTED--FIGURED KNOWIN' IT MIGHT HELP ME GET THE EDGE ON HIM.
JUST MADE ME SAD FOR THE GUY, THOUGH.
SEE...MY OLD MAN USED TO HIT ME TOO.
UNTIL I BEAT THE LIVING CRAP OUTTA HIM...
But there is another side to Geburah.

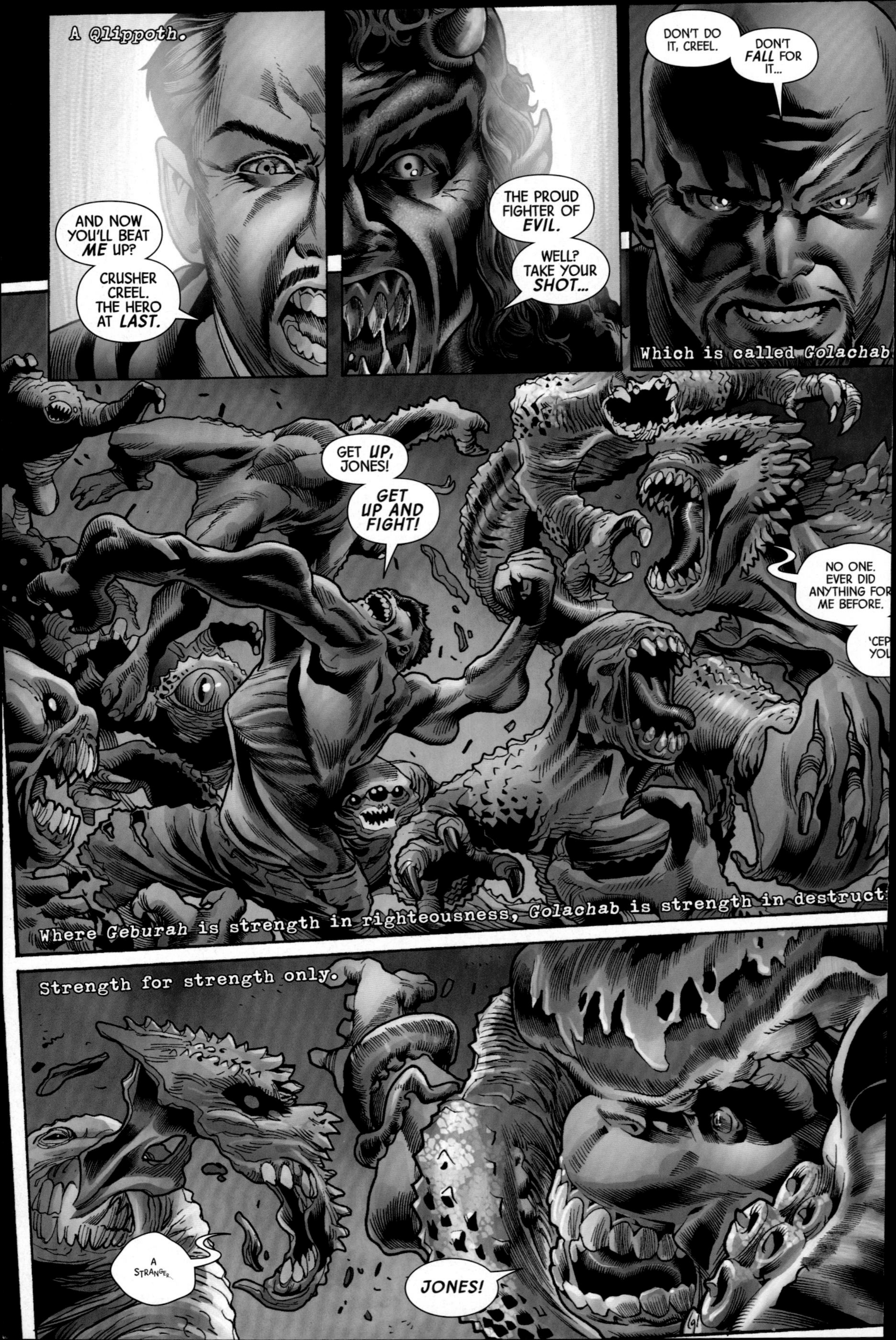
A Qlippoth.
AND NOW YOU'LL BEAT ME UP?
CRUSHER CREEL. THE HERO AT LAST.
THE PROUD FIGHTER OF EVIL.
WELL? TAKE YOUR SHOT...
DON'T DO IT, CREEL.
DON'T FALL FOR IT...
Which is called Golachab.
GET UP, JONES!
GET UP AND FIGHT!
NO ONE. EVER DID ANYTHING FOR ME BEFORE.
Where Geburah is strength in righteousness, Golachab is strength in destructi
Strength for strength only.
A STRANGER...
JONES!

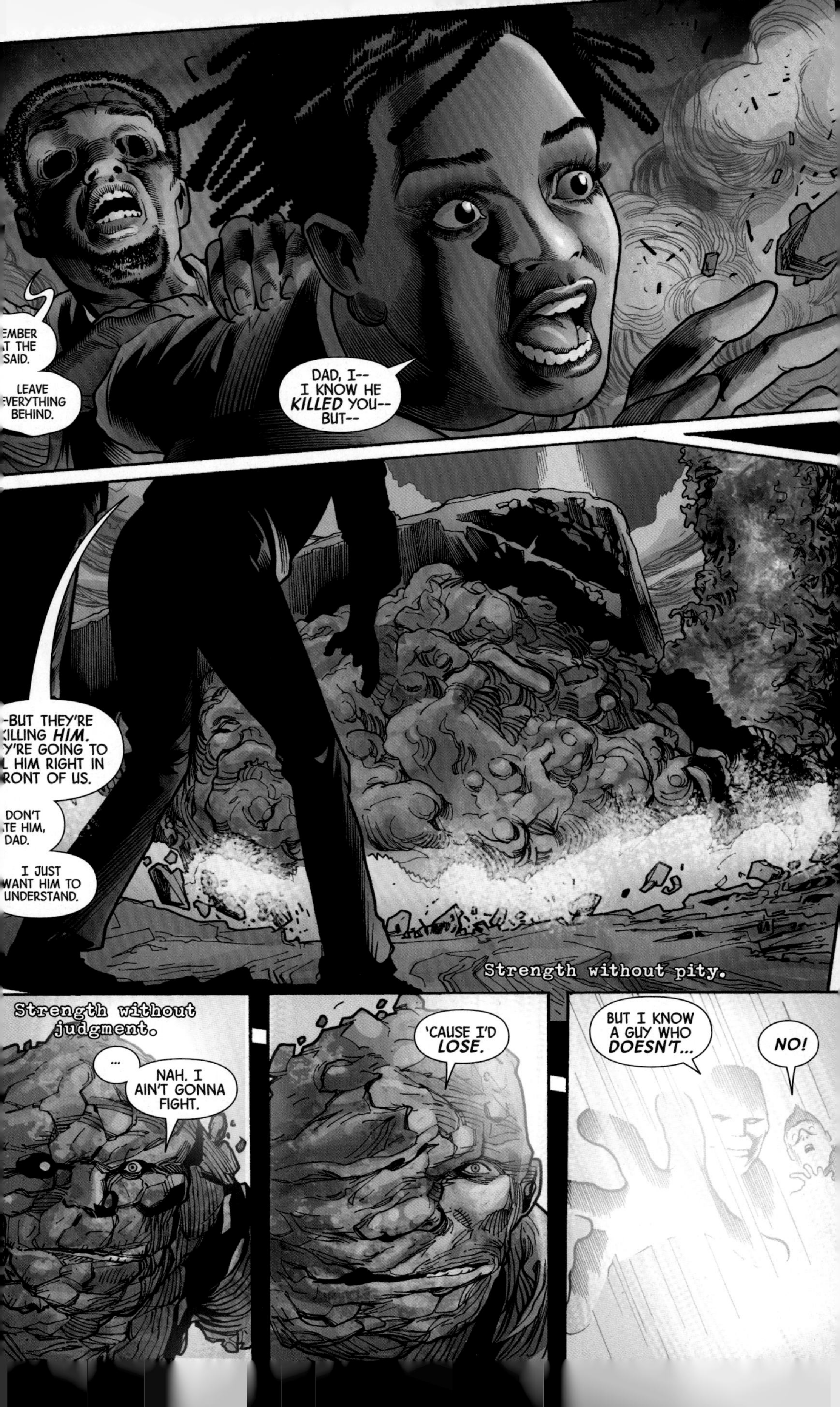
EMBER
T THE
SAID.
LEAVE
EVERYTHING
BEHIND.
DAD, I-- I KNOW HE KILLED YOU-- BUT--
-BUT THEY'RE
KILLING HIM.
Y'RE GOING TO
L HIM RIGHT IN
RONT OF US.
DON'T
TE HIM,
DAD.
I JUST WANT HIM TO UNDERSTAND.
Strength without pity.
Strength without judgment.
...
NAH. I AIN'T GONNA FIGHT.
'CAUSE I'D LOSE.
BUT I KNOW A GUY WHO DOESN'T...
NO!

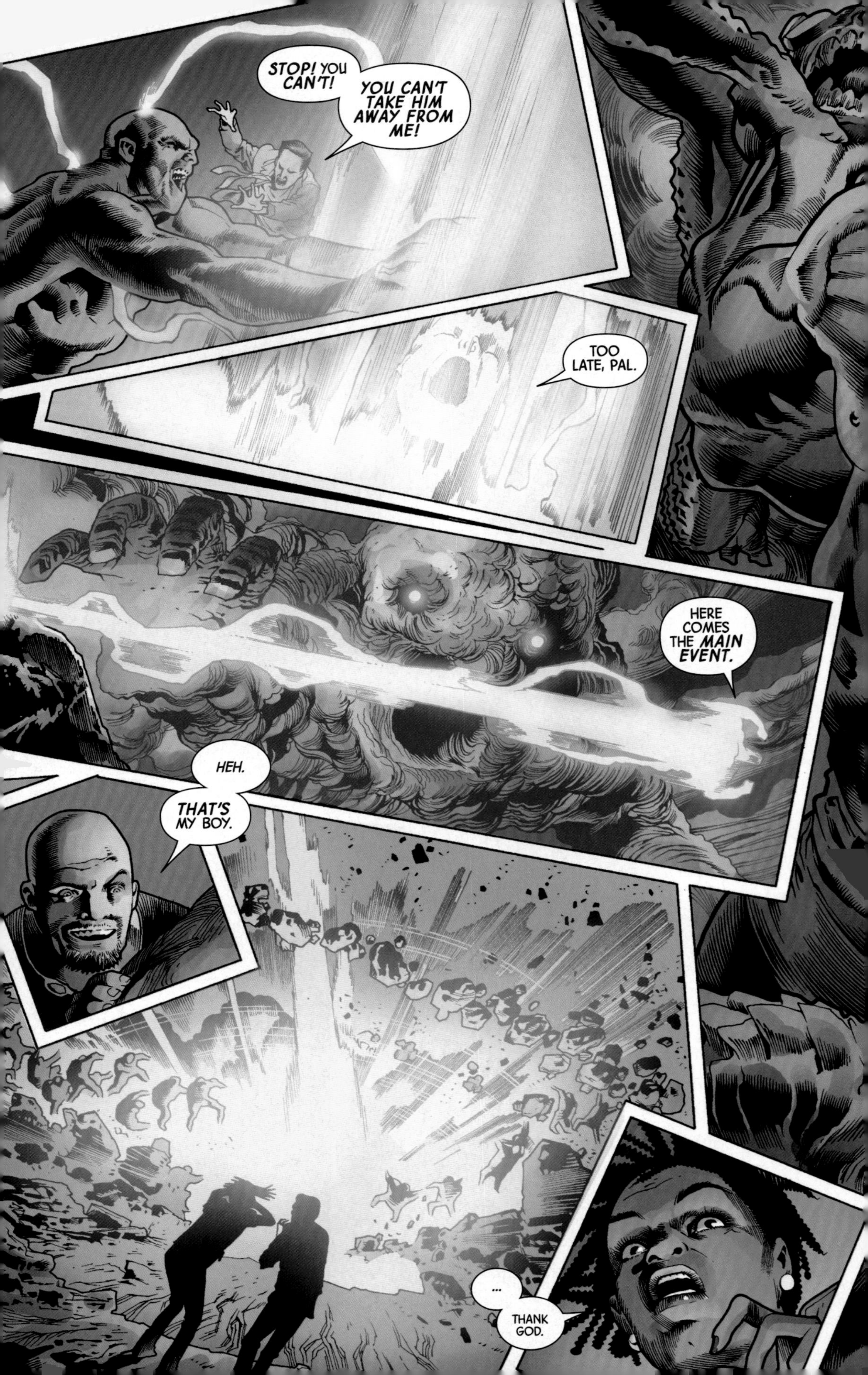
STOP! YOU CAN'T!
YOU CAN'T TAKE HIM AWAY FROM ME!
TOO LATE, PAL.
HERE COMES THE MAIN EVENT.
HEH.
THAT'S MY BOY.
...
THANK GOD.

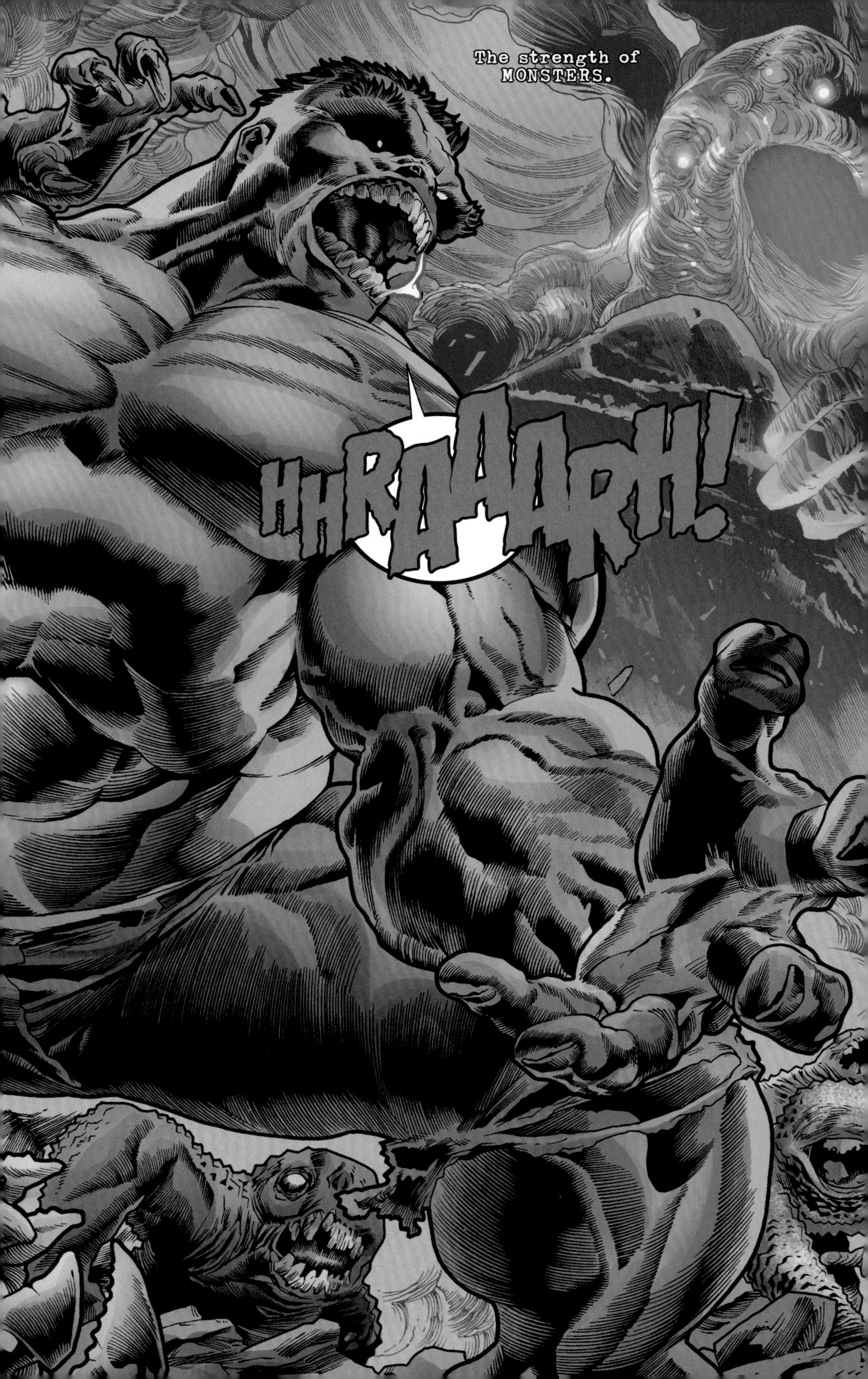
The strength of MONSTERS.
HHRAAAARH!

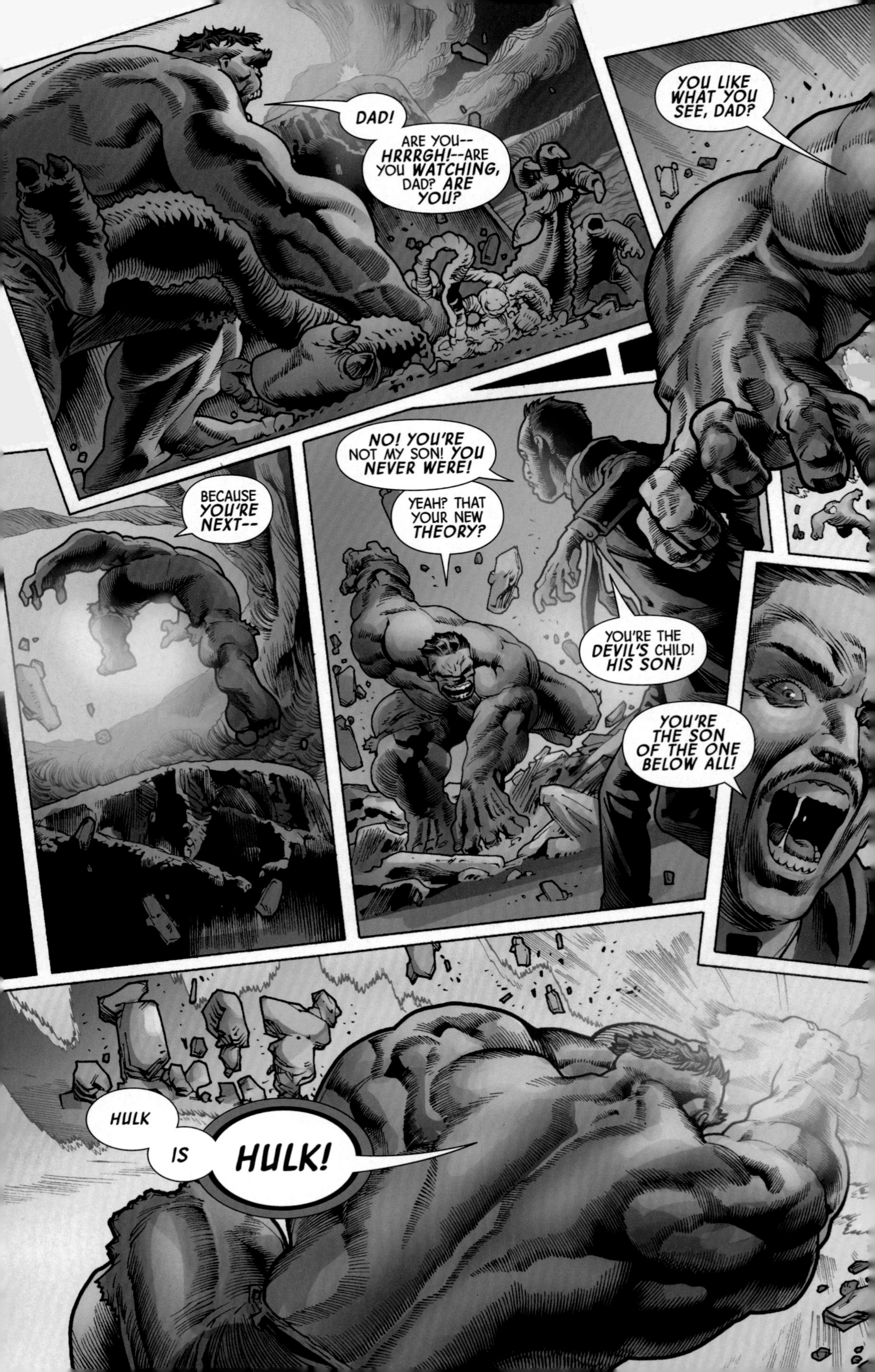
DAD!
ARE YOU-- HRRRGH!--ARE YOU WATCHING, DAD? ARE YOU?
YOU LIKE WHAT YOU SEE, DAD?
BECAUSE YOU'RE NEXT--
NO! YOU'RE NOT MY SON! YOU NEVER WERE!
YEAH? THAT YOUR NEW THEORY?
YOU'RE THE DEVIL'S CHILD! HIS SON!
YOU'RE THE SON OF THE ONE BELOW ALL!
HULK
IS
HULK!

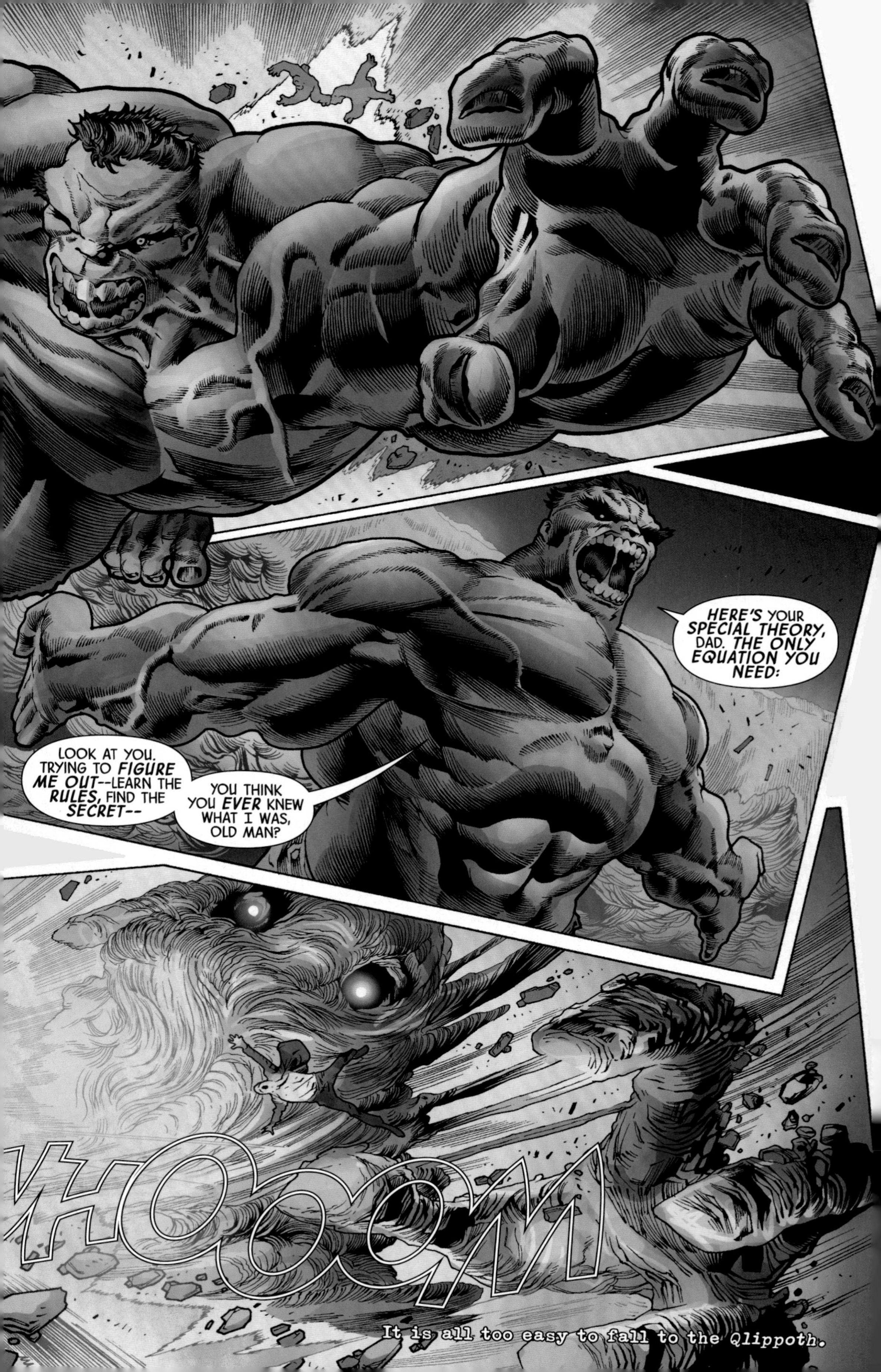
HERE'S YOUR SPECIAL THEORY, DAD. THE ONLY EQUATION YOU NEED:
LOOK AT YOU. TRYING TO FIGURE ME OUT--LEARN THE RULES, FIND THE SECRET--
YOU THINK YOU EVER KNEW WHAT I WAS, OLD MAN?
WHOOOM
It is all too easy to fall to the Qlippoth.

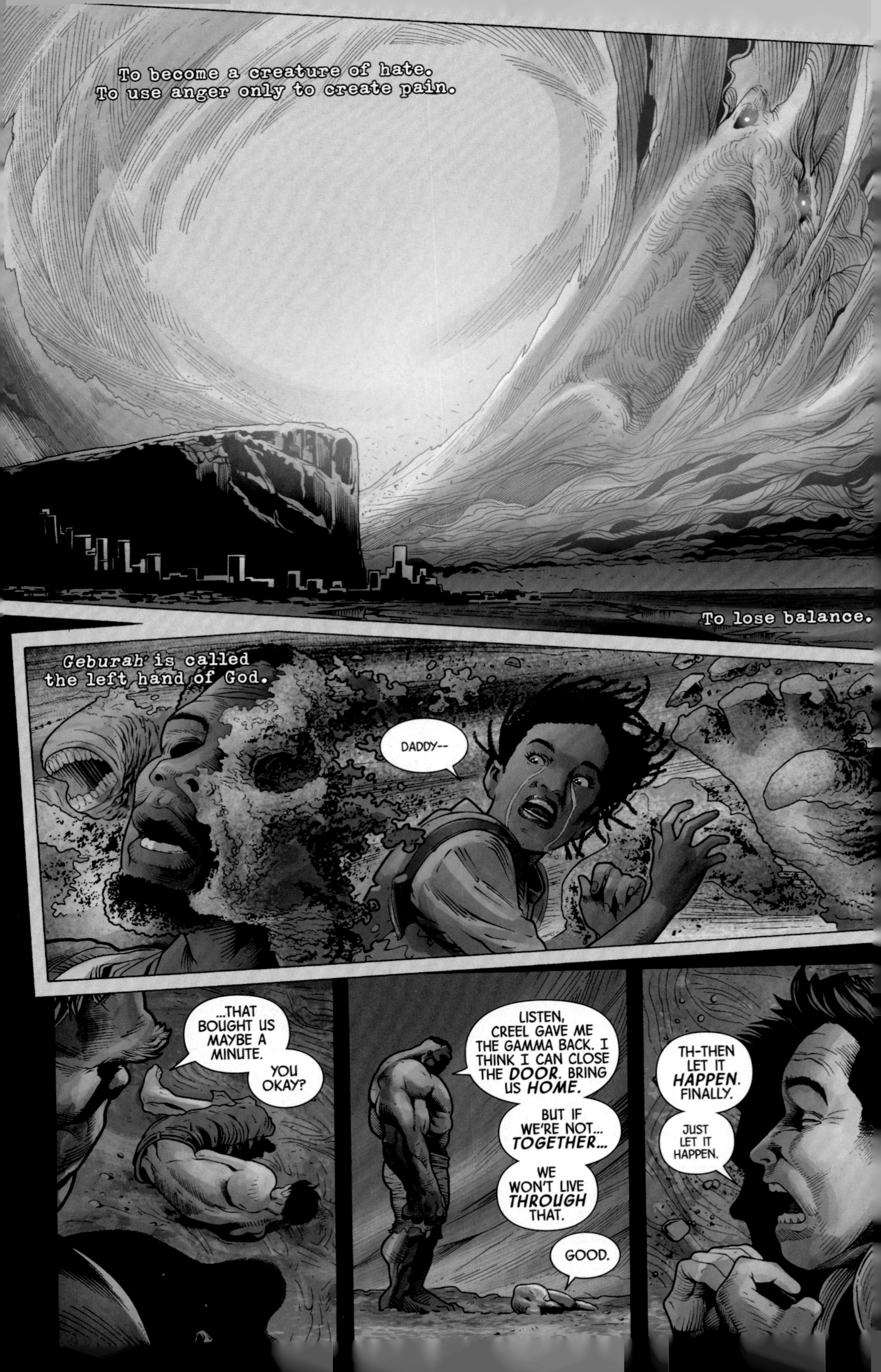
To become a creature of hate.
To use anger only to create pain.
To lose balance.
Geburah is called the left hand of God.
DADDY--
...THAT BOUGHT US MAYBE A MINUTE.
YOU OKAY?
LISTEN, CREEL GAVE ME THE GAMMA BACK. I THINK I CAN CLOSE THE DOOR. BRING US HOME.
BUT IF WE'RE NOT... TOGETHER...
WE WON'T LIVE THROUGH THAT.
GOOD.
TH-THEN LET IT HAPPEN. FINALLY.
JUST LET IT HAPPEN.

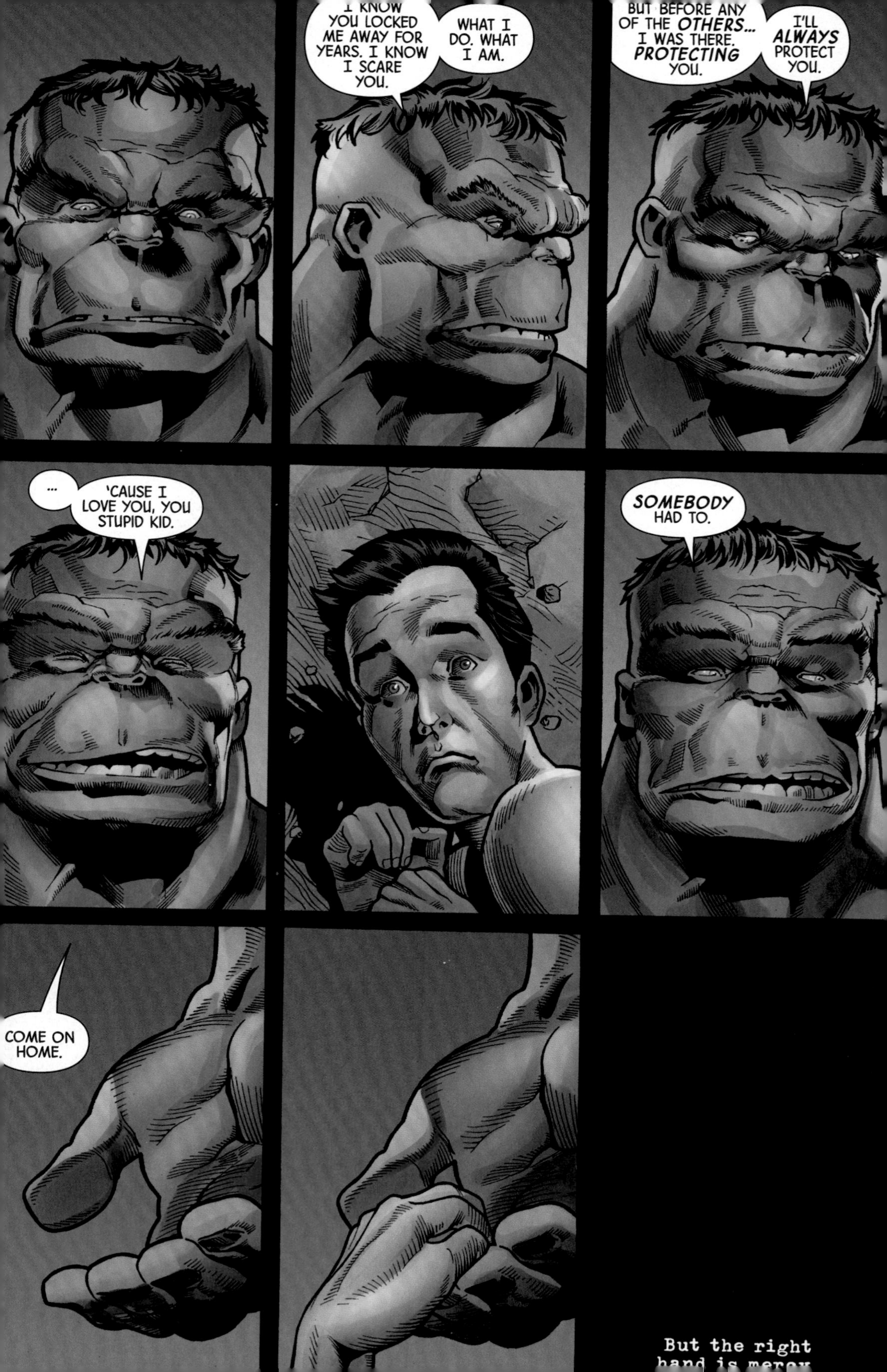

I KNOW YOU LOCKED ME AWAY FOR YEARS. I KNOW I SCARE YOU.
WHAT I DO. WHAT I AM.
BUT BEFORE ANY OF THE OTHERS... I WAS THERE. PROTECTING YOU.
I'LL ALWAYS PROTECT YOU.
...
'CAUSE I LOVE YOU, YOU STUPID KID.
SOMEBODY HAD TO.
COME ON HOME.
But the right hand is

And so I ask again.

What will the Hulk be?

What is the Hulk?

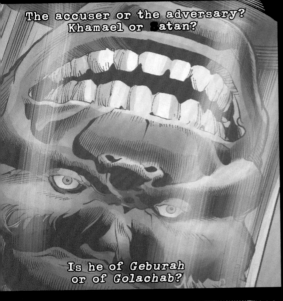

The accuser or the adversary?
Khamael or Satan?

Is he of *Geburah*
or of *Golachab*?

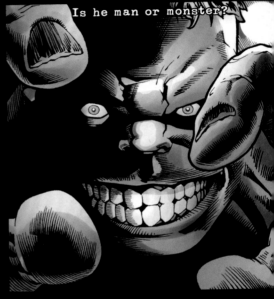

Is he man or monster?

What will you become,
Bruce Banner of Earth?

Who are you?

And who am I?

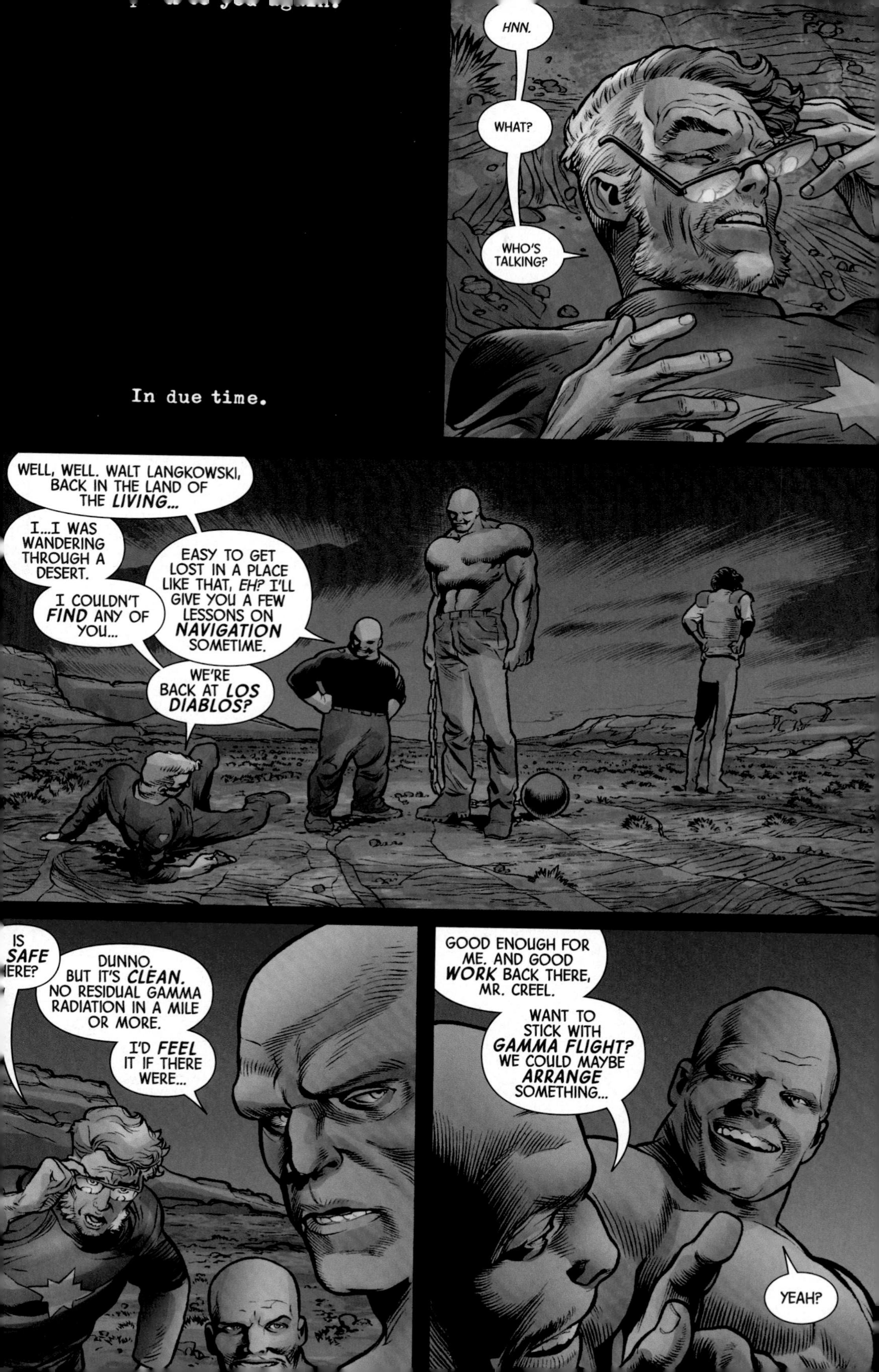

In due time.
HNN.
WHAT?
WHO'S TALKING?
WELL, WELL. WALT LANGKOWSKI, BACK IN THE LAND OF THE LIVING...
I...I WAS WANDERING THROUGH A DESERT.
EASY TO GET LOST IN A PLACE LIKE THAT, EH? I'LL GIVE YOU A FEW LESSONS ON NAVIGATION SOMETIME.
I COULDN'T FIND ANY OF YOU...
WE'RE BACK AT LOS DIABLOS?
IS SAFE ERE?
DUNNO. BUT IT'S CLEAN. NO RESIDUAL GAMMA RADIATION IN A MILE OR MORE.
I'D FEEL IT IF THERE WERE...
GOOD ENOUGH FOR ME. AND GOOD WORK BACK THERE, MR. CREEL.
WANT TO STICK WITH GAMMA FLIGHT? WE COULD MAYBE ARRANGE SOMETHING...
YEAH?

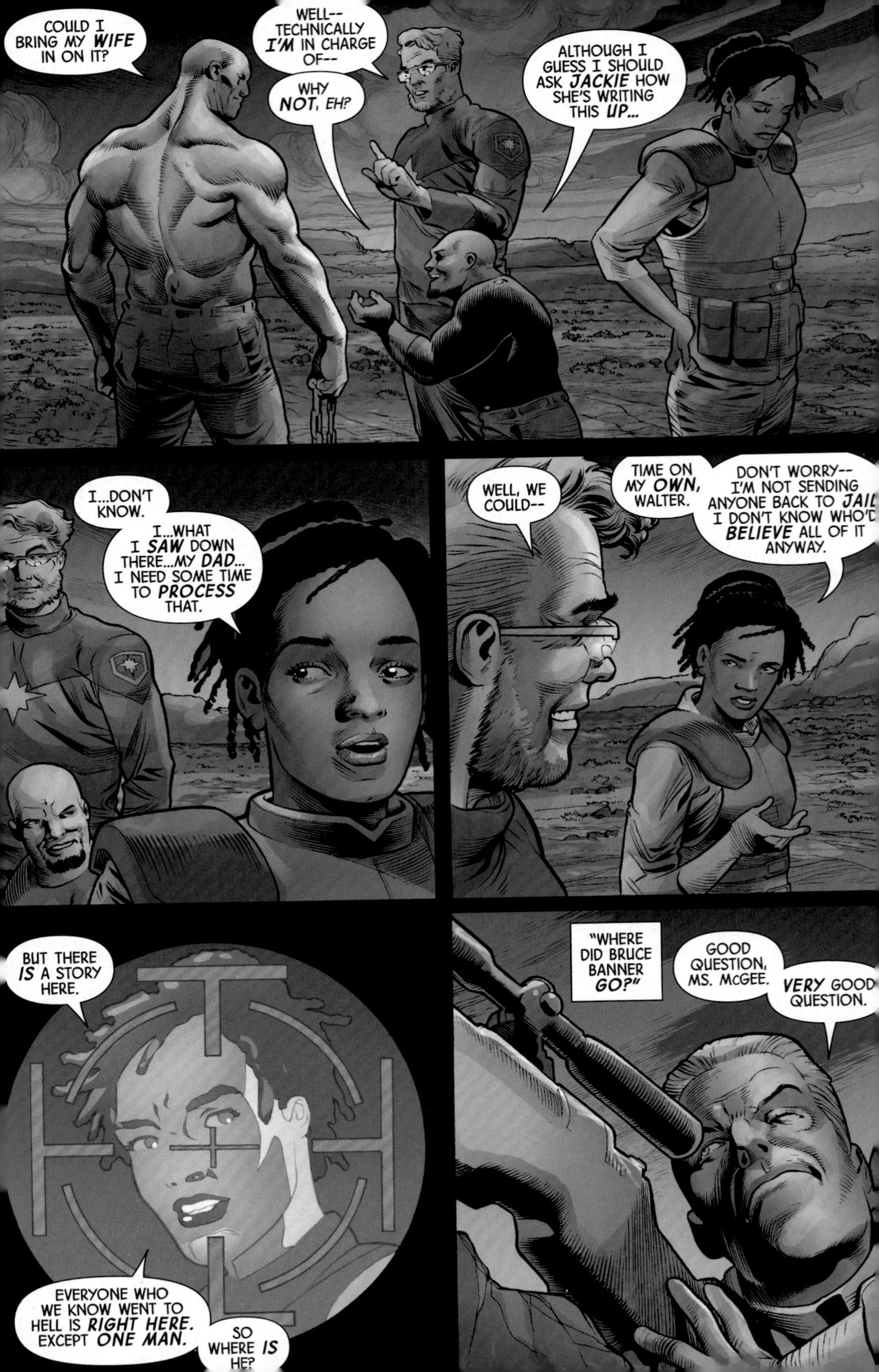
COULD I BRING MY WIFE IN ON IT?
WELL-- TECHNICALLY I'M IN CHARGE OF--
WHY NOT, EH?
ALTHOUGH I GUESS I SHOULD ASK JACKIE HOW SHE'S WRITING THIS UP...
I...DON'T KNOW.
I...WHAT I SAW DOWN THERE...MY DAD... I NEED SOME TIME TO PROCESS THAT.
WELL, WE COULD--
TIME ON MY OWN, WALTER.
DON'T WORRY-- I'M NOT SENDING ANYONE BACK TO JAIL I DON'T KNOW WHO'D BELIEVE ALL OF IT ANYWAY.
BUT THERE IS A STORY HERE.
EVERYONE WHO WE KNOW WENT TO HELL IS RIGHT HERE. EXCEPT ONE MAN.
SO WHERE IS HE?
"WHERE DID BRUCE BANNER GO?"
GOOD QUESTION, MS. McGEE.
VERY GOOD QUESTION.

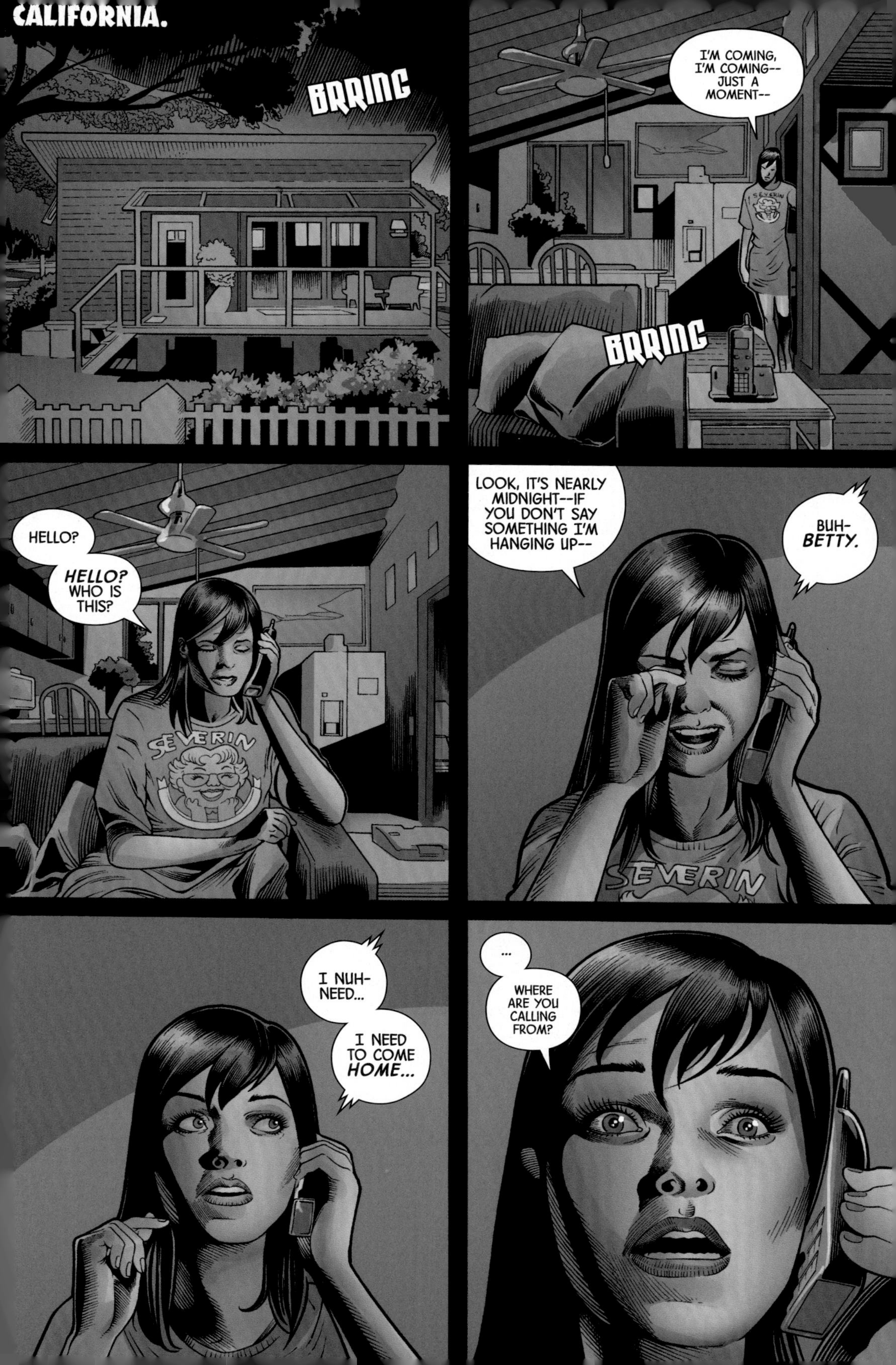
CALIFORNIA.
BRRING
I'M COMING, I'M COMING-- JUST A MOMENT--
BRRING
HELLO?
HELLO? WHO IS THIS?
SEVERIN
LOOK, IT'S NEARLY MIDNIGHT--IF YOU DON'T SAY SOMETHING I'M HANGING UP--
BUH-BETTY.
SEVERIN
I NUH-NEED...
I NEED TO COME HOME...
...
WHERE ARE YOU CALLING FROM?

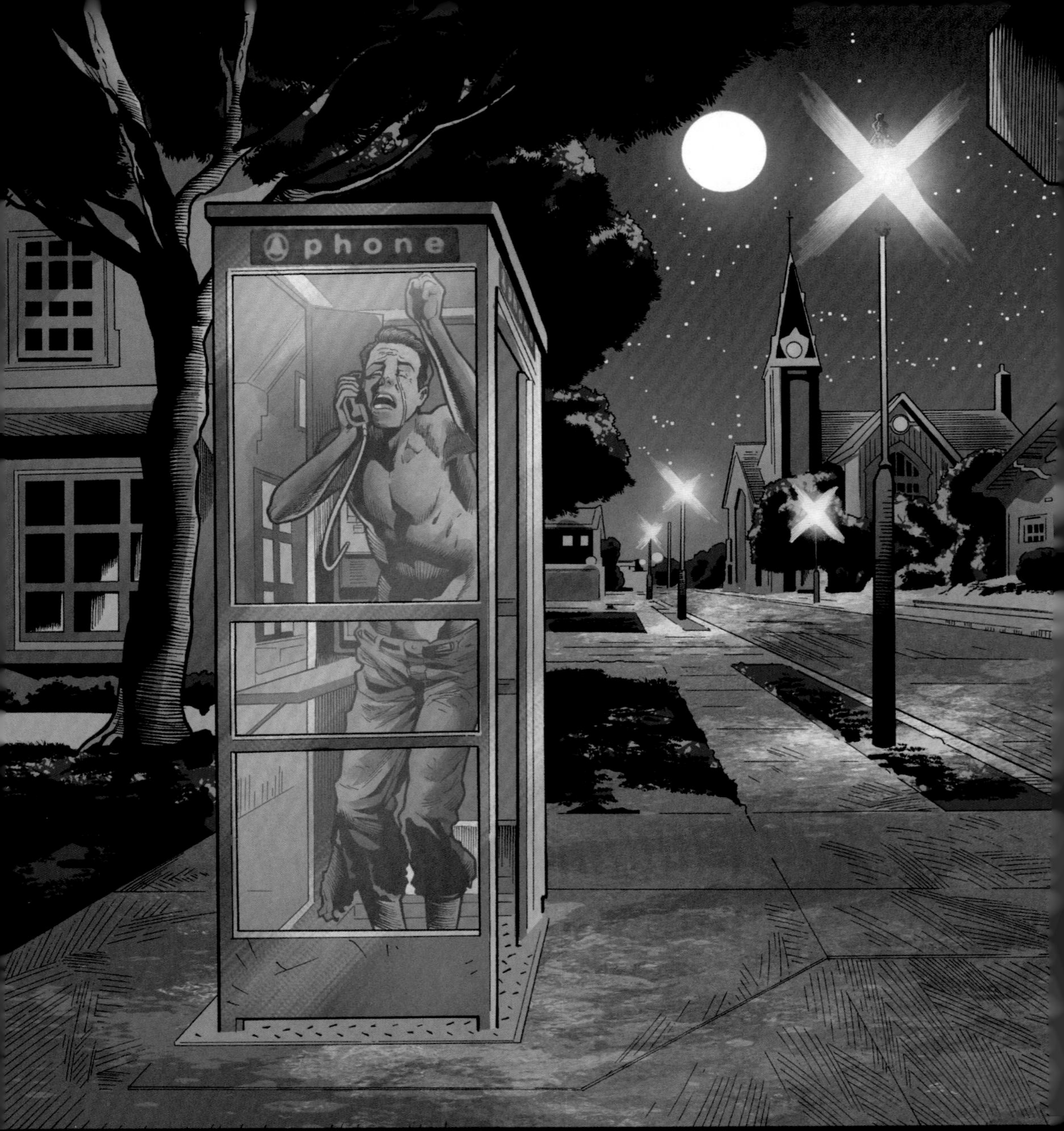
phone

A BOOTH IN THE MIDWEST

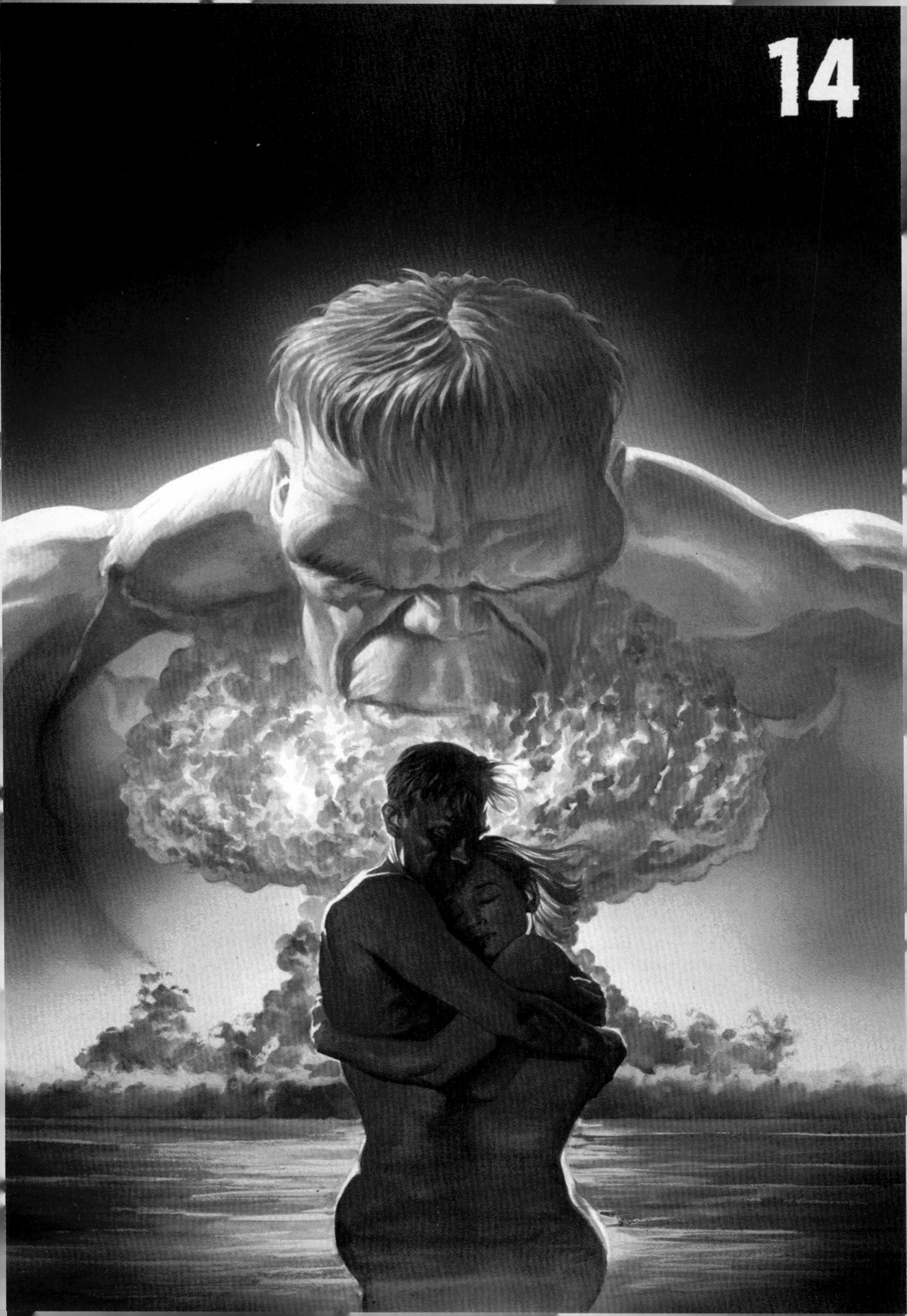
14

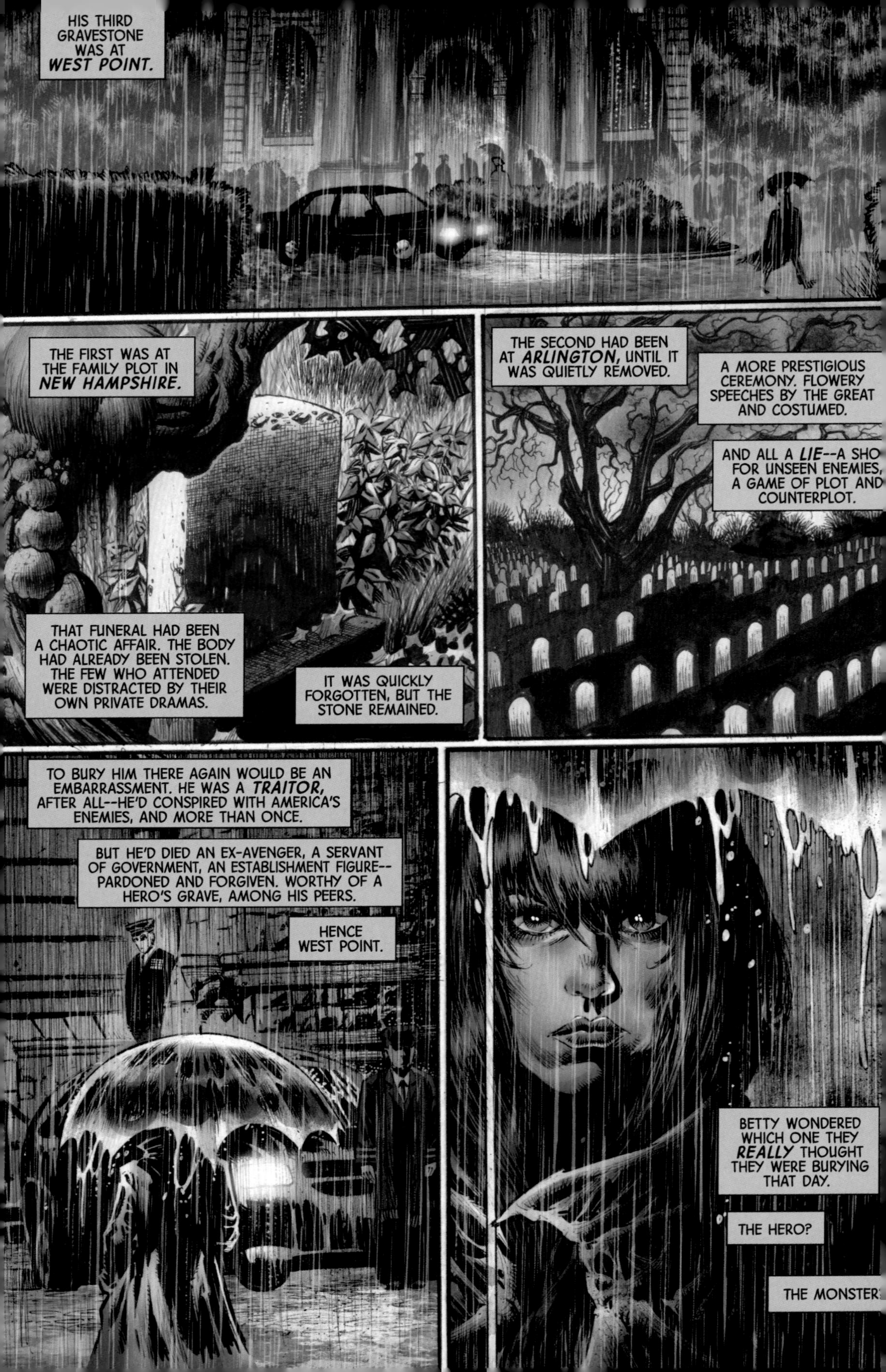
HIS THIRD GRAVESTONE WAS AT WEST POINT.
THE FIRST WAS AT THE FAMILY PLOT IN NEW HAMPSHIRE.
THAT FUNERAL HAD BEEN A CHAOTIC AFFAIR. THE BODY HAD ALREADY BEEN STOLEN. THE FEW WHO ATTENDED WERE DISTRACTED BY THEIR OWN PRIVATE DRAMAS.
IT WAS QUICKLY FORGOTTEN, BUT THE STONE REMAINED.
THE SECOND HAD BEEN AT ARLINGTON, UNTIL IT WAS QUIETLY REMOVED.
A MORE PRESTIGIOUS CEREMONY. FLOWERY SPEECHES BY THE GREAT AND COSTUMED.
AND ALL A LIE--A SHO FOR UNSEEN ENEMIES, A GAME OF PLOT AND COUNTERPLOT.
TO BURY HIM THERE AGAIN WOULD BE AN EMBARRASSMENT. HE WAS A TRAITOR, AFTER ALL--HE'D CONSPIRED WITH AMERICA'S ENEMIES, AND MORE THAN ONCE.
BUT HE'D DIED AN EX-AVENGER, A SERVANT OF GOVERNMENT, AN ESTABLISHMENT FIGURE--PARDONED AND FORGIVEN. WORTHY OF A HERO'S GRAVE, AMONG HIS PEERS.
HENCE WEST POINT.
BETTY WONDERED WHICH ONE THEY REALLY THOUGHT THEY WERE BURYING THAT DAY.
THE HERO?
THE MONSTER

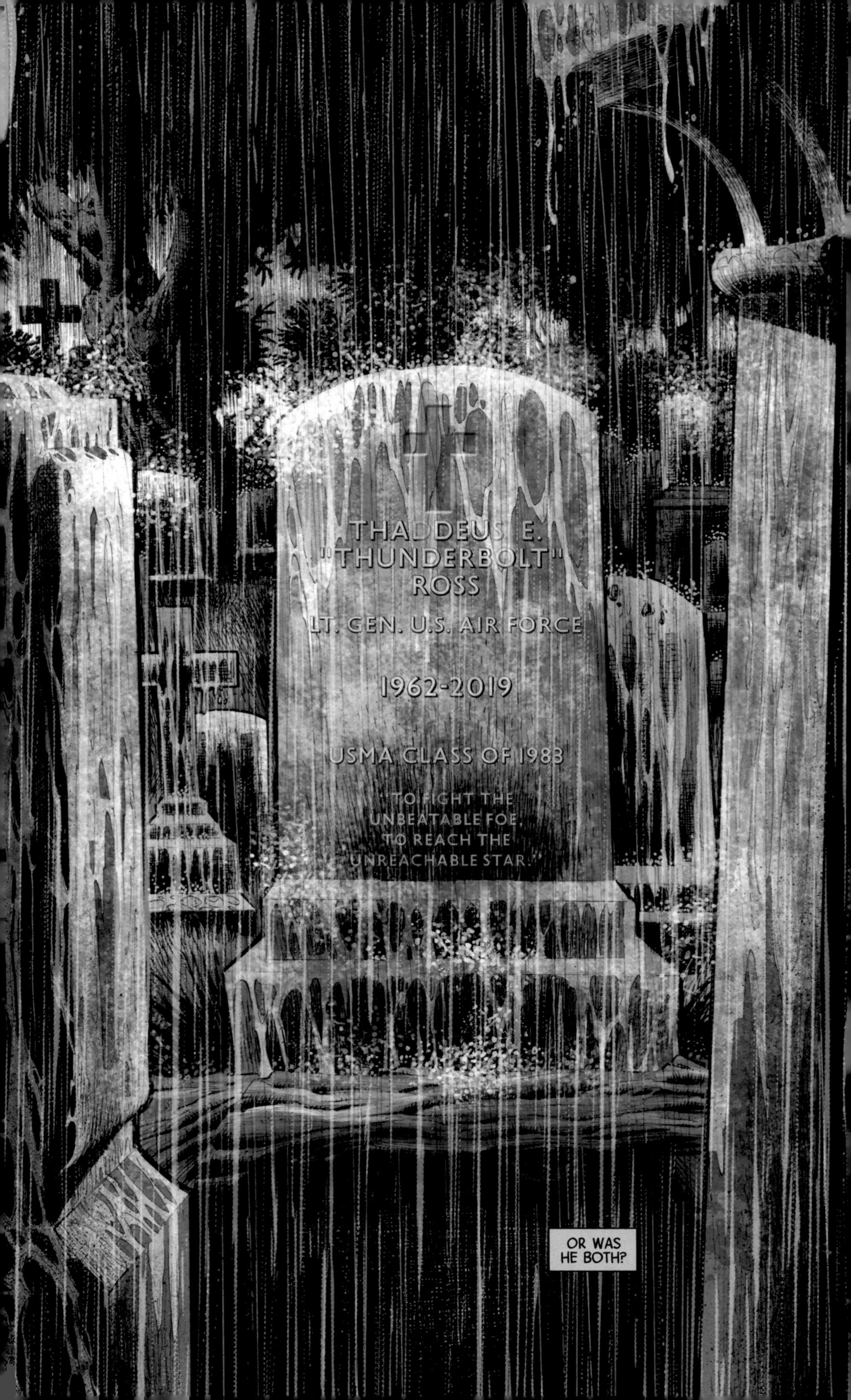
THADDEUS E.
"THUNDERBOLT"
ROSS
LT. GEN. U.S. AIR FORCE
1962-2019
USMA CLASS OF 1983
"TO FIGHT THE
UNBEATABLE FOE.
TO REACH THE
UNREACHABLE STAR."
OR WAS
HE BOTH?

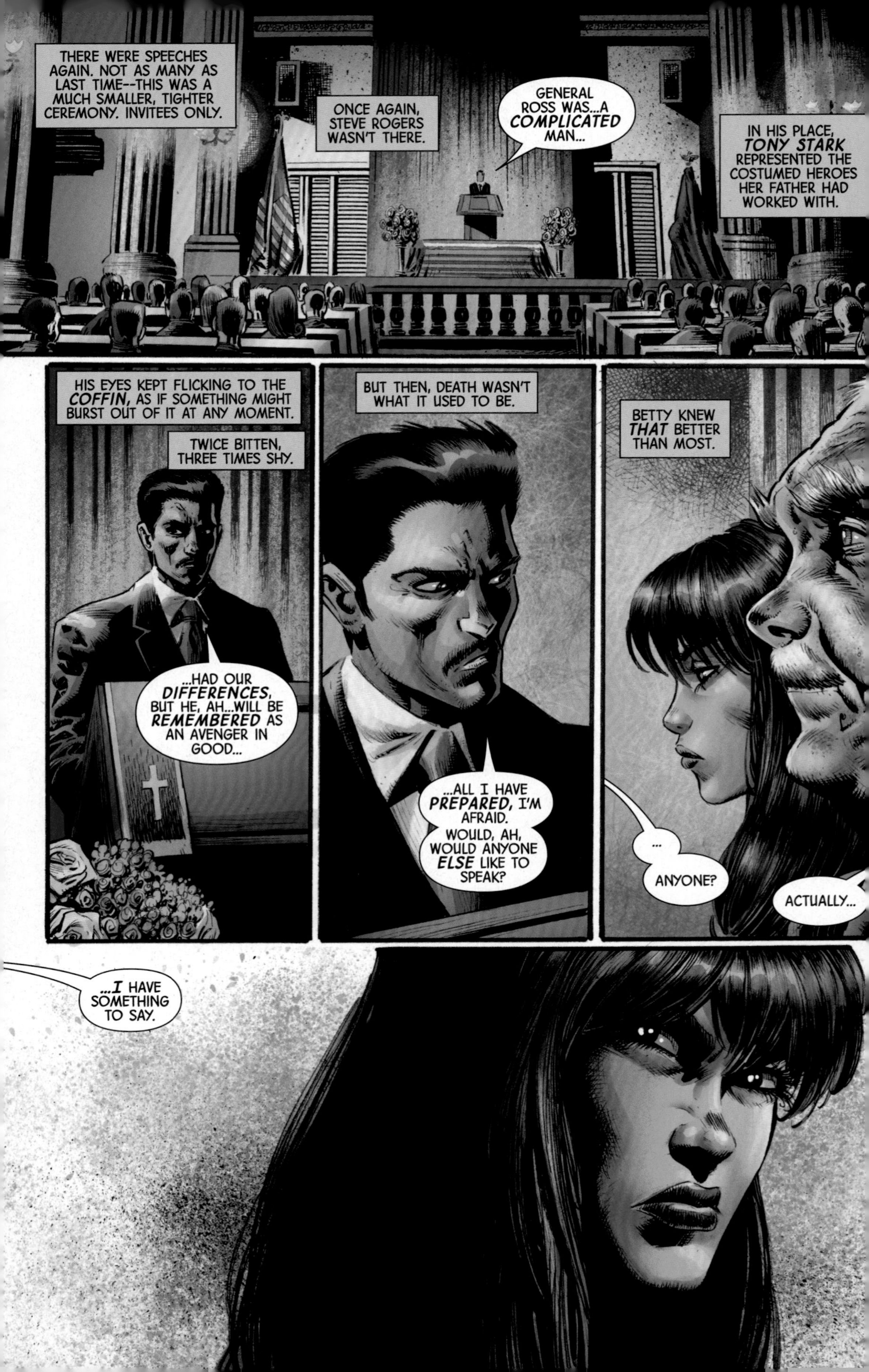

THERE WERE SPEECHES AGAIN. NOT AS MANY AS LAST TIME--THIS WAS A MUCH SMALLER, TIGHTER CEREMONY. INVITEES ONLY.
ONCE AGAIN, STEVE ROGERS WASN'T THERE.
GENERAL ROSS WAS...A COMPLICATED MAN...
IN HIS PLACE, TONY STARK REPRESENTED THE COSTUMED HEROES HER FATHER HAD WORKED WITH.
HIS EYES KEPT FLICKING TO THE COFFIN, AS IF SOMETHING MIGHT BURST OUT OF IT AT ANY MOMENT.
TWICE BITTEN, THREE TIMES SHY.
...HAD OUR DIFFERENCES, BUT HE, AH...WILL BE REMEMBERED AS AN AVENGER IN GOOD...
BUT THEN, DEATH WASN'T WHAT IT USED TO BE.
...ALL I HAVE PREPARED, I'M AFRAID. WOULD, AH, WOULD ANYONE ELSE LIKE TO SPEAK?
BETTY KNEW THAT BETTER THAN MOST.
...
ANYONE?
ACTUALLY...
...I HAVE SOMETHING TO SAY.

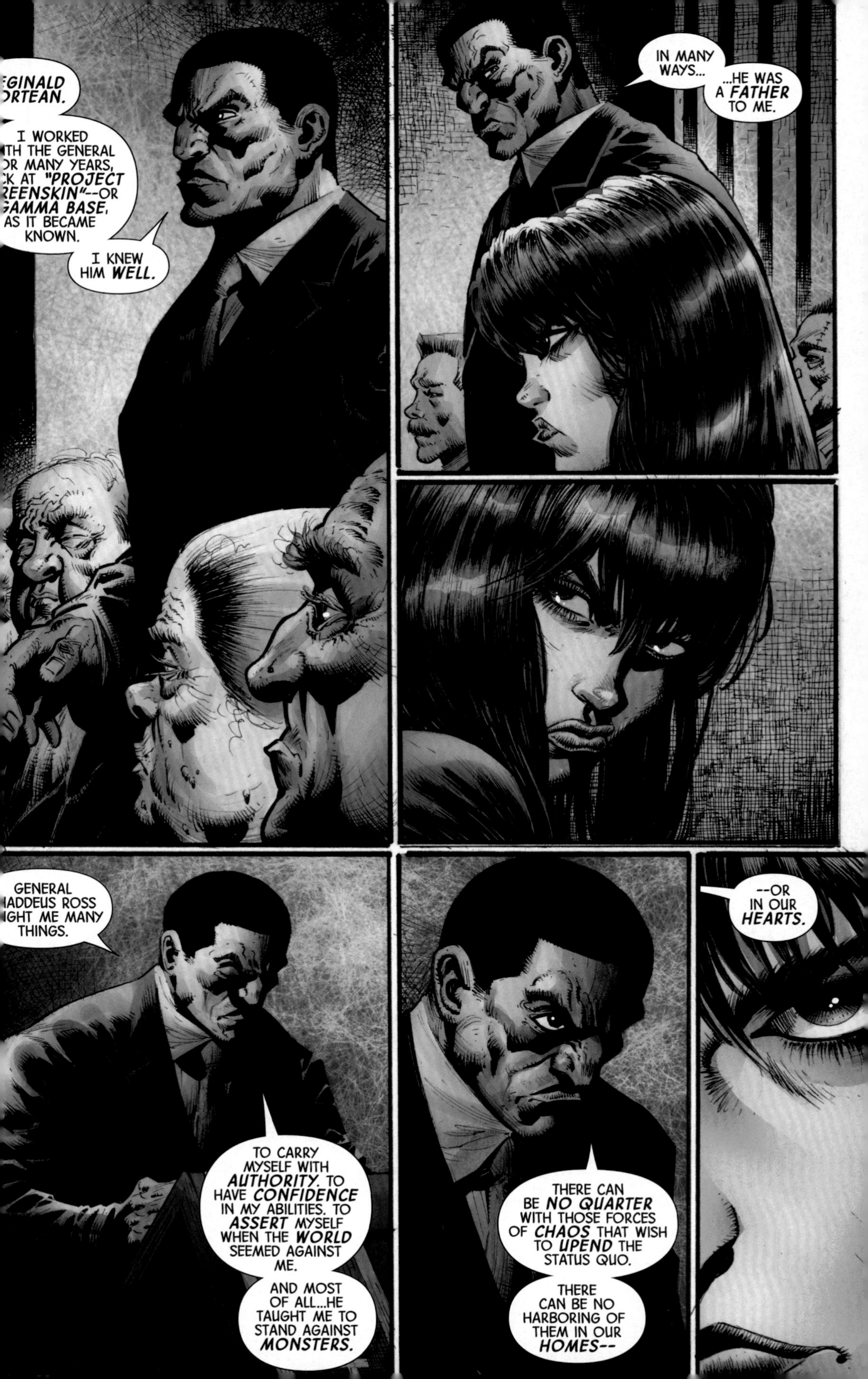
EGINALD ORTEAN.
I WORKED ITH THE GENERAL OR MANY YEARS, CK AT "PROJECT REENSKIN"--OR GAMMA BASE, AS IT BECAME KNOWN.
I KNEW HIM WELL.
IN MANY WAYS...
...HE WAS A FATHER TO ME.
GENERAL ADDEUS ROSS IGHT ME MANY THINGS.
TO CARRY MYSELF WITH AUTHORITY. TO HAVE CONFIDENCE IN MY ABILITIES. TO ASSERT MYSELF WHEN THE WORLD SEEMED AGAINST ME.
AND MOST OF ALL...HE TAUGHT ME TO STAND AGAINST MONSTERS.
THERE CAN BE NO QUARTER WITH THOSE FORCES OF CHAOS THAT WISH TO UPEND THE STATUS QUO.
THERE CAN BE NO HARBORING OF THEM IN OUR HOMES--
--OR IN OUR HEARTS.

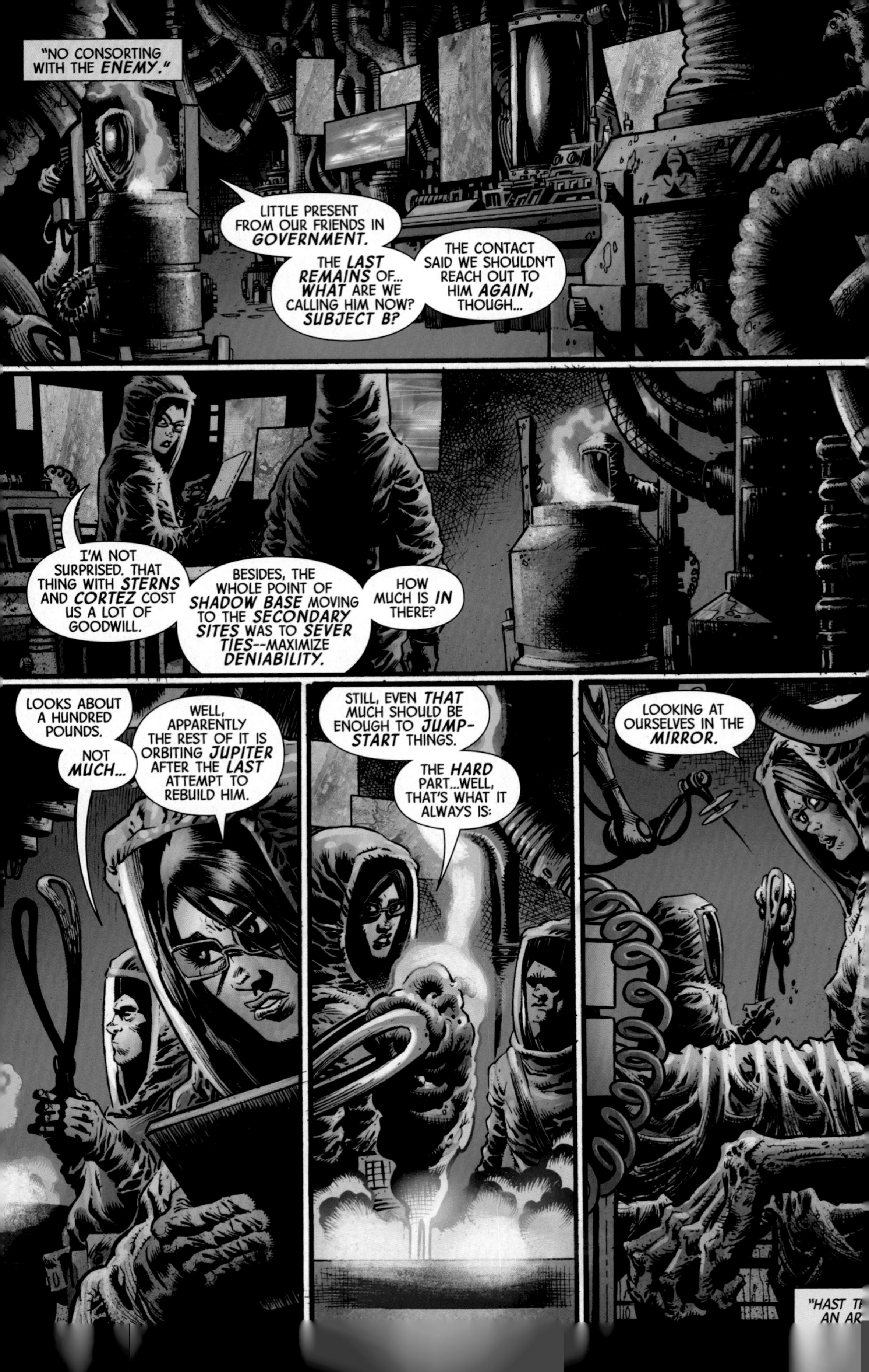
"NO CONSORTING WITH THE ENEMY."
LITTLE PRESENT FROM OUR FRIENDS IN GOVERNMENT.
THE LAST REMAINS OF... WHAT ARE WE CALLING HIM NOW? SUBJECT B?
THE CONTACT SAID WE SHOULDN'T REACH OUT TO HIM AGAIN, THOUGH...
I'M NOT SURPRISED. THAT THING WITH STERNS AND CORTEZ COST US A LOT OF GOODWILL.
BESIDES, THE WHOLE POINT OF SHADOW BASE MOVING TO THE SECONDARY SITES WAS TO SEVER TIES--MAXIMIZE DENIABILITY.
HOW MUCH IS IN THERE?
LOOKS ABOUT A HUNDRED POUNDS.
NOT MUCH...
WELL, APPARENTLY THE REST OF IT IS ORBITING JUPITER AFTER THE LAST ATTEMPT TO REBUILD HIM.
STILL, EVEN THAT MUCH SHOULD BE ENOUGH TO JUMP-START THINGS.
THE HARD PART...WELL, THAT'S WHAT IT ALWAYS IS:
LOOKING AT OURSELVES IN THE MIRROR.

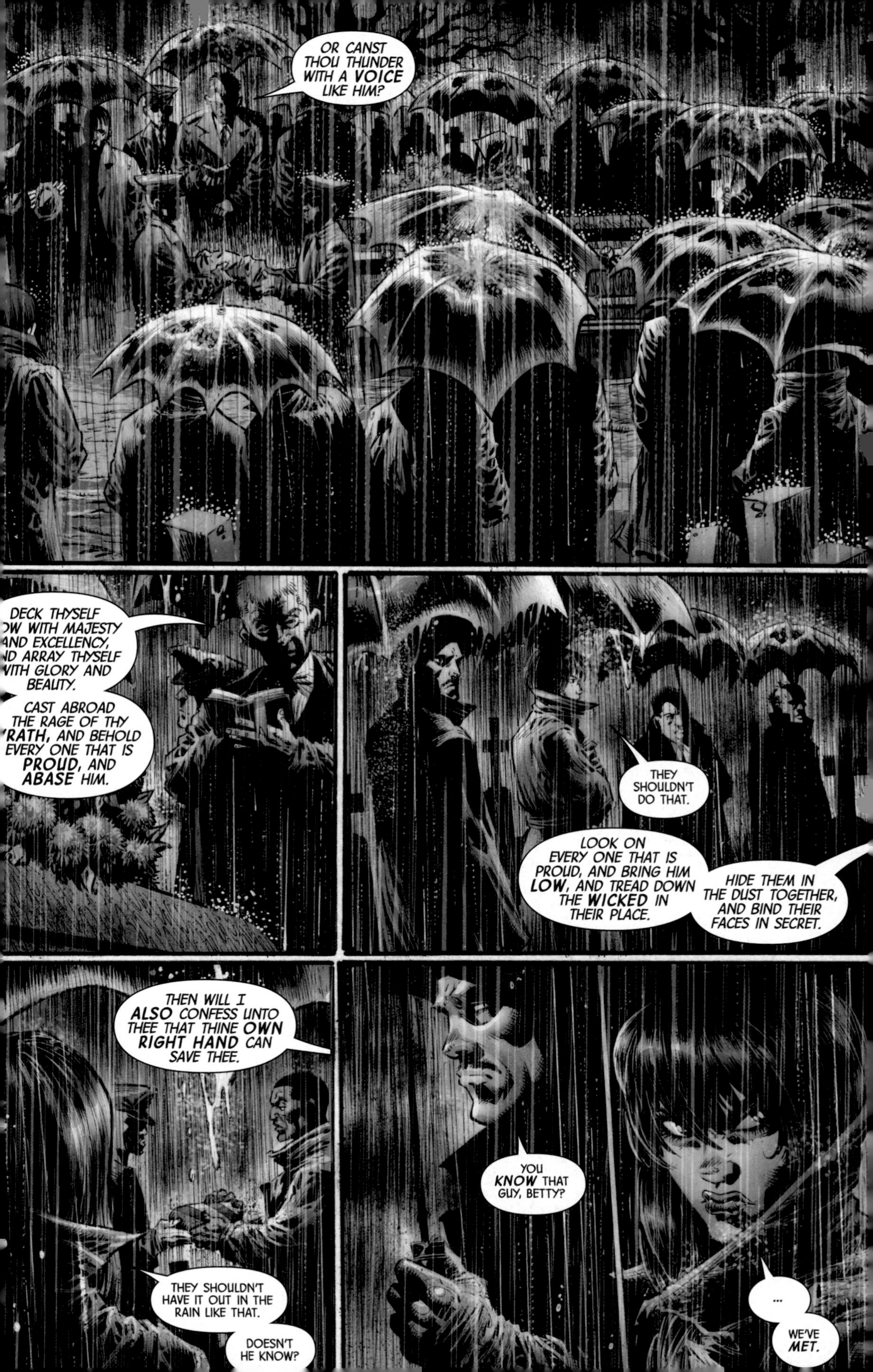

OR CANST THOU THUNDER WITH A VOICE LIKE HIM?
DECK THYSELF OW WITH MAJESTY AND EXCELLENCY, ND ARRAY THYSELF VITH GLORY AND BEAUTY.
CAST ABROAD THE RAGE OF THY RATH, AND BEHOLD EVERY ONE THAT IS PROUD, AND ABASE HIM.
THEY SHOULDN'T DO THAT.
LOOK ON EVERY ONE THAT IS PROUD, AND BRING HIM LOW, AND TREAD DOWN THE WICKED IN THEIR PLACE.
HIDE THEM IN THE DUST TOGETHER, AND BIND THEIR FACES IN SECRET.
THEN WILL I ALSO CONFESS UNTO THEE THAT THINE OWN RIGHT HAND CAN SAVE THEE.
THEY SHOULDN'T HAVE IT OUT IN THE RAIN LIKE THAT.
DOESN'T HE KNOW?
YOU KNOW THAT GUY, BETTY?
...
WE'VE MET.

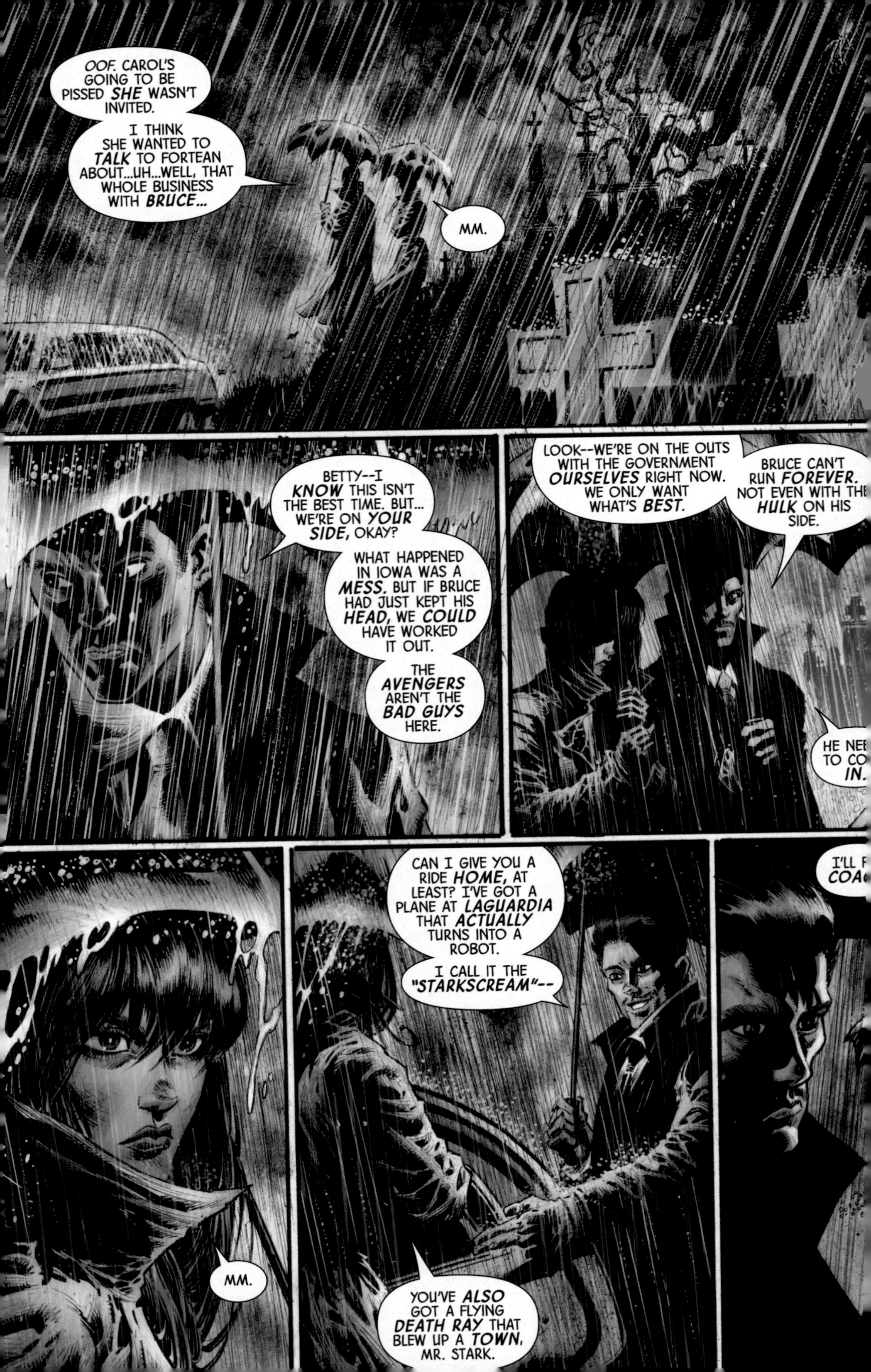
OOF. CAROL'S GOING TO BE PISSED SHE WASN'T INVITED.
I THINK SHE WANTED TO TALK TO FORTEAN ABOUT...UH...WELL, THAT WHOLE BUSINESS WITH BRUCE...
MM.
BETTY--I KNOW THIS ISN'T THE BEST TIME. BUT... WE'RE ON YOUR SIDE, OKAY?
WHAT HAPPENED IN IOWA WAS A MESS. BUT IF BRUCE HAD JUST KEPT HIS HEAD, WE COULD HAVE WORKED IT OUT.
THE AVENGERS AREN'T THE BAD GUYS HERE.
LOOK--WE'RE ON THE OUTS WITH THE GOVERNMENT OURSELVES RIGHT NOW. WE ONLY WANT WHAT'S BEST.
BRUCE CAN'T RUN FOREVER. NOT EVEN WITH THE HULK ON HIS SIDE.
MM.
CAN I GIVE YOU A RIDE HOME, AT LEAST? I'VE GOT A PLANE AT LAGUARDIA THAT ACTUALLY TURNS INTO A ROBOT.
I CALL IT THE "STARKSCREAM"--
YOU'VE ALSO GOT A FLYING DEATH RAY THAT BLEW UP A TOWN, MR. STARK.

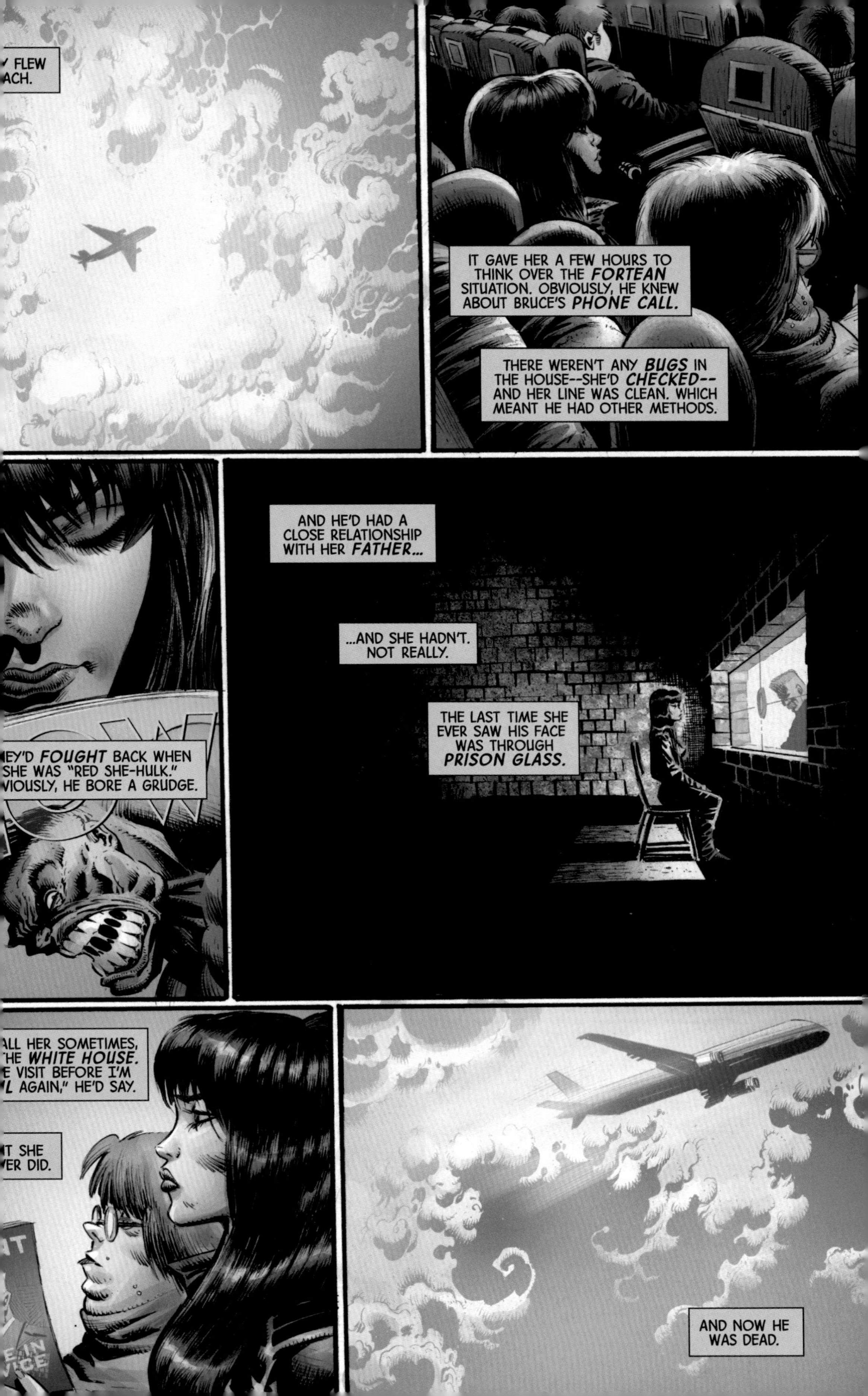

Y FLEW
ACH.
IT GAVE HER A FEW HOURS TO THINK OVER THE FORTEAN SITUATION. OBVIOUSLY, HE KNEW ABOUT BRUCE'S PHONE CALL.
THERE WEREN'T ANY BUGS IN THE HOUSE--SHE'D CHECKED--AND HER LINE WAS CLEAN. WHICH MEANT HE HAD OTHER METHODS.
EY'D FOUGHT BACK WHEN SHE WAS "RED SHE-HULK." VIOUSLY, HE BORE A GRUDGE.
AND HE'D HAD A CLOSE RELATIONSHIP WITH HER FATHER...
...AND SHE HADN'T. NOT REALLY.
THE LAST TIME SHE EVER SAW HIS FACE WAS THROUGH PRISON GLASS.
ALL HER SOMETIMES, HE WHITE HOUSE. E VISIT BEFORE I'M L AGAIN," HE'D SAY.
T SHE ER DID.
AND NOW HE WAS DEAD.

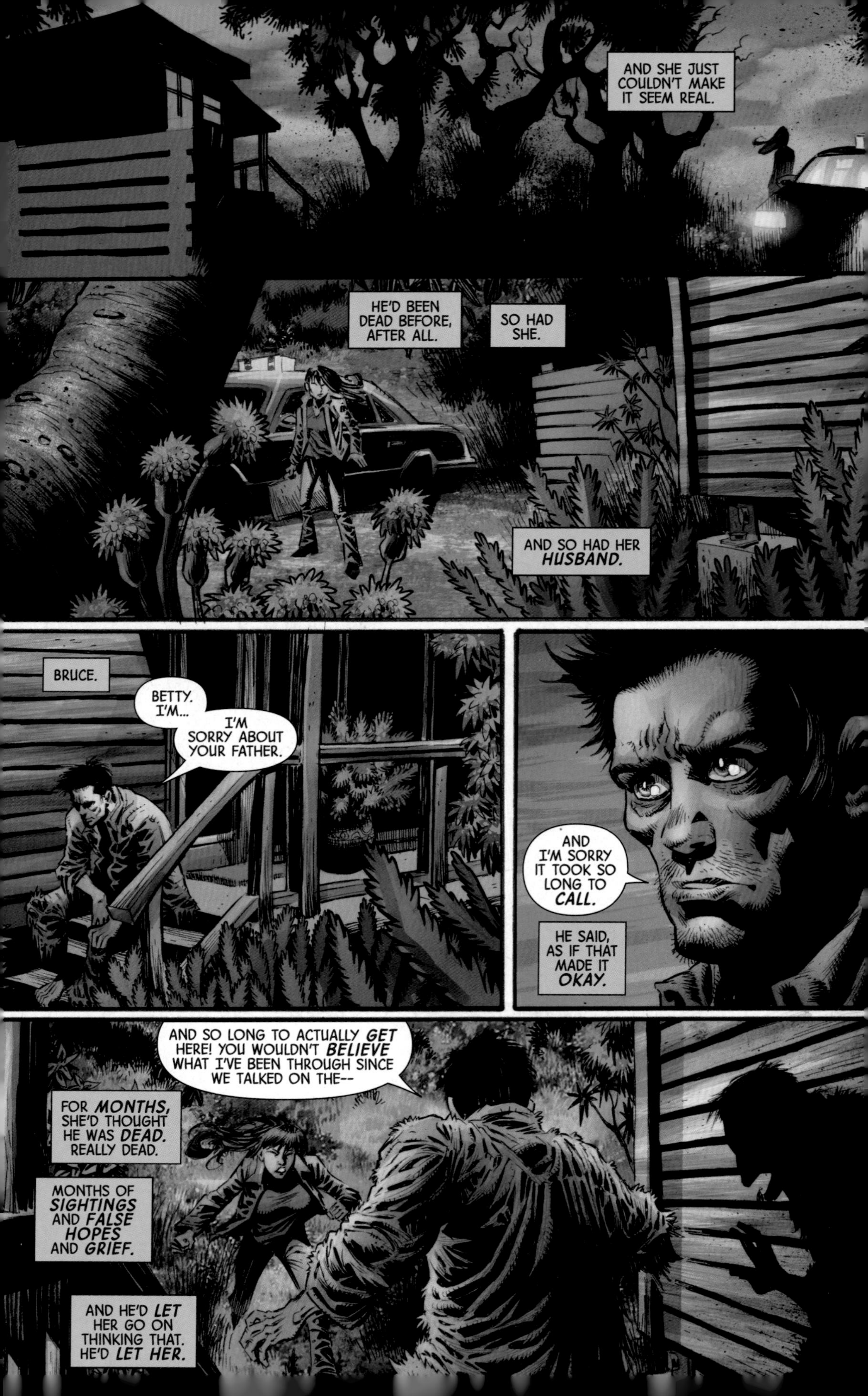
AND SHE JUST COULDN'T MAKE IT SEEM REAL.
HE'D BEEN DEAD BEFORE, AFTER ALL.
SO HAD SHE.
AND SO HAD HER *HUSBAND.*
BRUCE.
BETTY. I'M...
I'M SORRY ABOUT YOUR FATHER.
AND I'M SORRY IT TOOK SO LONG TO *CALL.*
HE SAID, AS IF THAT MADE IT *OKAY.*
AND SO LONG TO ACTUALLY *GET* HERE! YOU WOULDN'T *BELIEVE* WHAT I'VE BEEN THROUGH SINCE WE TALKED ON THE--
FOR *MONTHS,* SHE'D THOUGHT HE WAS *DEAD.* REALLY DEAD.
MONTHS OF *SIGHTINGS* AND *FALSE HOPES* AND *GRIEF.*
AND HE'D *LET* HER GO ON THINKING THAT. HE'D *LET HER.*

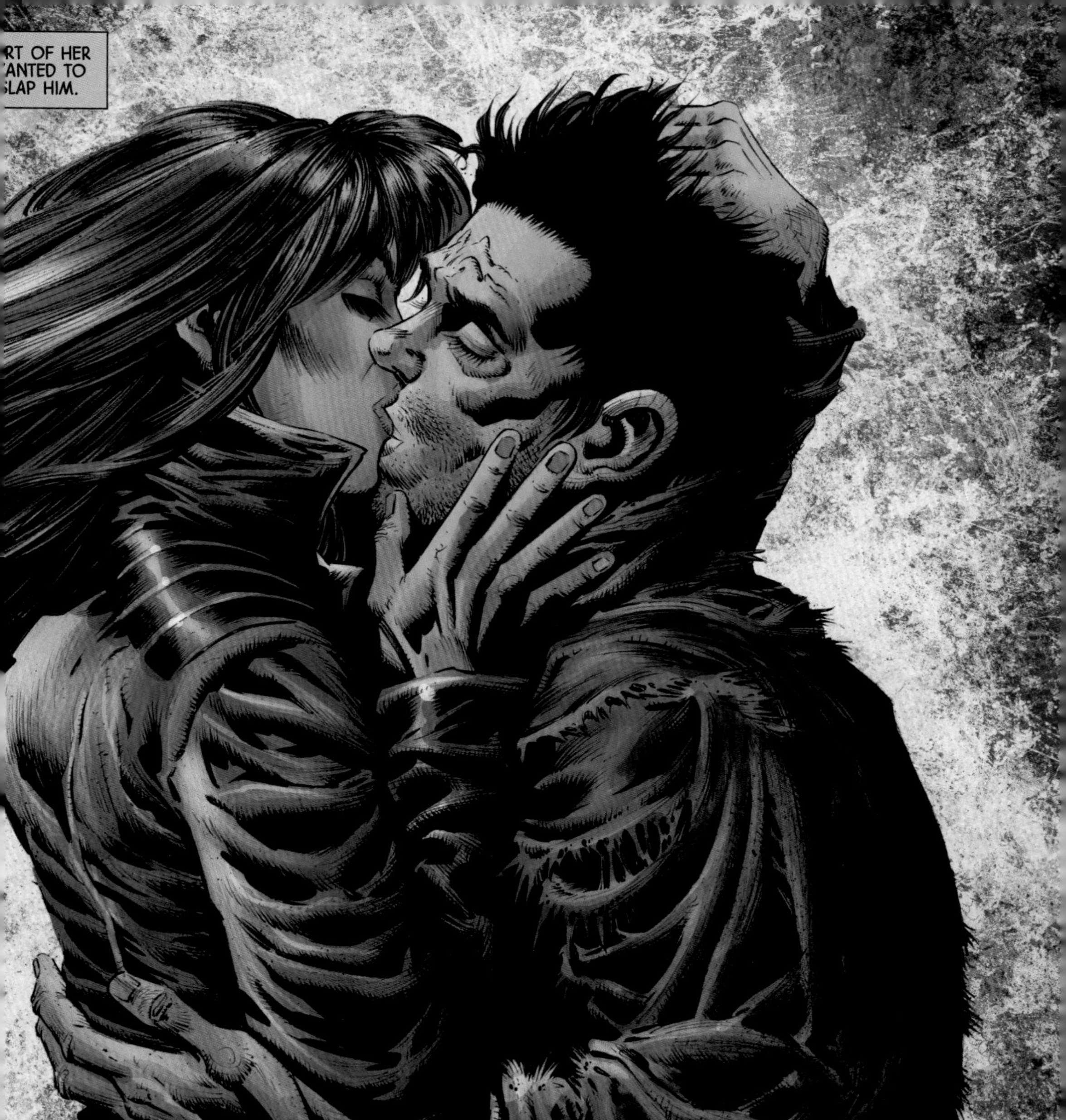
RT OF HER
ANTED TO
SLAP HIM.

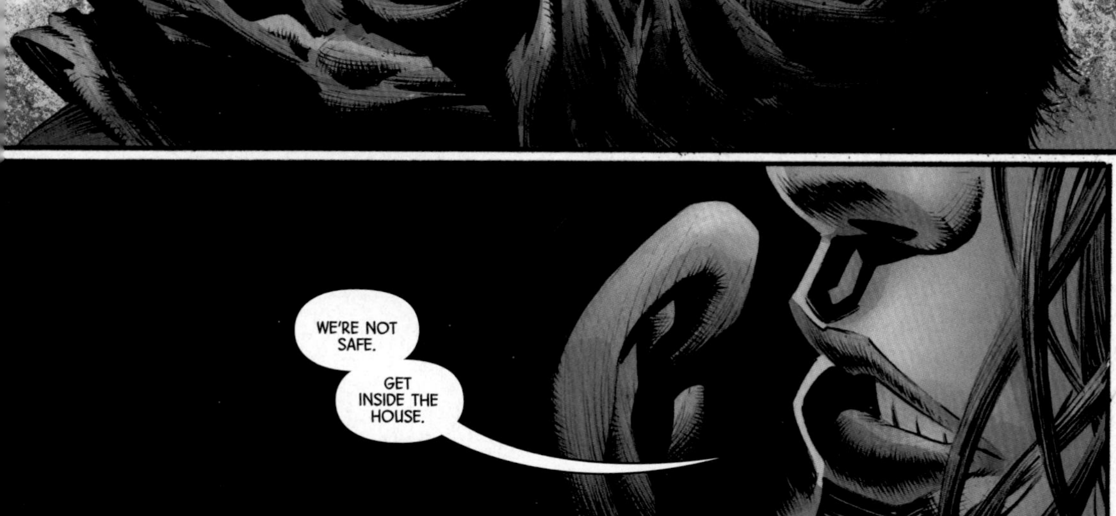
WE'RE NOT SAFE.
GET INSIDE THE HOUSE.

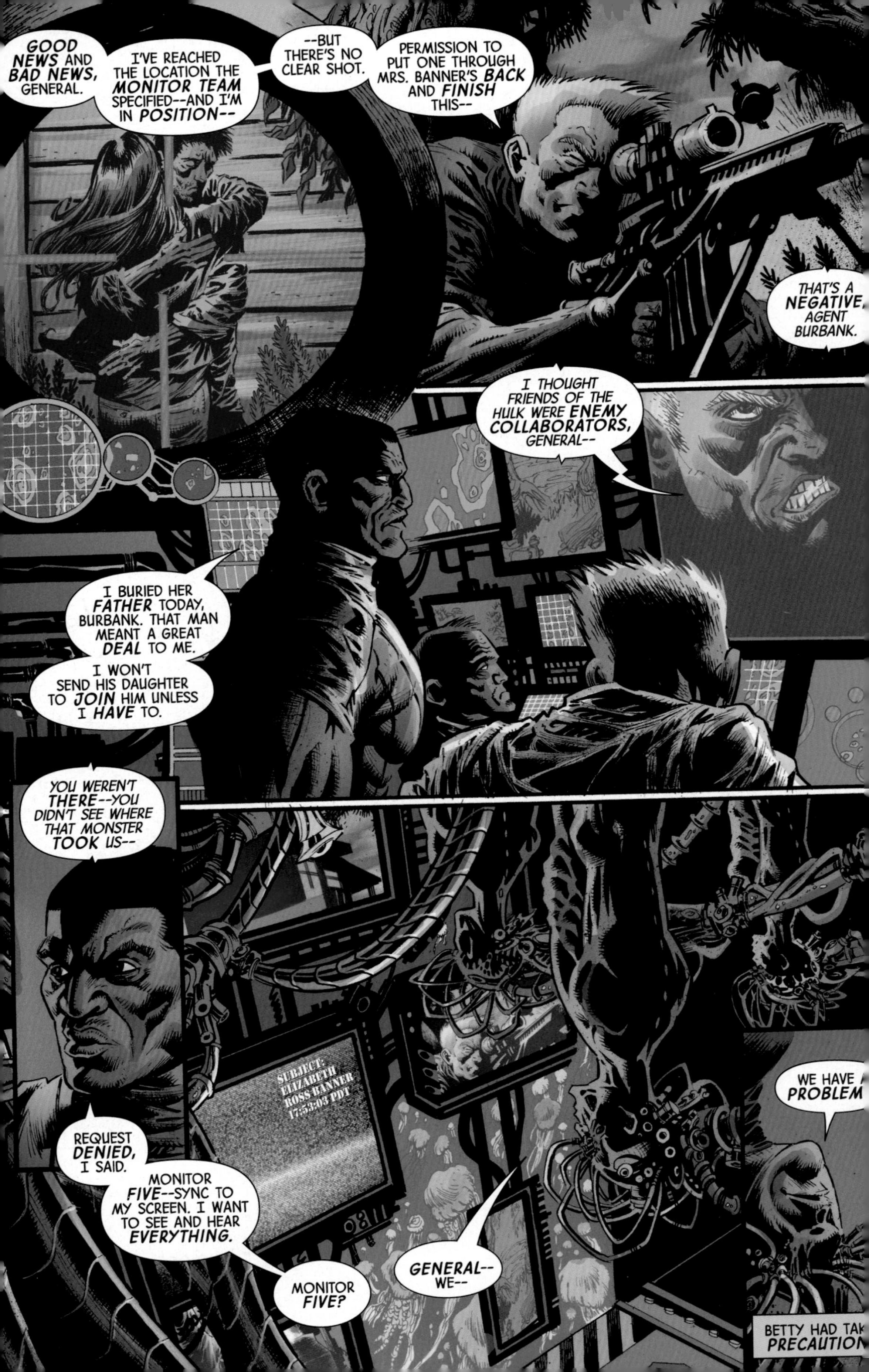
GOOD NEWS AND BAD NEWS, GENERAL.
I'VE REACHED THE LOCATION THE MONITOR TEAM SPECIFIED--AND I'M IN POSITION--
--BUT THERE'S NO CLEAR SHOT.
PERMISSION TO PUT ONE THROUGH MRS. BANNER'S BACK AND FINISH THIS--
THAT'S A NEGATIVE, AGENT BURBANK.
I THOUGHT FRIENDS OF THE HULK WERE ENEMY COLLABORATORS, GENERAL--
I BURIED HER FATHER TODAY, BURBANK. THAT MAN MEANT A GREAT DEAL TO ME.
I WON'T SEND HIS DAUGHTER TO JOIN HIM UNLESS I HAVE TO.
YOU WEREN'T THERE--YOU DIDN'T SEE WHERE THAT MONSTER TOOK US--
SUBJECT: ELIZABETH ROSS-BANNER 17:53:03 PDT
REQUEST DENIED, I SAID.
MONITOR FIVE--SYNC TO MY SCREEN. I WANT TO SEE AND HEAR EVERYTHING.
MONITOR FIVE?
GENERAL-- WE--
WE HAVE
PROBLEM
BETTY HAD TAK
PRECAUTION

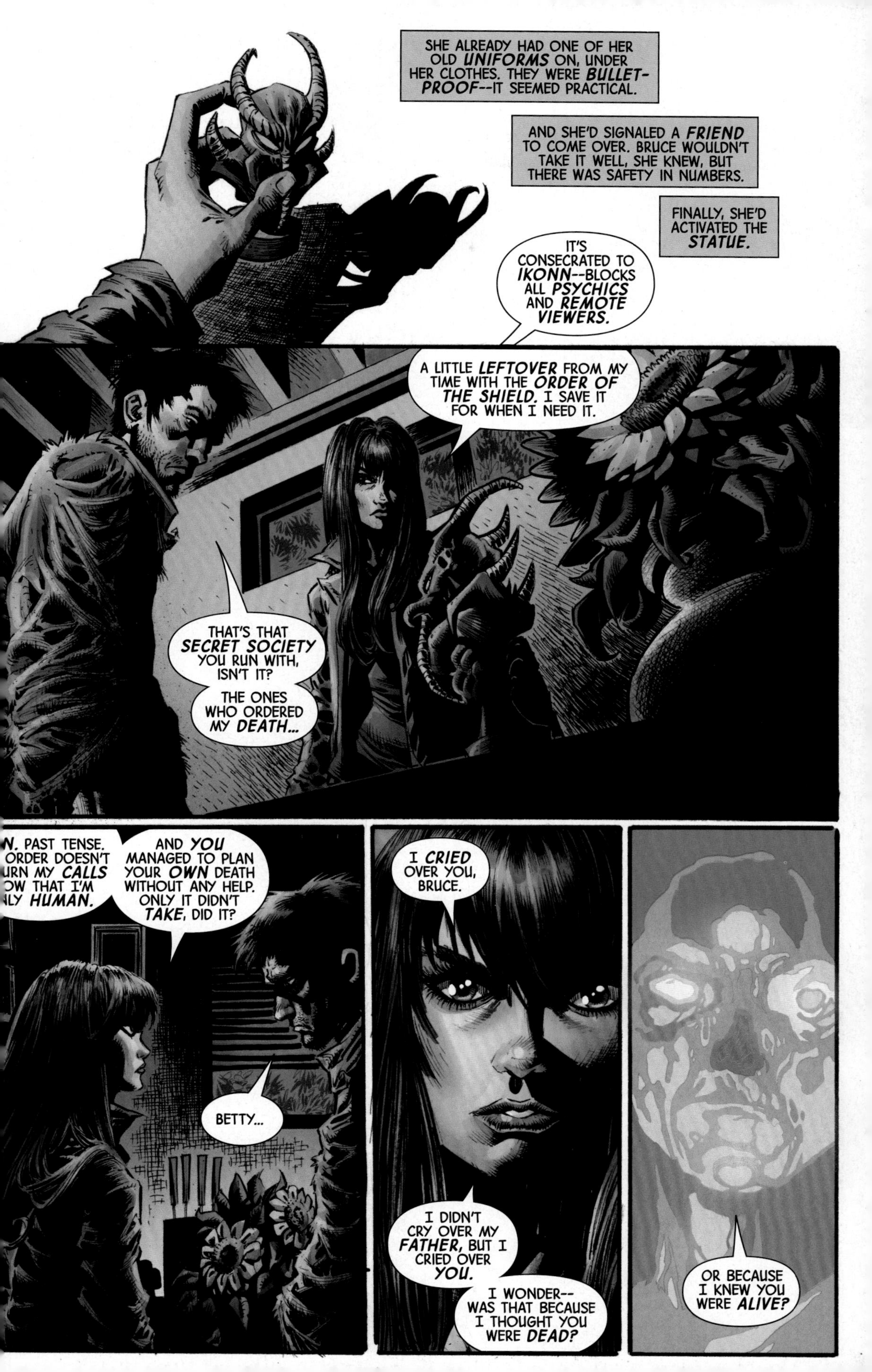
SHE ALREADY HAD ONE OF HER OLD UNIFORMS ON, UNDER HER CLOTHES. THEY WERE BULLET-PROOF--IT SEEMED PRACTICAL.
AND SHE'D SIGNALED A FRIEND TO COME OVER. BRUCE WOULDN'T TAKE IT WELL, SHE KNEW, BUT THERE WAS SAFETY IN NUMBERS.
FINALLY, SHE'D ACTIVATED THE STATUE.
IT'S CONSECRATED TO IKONN--BLOCKS ALL PSYCHICS AND REMOTE VIEWERS.
A LITTLE LEFTOVER FROM MY TIME WITH THE ORDER OF THE SHIELD. I SAVE IT FOR WHEN I NEED IT.
THAT'S THAT SECRET SOCIETY YOU RUN WITH, ISN'T IT?
THE ONES WHO ORDERED MY DEATH...
N. PAST TENSE. ORDER DOESN'T URN MY CALLS OW THAT I'M LY HUMAN.
AND YOU MANAGED TO PLAN YOUR OWN DEATH WITHOUT ANY HELP. ONLY IT DIDN'T TAKE, DID IT?
BETTY...
I CRIED OVER YOU, BRUCE.
I DIDN'T CRY OVER MY FATHER, BUT I CRIED OVER YOU.
I WONDER-- WAS THAT BECAUSE I THOUGHT YOU WERE DEAD?
OR BECAUSE I KNEW YOU WERE ALIVE?

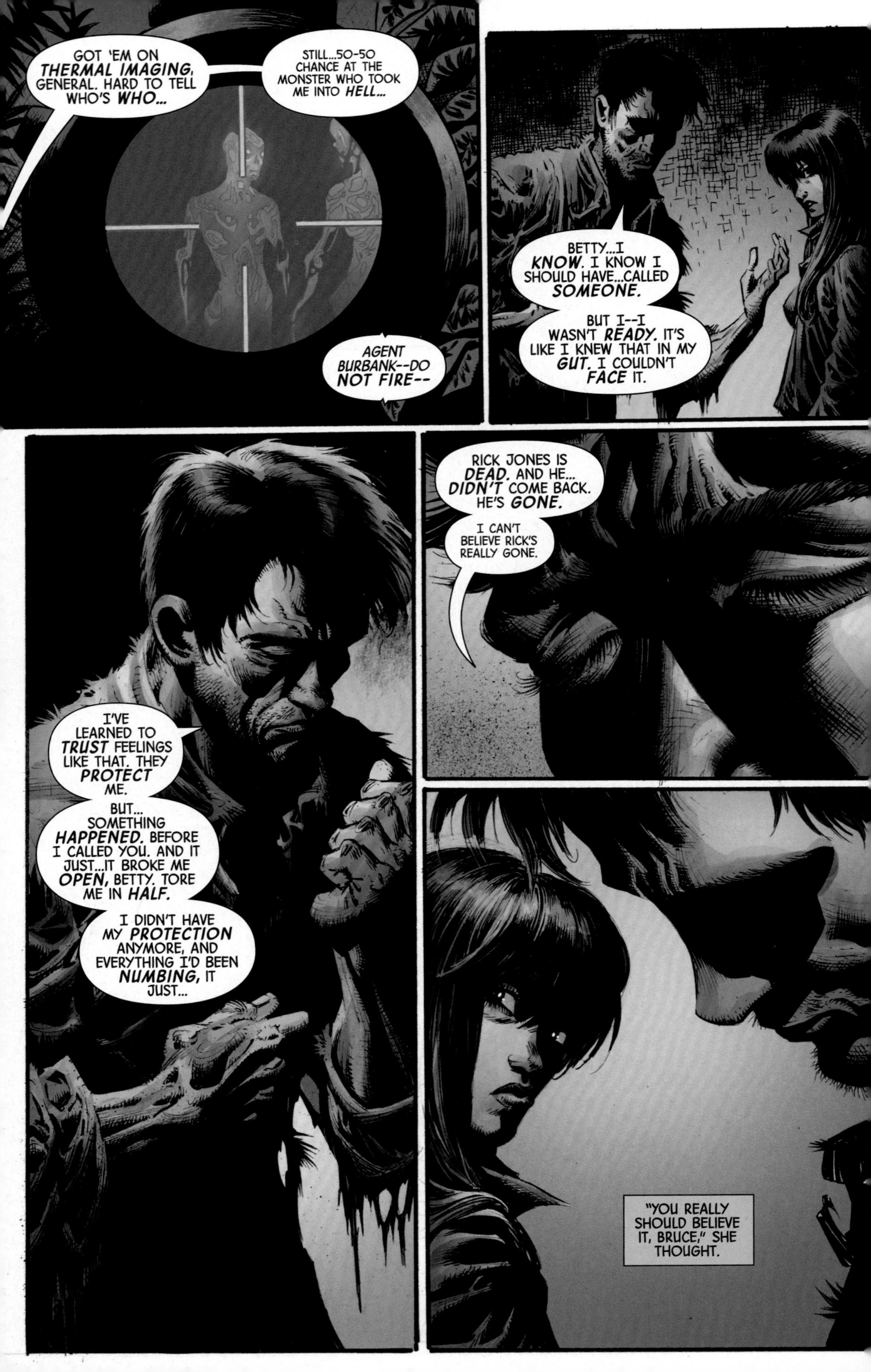
GOT 'EM ON THERMAL IMAGING, GENERAL. HARD TO TELL WHO'S WHO...
STILL...50-50 CHANCE AT THE MONSTER WHO TOOK ME INTO HELL...
AGENT BURBANK--DO NOT FIRE--
BETTY...I KNOW. I KNOW I SHOULD HAVE...CALLED SOMEONE.
BUT I--I WASN'T READY. IT'S LIKE I KNEW THAT IN MY GUT. I COULDN'T FACE IT.
I'VE LEARNED TO TRUST FEELINGS LIKE THAT. THEY PROTECT ME.
BUT... SOMETHING HAPPENED. BEFORE I CALLED YOU. AND IT JUST...IT BROKE ME OPEN, BETTY. TORE ME IN HALF.
I DIDN'T HAVE MY PROTECTION ANYMORE, AND EVERYTHING I'D BEEN NUMBING, IT JUST...
RICK JONES IS DEAD. AND HE... DIDN'T COME BACK. HE'S GONE.
I CAN'T BELIEVE RICK'S REALLY GONE.
"YOU REALLY SHOULD BELIEVE IT, BRUCE," SHE THOUGHT.

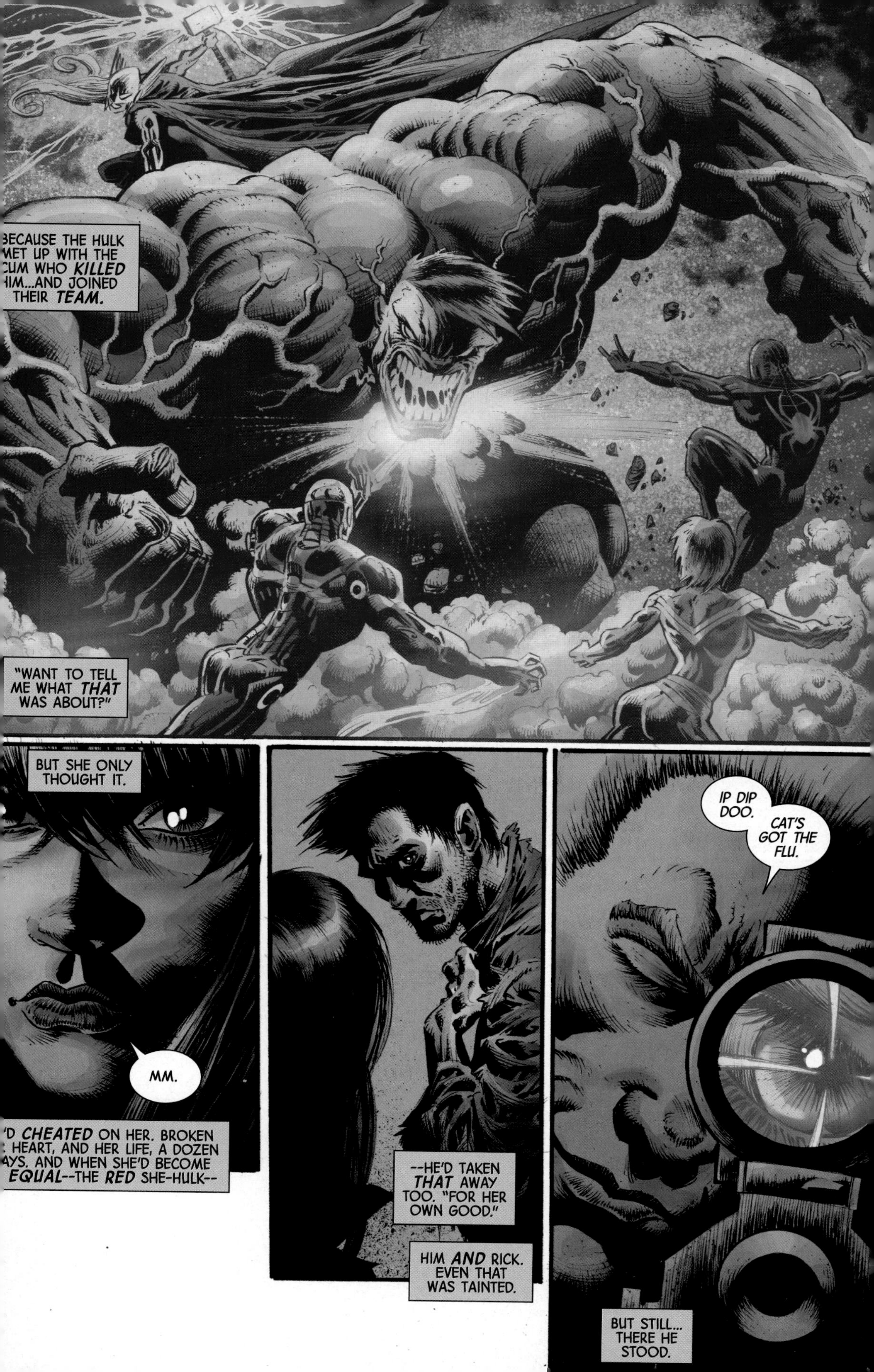
BECAUSE THE HULK MET UP WITH THE SCUM WHO KILLED HIM...AND JOINED THEIR TEAM.
"WANT TO TELL ME WHAT THAT WAS ABOUT?"
BUT SHE ONLY THOUGHT IT.
MM.
'D CHEATED ON HER. BROKEN HEART, AND HER LIFE, A DOZEN AYS. AND WHEN SHE'D BECOME EQUAL--THE RED SHE-HULK--
--HE'D TAKEN THAT AWAY TOO. "FOR HER OWN GOOD."
HIM AND RICK. EVEN THAT WAS TAINTED.
IP DIP DOO.
CAT'S GOT THE FLU.
BUT STILL... THERE HE STOOD.

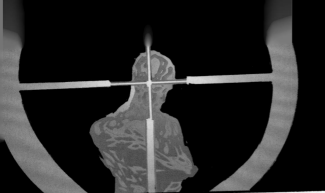

AN *OPEN WOUND* IN THE SHAPE OF A MAN.

DOG'S GOT THE CHICKEN POX.

A BEATEN *DOG.* AND SHE JUST COULDN'T DO IT. SHE COULD *NEVER* DO IT.

NEVER *HURT* HIM.

EVEN WITH THE TRUTH.

AGENT BURBANK! *STAND DOWN NOW!* THAT IS AN *ORDER!*

THE *SUN'S GONE DOWN--*

HER FATHER HAD CALLED HIM A "MILKSOP."

SHE'D *LOVED* THAT VULNERABILITY...

...BUT NOW IT SEEMED, SOMEHOW, AS *MANAGED* AS THE *RAGE* THAT SMASHED CITIES AND LEFT NO BODY COUNT.

BETTY... I REALLY AM *SO* SORRY.

AS CAREFULLY *CALCULATED.*

SO OUT GOES YOU.

IN THAT MOMENT, SHE KNEW *WHY* HER FATHER HAD HATED HIM.

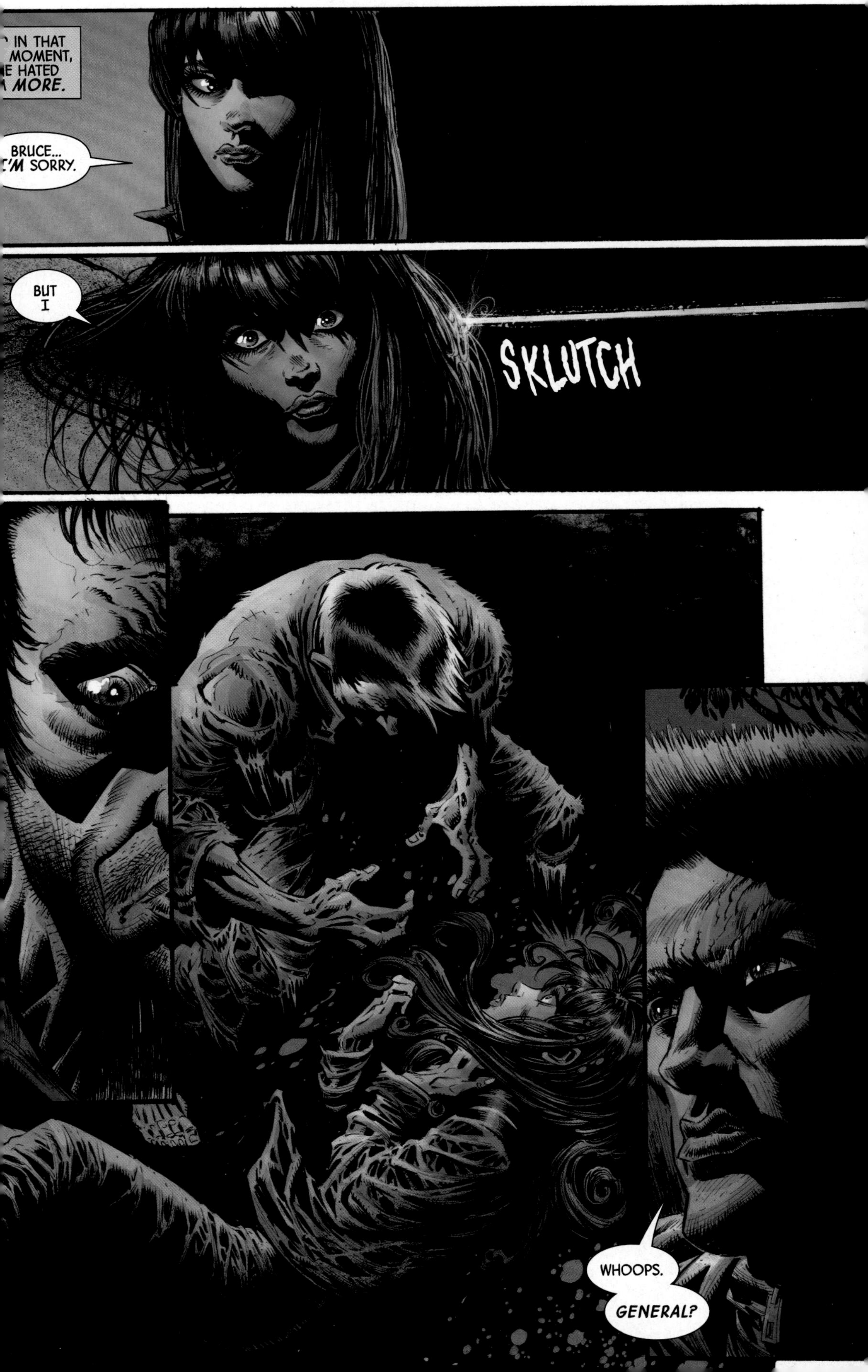
IN THAT MOMENT, E HATED MORE.
BRUCE... 'M SORRY.
BUT I
SKLUTCH
WHOOPS.
GENERAL?

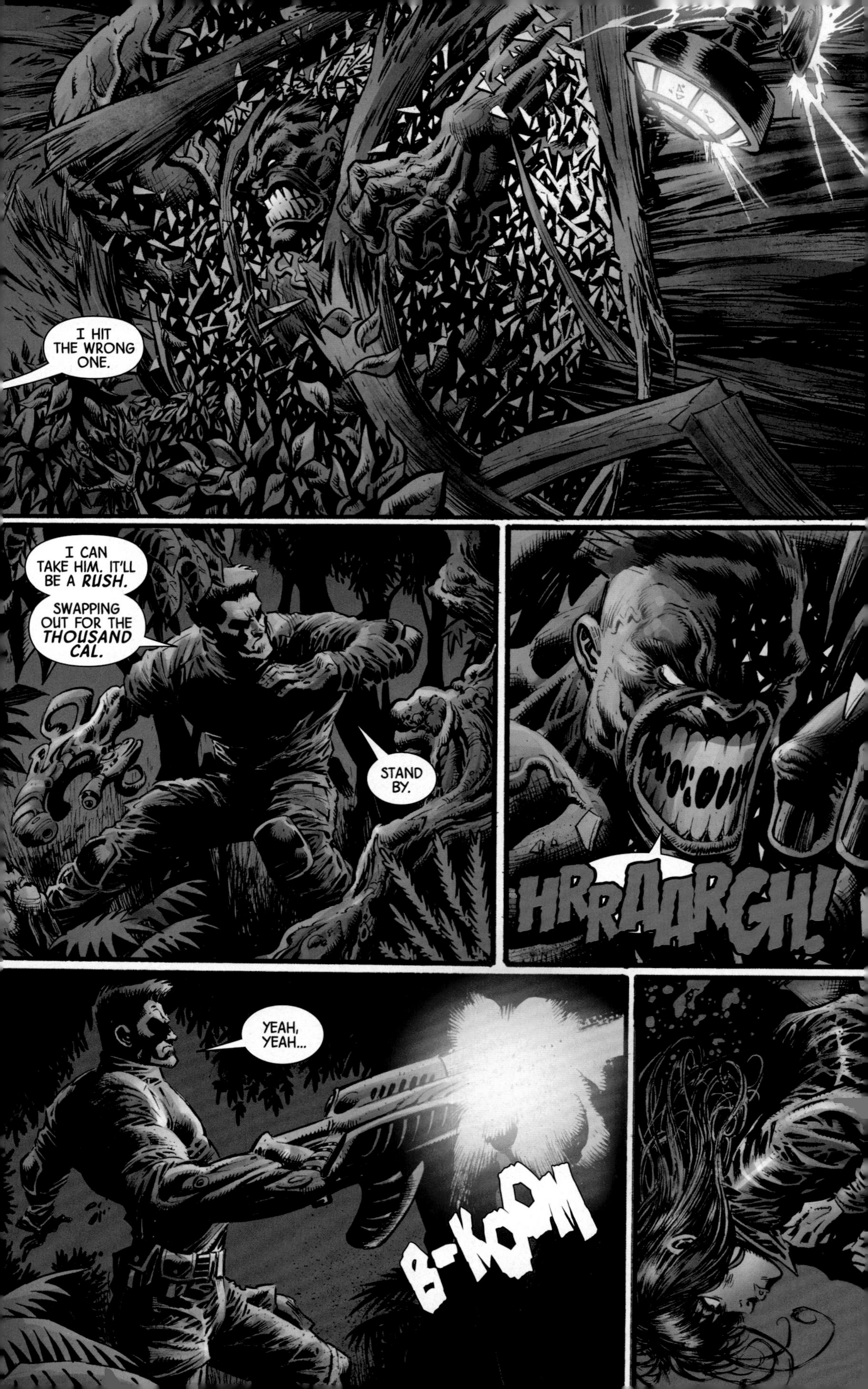

I HIT THE WRONG ONE.
I CAN TAKE HIM. IT'LL BE A *RUSH.*
SWAPPING OUT FOR THE *THOUSAND CAL.*
STAND BY.
HRRAARGH!
YEAH, YEAH...
B-KOOM

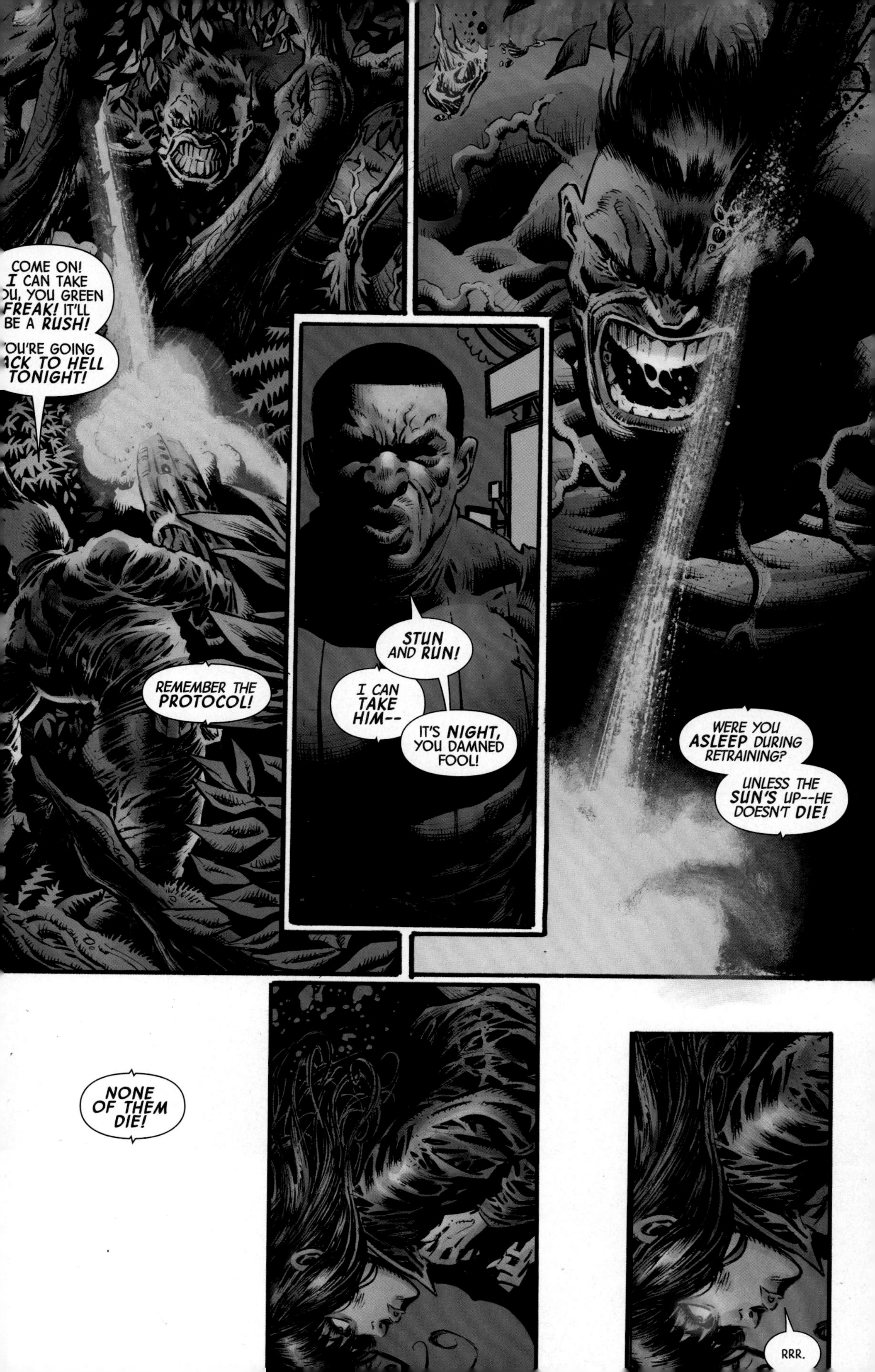

COME ON! I CAN TAKE OU, YOU GREEN FREAK! IT'LL BE A RUSH!
OU'RE GOING ACK TO HELL TONIGHT!
REMEMBER THE PROTOCOL!
STUN AND RUN!
I CAN TAKE HIM--
IT'S NIGHT, YOU DAMNED FOOL!
WERE YOU ASLEEP DURING RETRAINING?
UNLESS THE SUN'S UP--HE DOESN'T DIE!
NONE OF THEM DIE!
RRR.

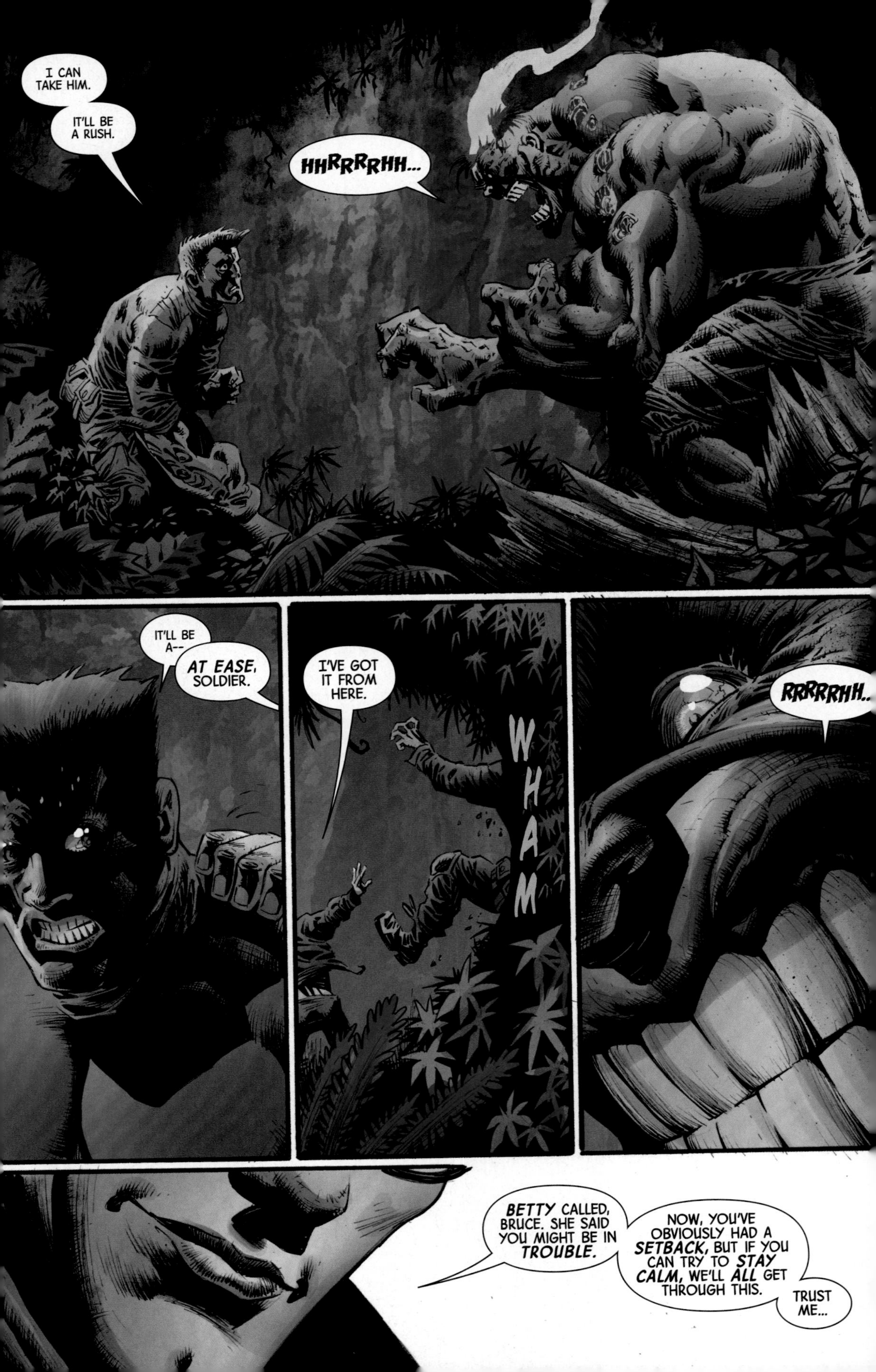
I CAN TAKE HIM.
IT'LL BE A RUSH.
HHRRRRHH...
IT'LL BE A--
AT EASE, SOLDIER.
I'VE GOT IT FROM HERE.
WHAM
RRRRRHH..
BETTY CALLED, BRUCE. SHE SAID YOU MIGHT BE IN TROUBLE.
NOW, YOU'VE OBVIOUSLY HAD A SETBACK, BUT IF YOU CAN TRY TO STAY CALM, WE'LL ALL GET THROUGH THIS.
TRUST ME...

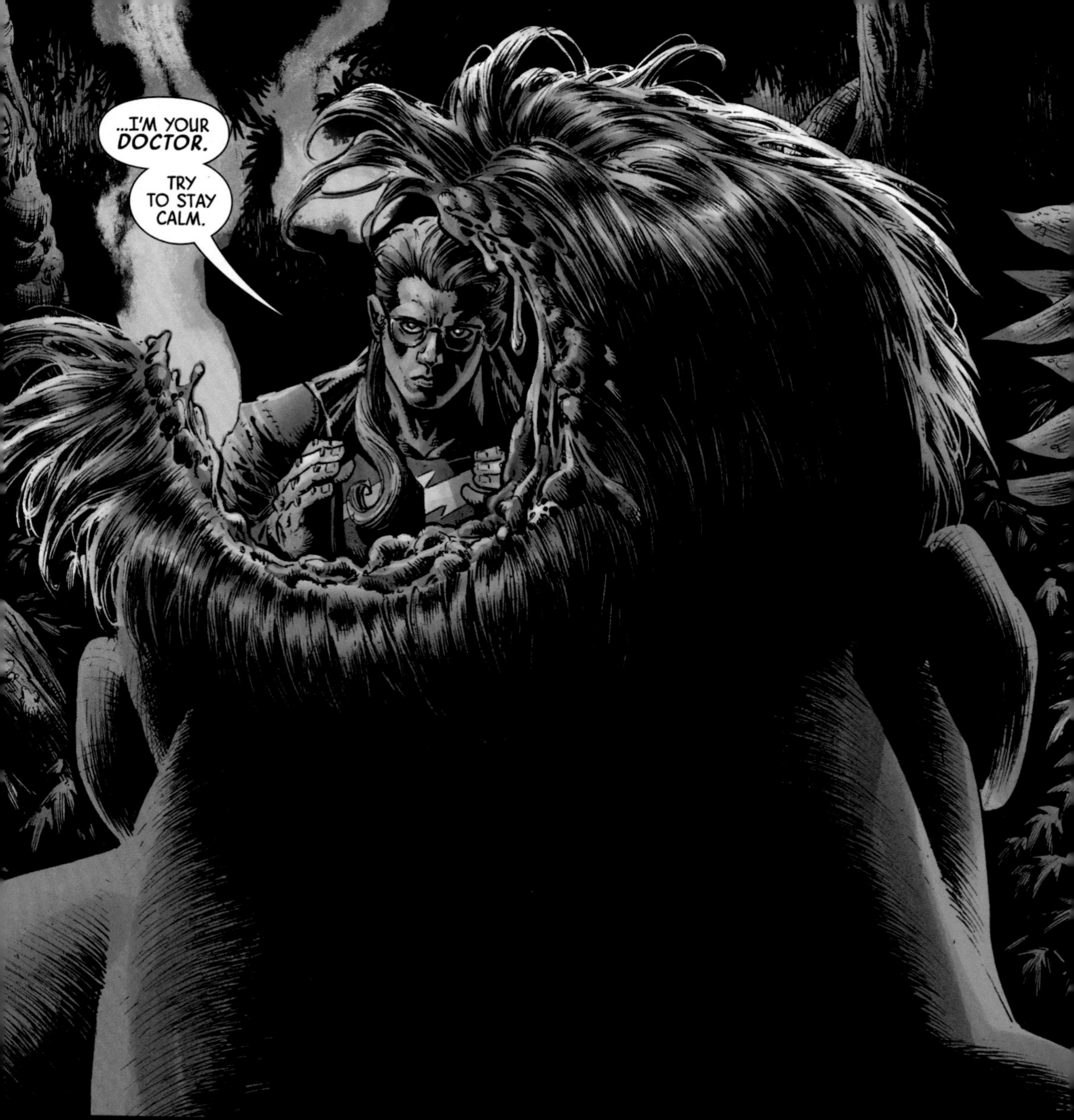
...I'M YOUR DOCTOR.
TRY TO STAY CALM.

WE ONLY MEET AT FUNERALS

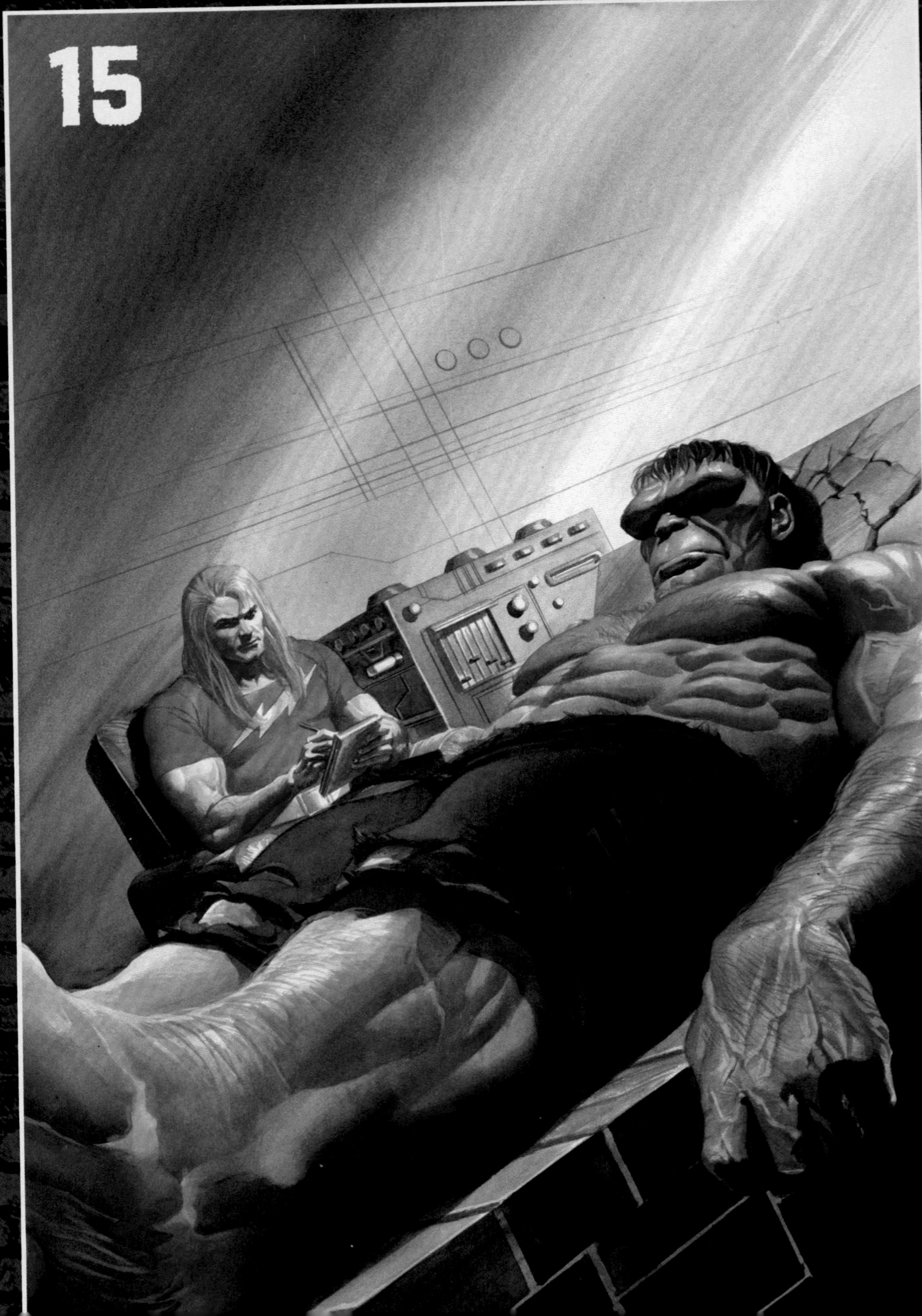
15

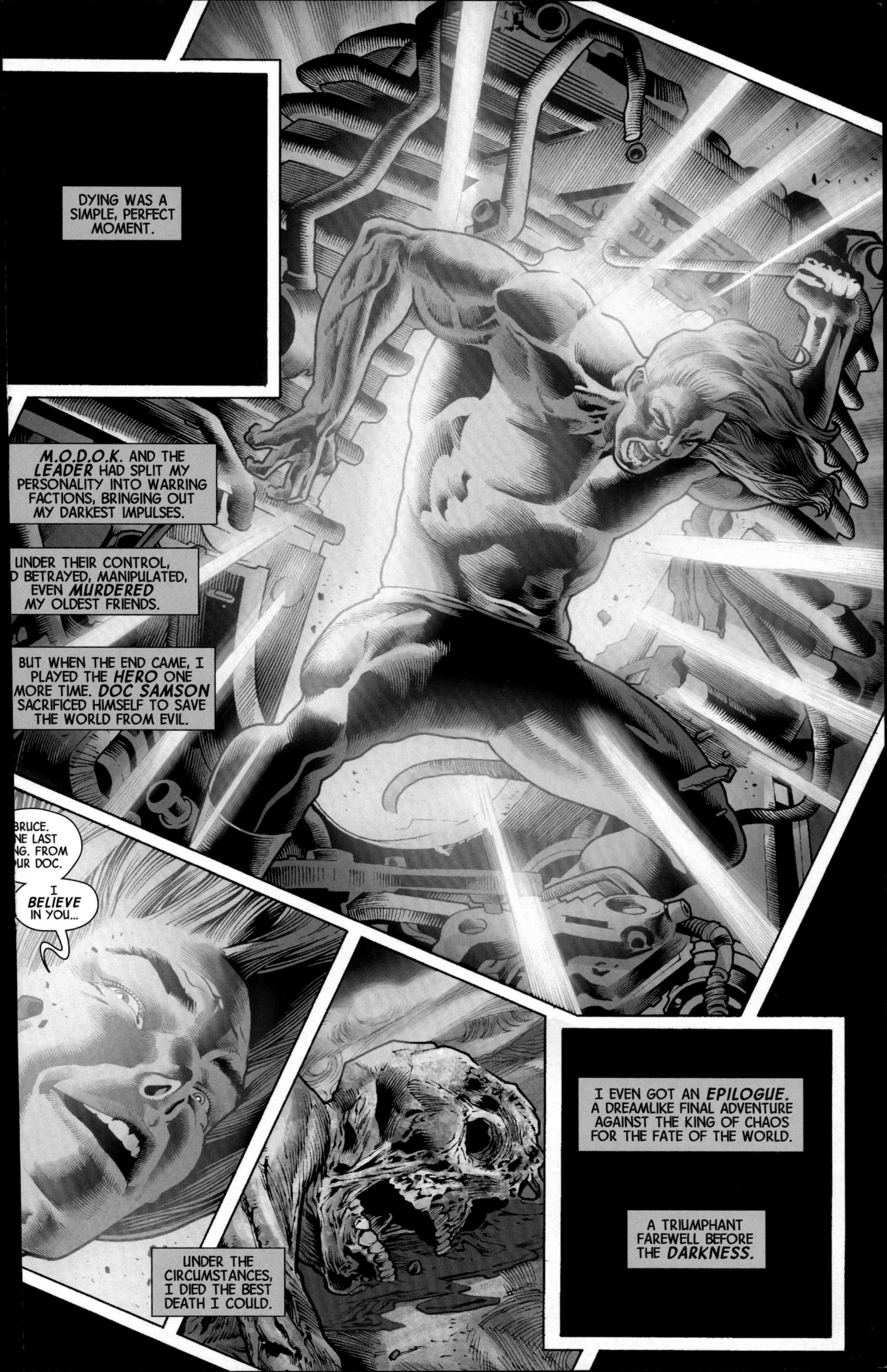
DYING WAS A SIMPLE, PERFECT MOMENT.
M.O.D.O.K. AND THE LEADER HAD SPLIT MY PERSONALITY INTO WARRING FACTIONS, BRINGING OUT MY DARKEST IMPULSES.
UNDER THEIR CONTROL, D BETRAYED, MANIPULATED, EVEN MURDERED MY OLDEST FRIENDS.
BUT WHEN THE END CAME, I PLAYED THE HERO ONE MORE TIME. DOC SAMSON SACRIFICED HIMSELF TO SAVE THE WORLD FROM EVIL.
BRUCE. NE LAST NG. FROM UR DOC.
I BELIEVE IN YOU...
UNDER THE CIRCUMSTANCES, I DIED THE BEST DEATH I COULD.
I EVEN GOT AN EPILOGUE. A DREAMLIKE FINAL ADVENTURE AGAINST THE KING OF CHAOS FOR THE FATE OF THE WORLD.
A TRIUMPHANT FAREWELL BEFORE THE DARKNESS.

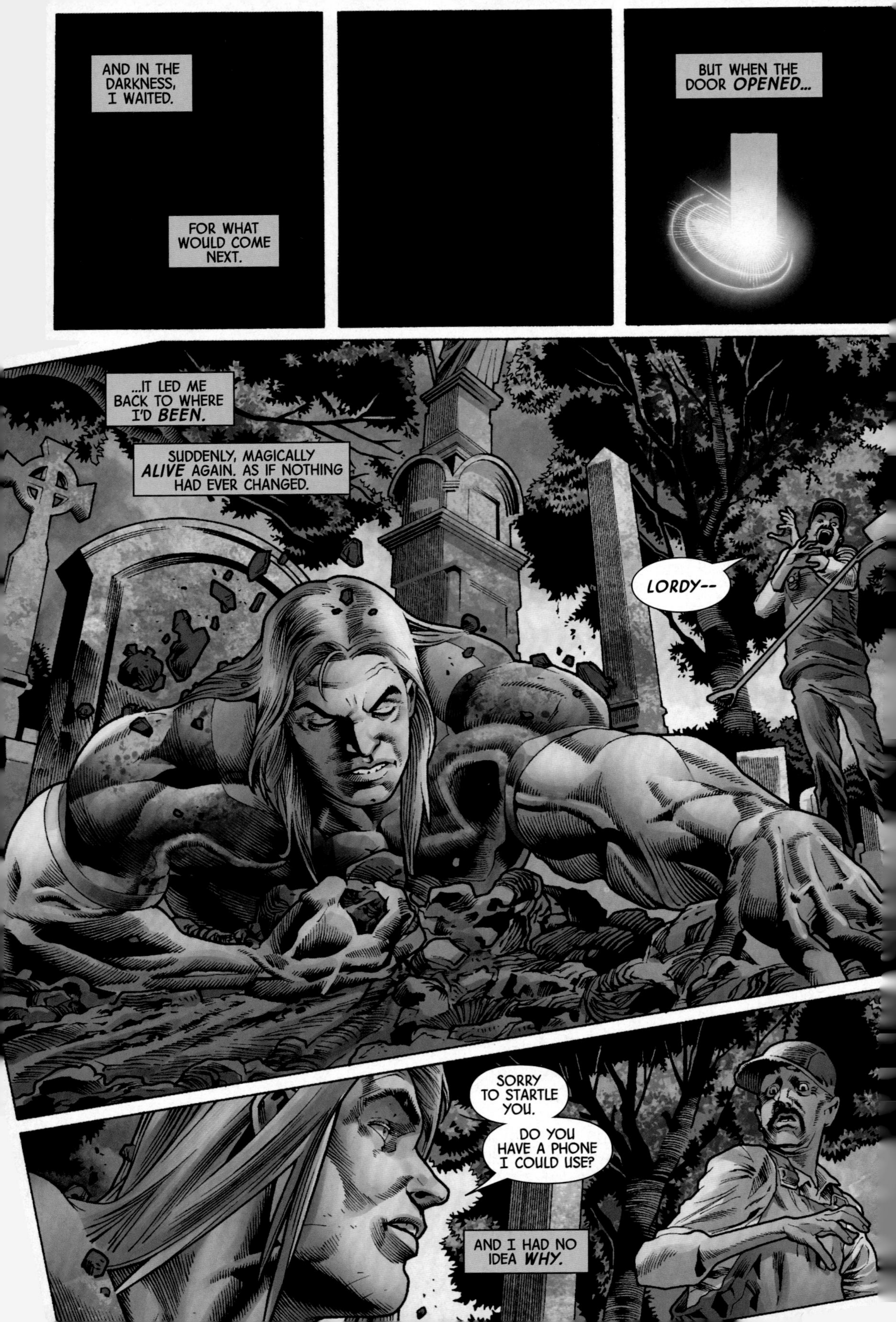
AND IN THE DARKNESS, I WAITED.
FOR WHAT WOULD COME NEXT.
BUT WHEN THE DOOR OPENED...
...IT LED ME BACK TO WHERE I'D BEEN.
SUDDENLY, MAGICALLY ALIVE AGAIN. AS IF NOTHING HAD EVER CHANGED.
LORDY--
SORRY TO STARTLE YOU.
DO YOU HAVE A PHONE I COULD USE?
AND I HAD NO IDEA WHY.

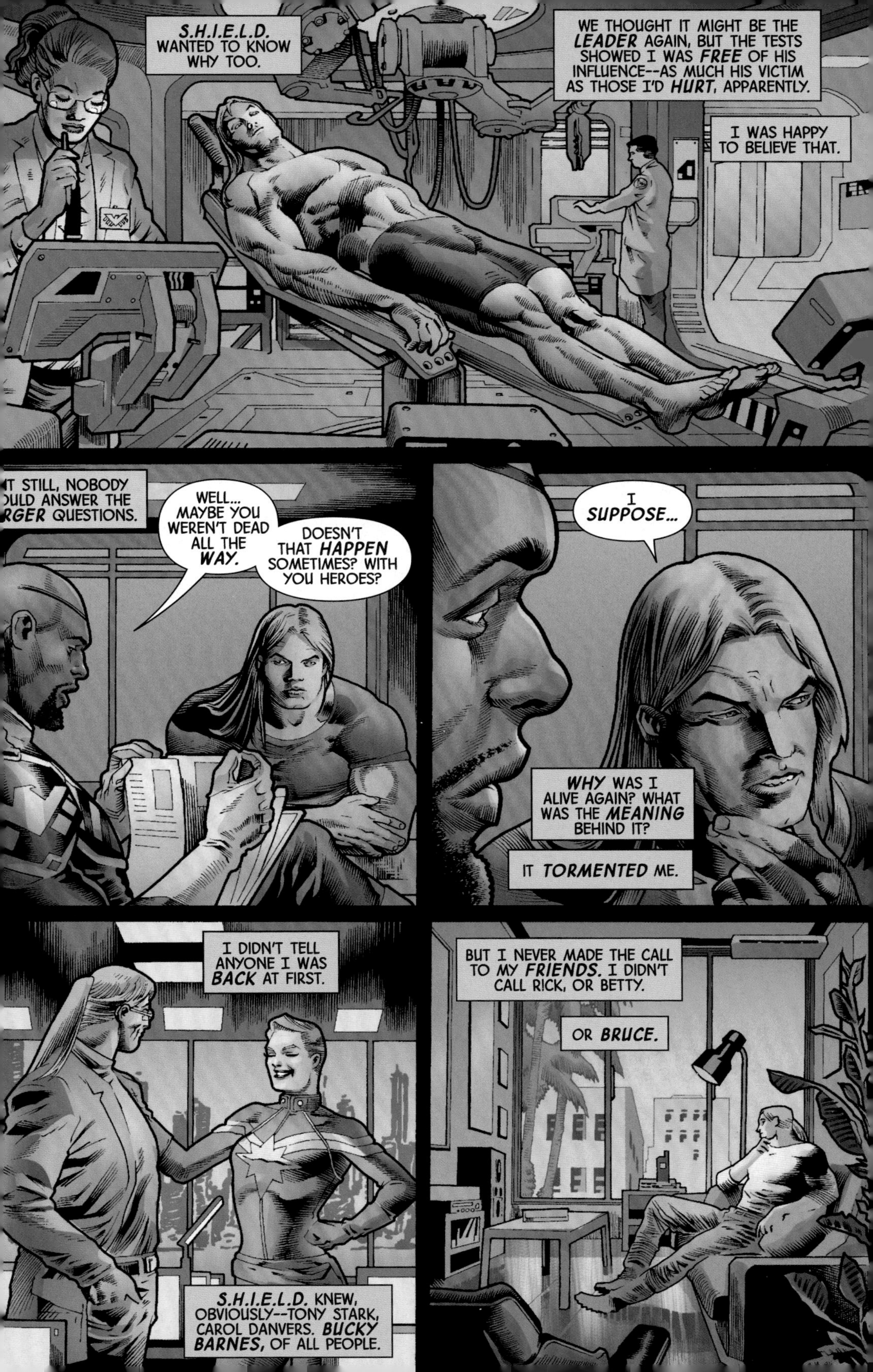

S.H.I.E.L.D. WANTED TO KNOW WHY TOO.
WE THOUGHT IT MIGHT BE THE LEADER AGAIN, BUT THE TESTS SHOWED I WAS FREE OF HIS INFLUENCE--AS MUCH HIS VICTIM AS THOSE I'D HURT, APPARENTLY.
I WAS HAPPY TO BELIEVE THAT.
T STILL, NOBODY OULD ANSWER THE RGER QUESTIONS.
WELL... MAYBE YOU WEREN'T DEAD ALL THE WAY.
DOESN'T THAT HAPPEN SOMETIMES? WITH YOU HEROES?
I SUPPOSE...
WHY WAS I ALIVE AGAIN? WHAT WAS THE MEANING BEHIND IT?
IT TORMENTED ME.
I DIDN'T TELL ANYONE I WAS BACK AT FIRST.
S.H.I.E.L.D. KNEW, OBVIOUSLY--TONY STARK, CAROL DANVERS. BUCKY BARNES, OF ALL PEOPLE.
BUT I NEVER MADE THE CALL TO MY FRIENDS. I DIDN'T CALL RICK, OR BETTY.
OR BRUCE.

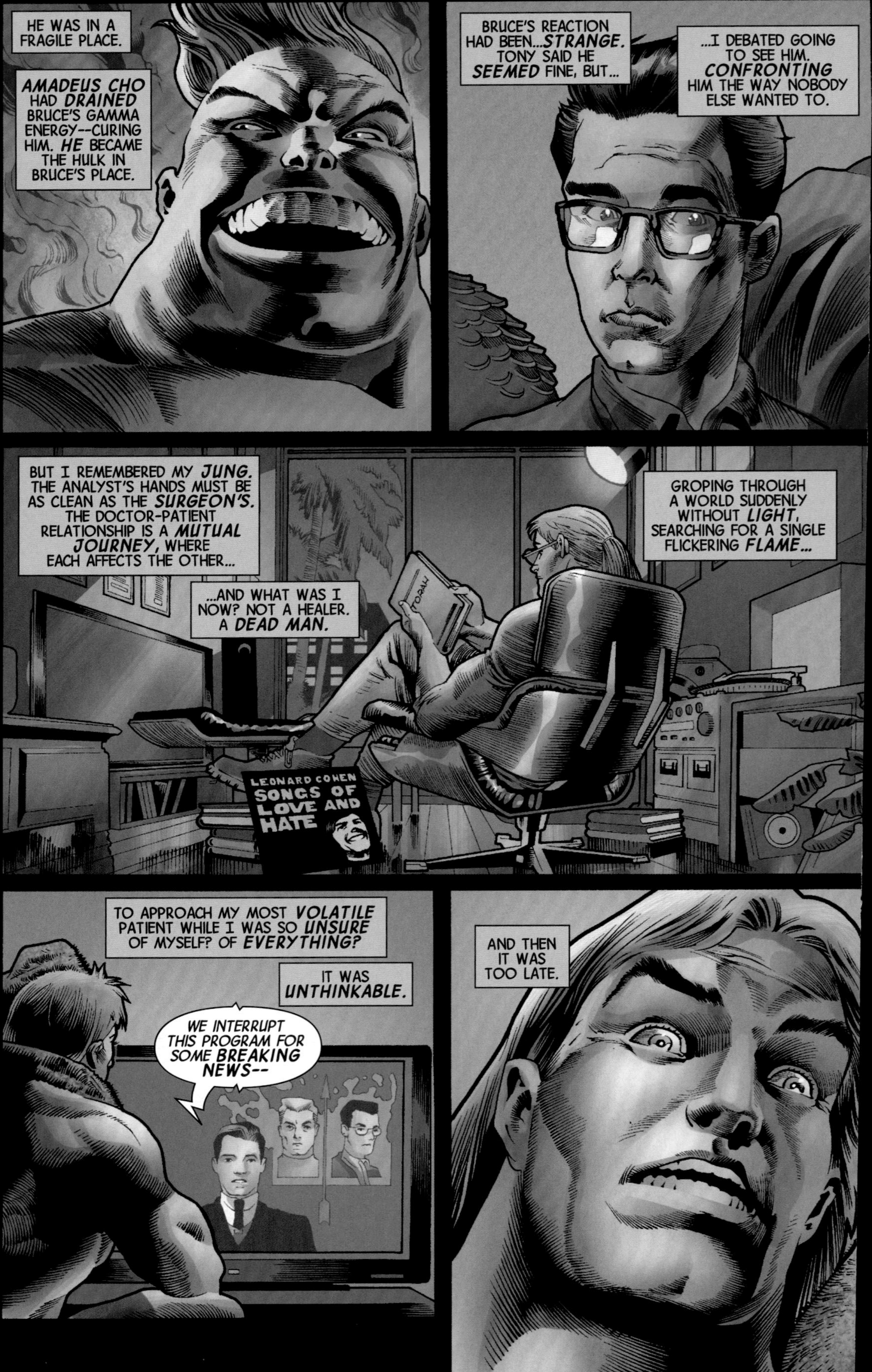

HE WAS IN A FRAGILE PLACE.
AMADEUS CHO HAD DRAINED BRUCE'S GAMMA ENERGY--CURING HIM. HE BECAME THE HULK IN BRUCE'S PLACE.
BRUCE'S REACTION HAD BEEN...STRANGE. TONY SAID HE SEEMED FINE, BUT...
...I DEBATED GOING TO SEE HIM. CONFRONTING HIM THE WAY NOBODY ELSE WANTED TO.
BUT I REMEMBERED MY JUNG. THE ANALYST'S HANDS MUST BE AS CLEAN AS THE SURGEON'S. THE DOCTOR-PATIENT RELATIONSHIP IS A MUTUAL JOURNEY, WHERE EACH AFFECTS THE OTHER...
...AND WHAT WAS I NOW? NOT A HEALER. A DEAD MAN.
GROPING THROUGH A WORLD SUDDENLY WITHOUT LIGHT, SEARCHING FOR A SINGLE FLICKERING FLAME...
TORAH
LEONARD COHEN
SONGS OF LOVE AND HATE
TO APPROACH MY MOST VOLATILE PATIENT WHILE I WAS SO UNSURE OF MYSELF? OF EVERYTHING?
IT WAS UNTHINKABLE.
WE INTERRUPT THIS PROGRAM FOR SOME BREAKING NEWS--
AND THEN IT WAS TOO LATE.

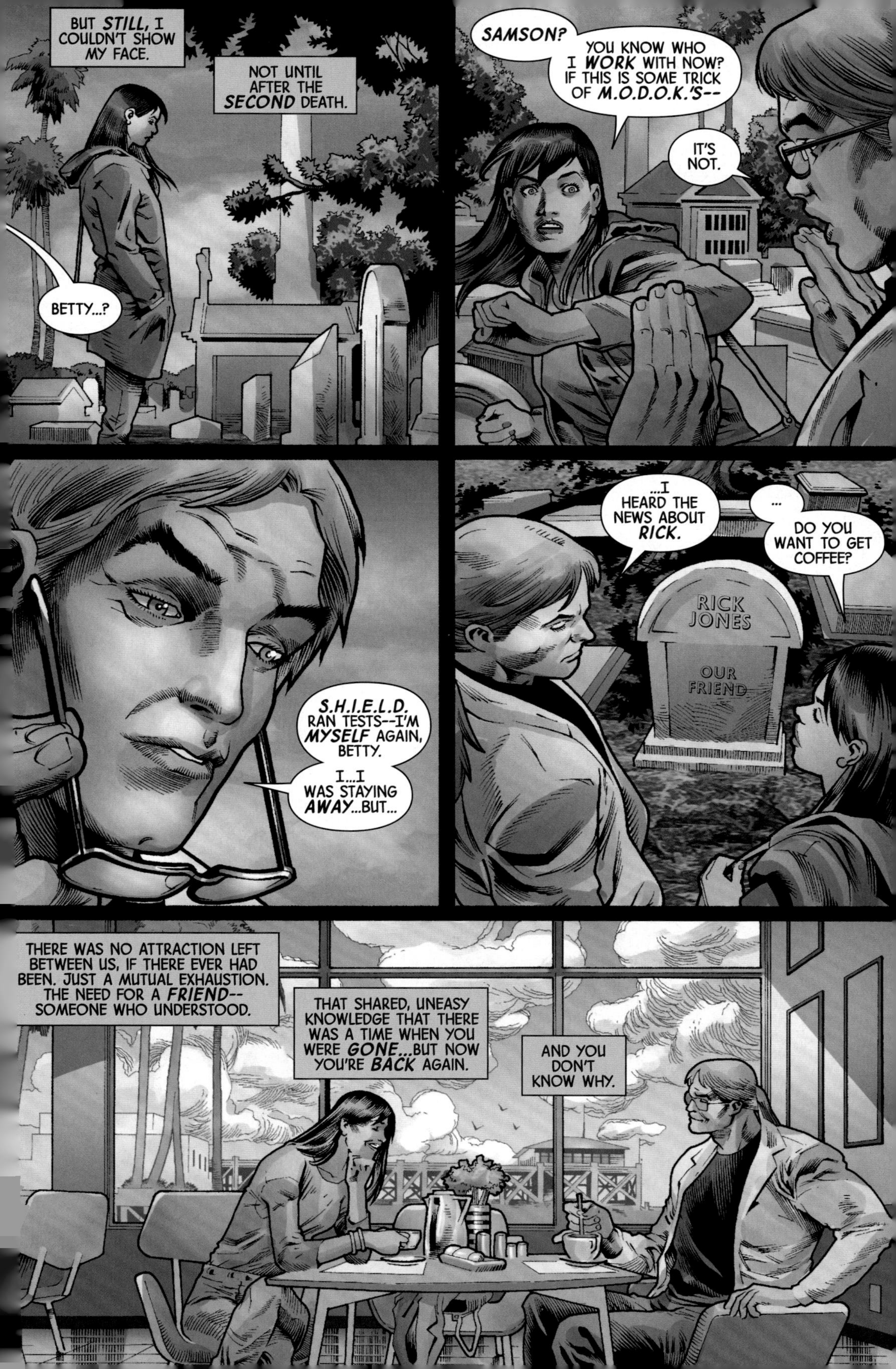
BUT STILL, I COULDN'T SHOW MY FACE.
NOT UNTIL AFTER THE SECOND DEATH.
BETTY...?
SAMSON?
YOU KNOW WHO I WORK WITH NOW? IF THIS IS SOME TRICK OF M.O.D.O.K.'S--
IT'S NOT.
S.H.I.E.L.D. RAN TESTS--I'M MYSELF AGAIN, BETTY.
I...I WAS STAYING AWAY...BUT...
...I HEARD THE NEWS ABOUT RICK.
...
DO YOU WANT TO GET COFFEE?
RICK JONES
OUR FRIEND
THERE WAS NO ATTRACTION LEFT BETWEEN US, IF THERE EVER HAD BEEN. JUST A MUTUAL EXHAUSTION. THE NEED FOR A FRIEND-- SOMEONE WHO UNDERSTOOD.
THAT SHARED, UNEASY KNOWLEDGE THAT THERE WAS A TIME WHEN YOU WERE GONE...BUT NOW YOU'RE BACK AGAIN.
AND YOU DON'T KNOW WHY.

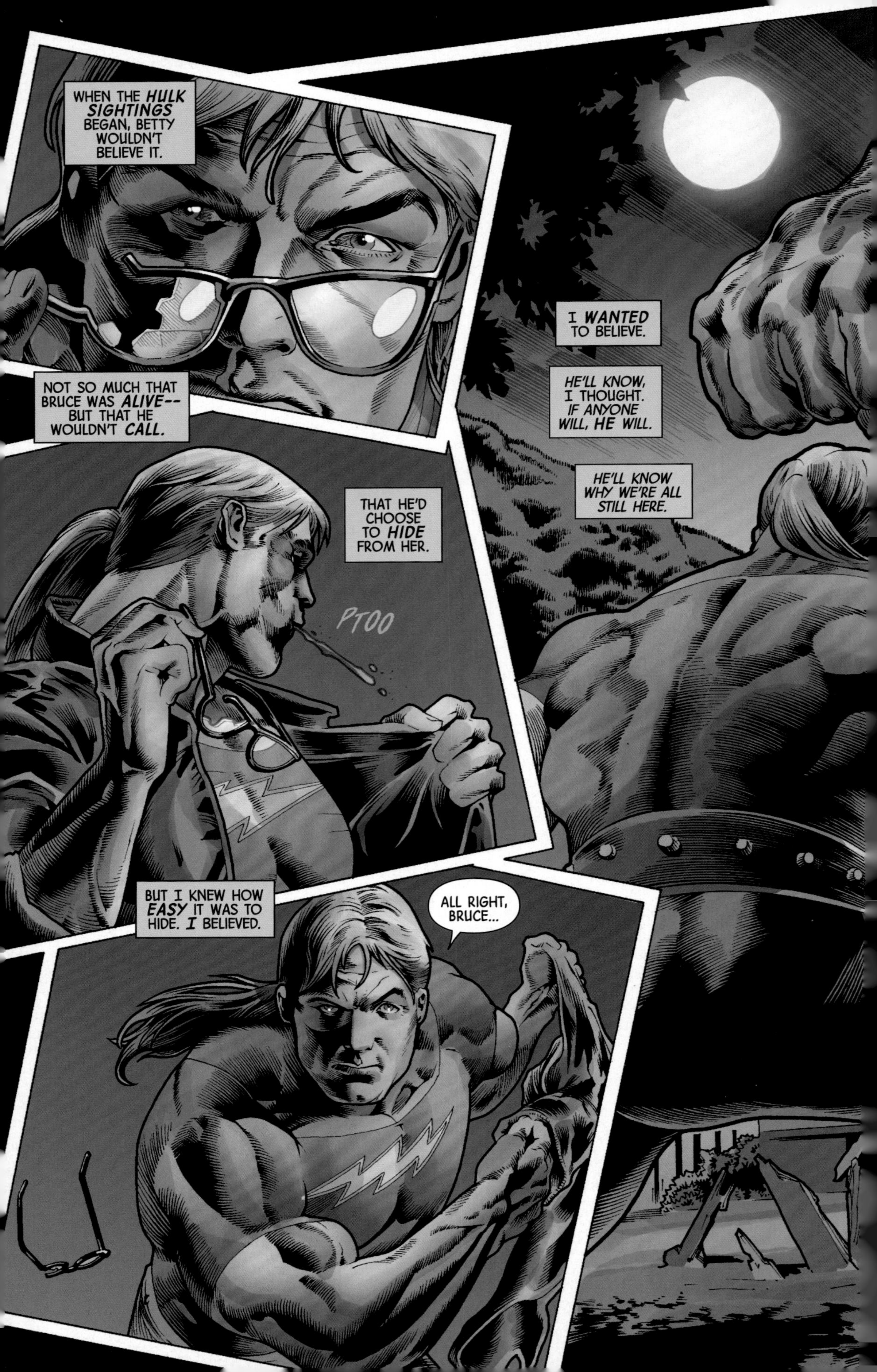
WHEN THE HULK SIGHTINGS BEGAN, BETTY WOULDN'T BELIEVE IT.
NOT SO MUCH THAT BRUCE WAS ALIVE-- BUT THAT HE WOULDN'T CALL.
THAT HE'D CHOOSE TO HIDE FROM HER.
PTOO
BUT I KNEW HOW EASY IT WAS TO HIDE. I BELIEVED.
ALL RIGHT, BRUCE...
I WANTED TO BELIEVE.
HE'LL KNOW, I THOUGHT. IF ANYONE WILL, HE WILL.
HE'LL KNOW WHY WE'RE ALL STILL HERE.

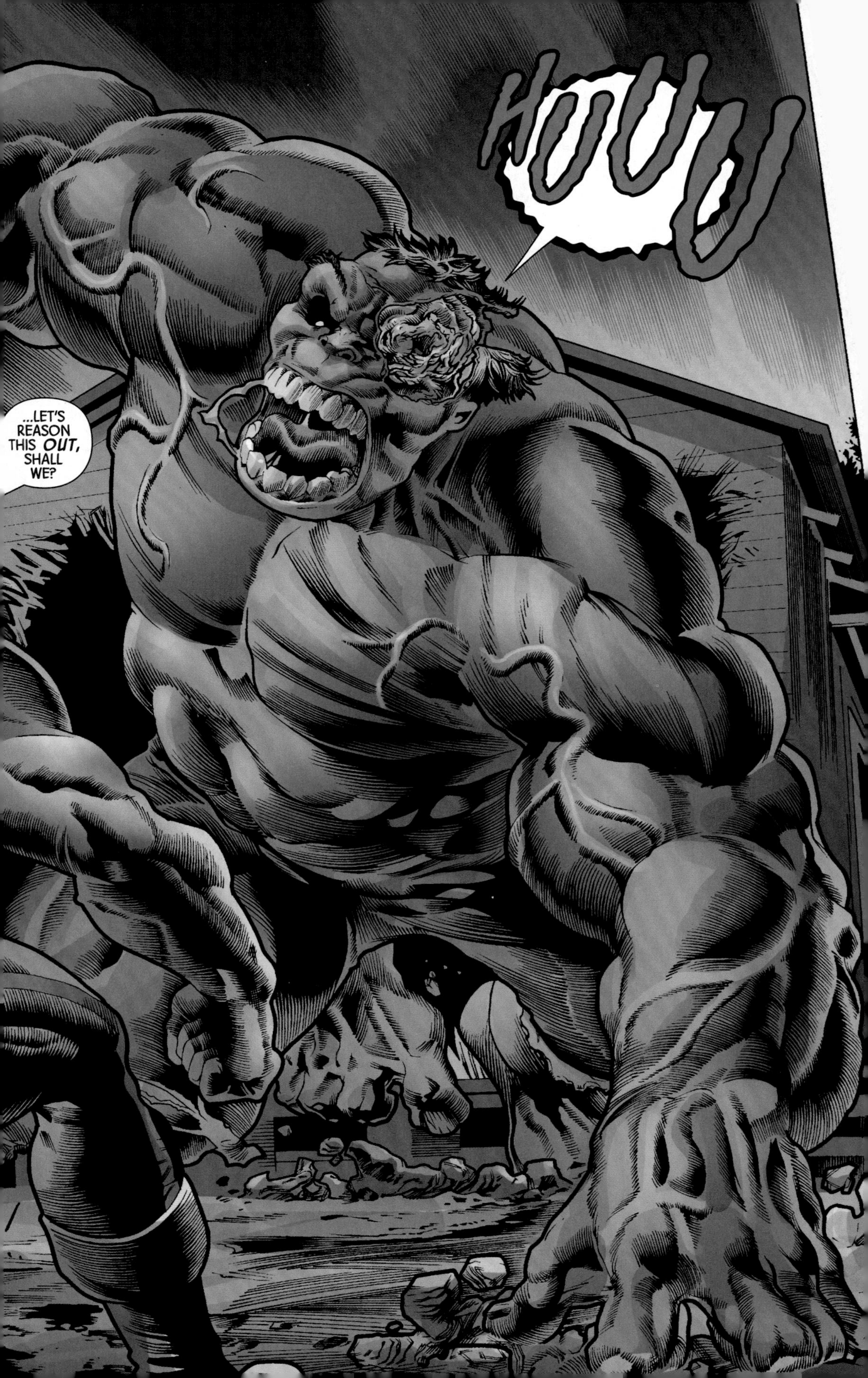
HUUUU
...LET'S REASON THIS OUT, SHALL WE?

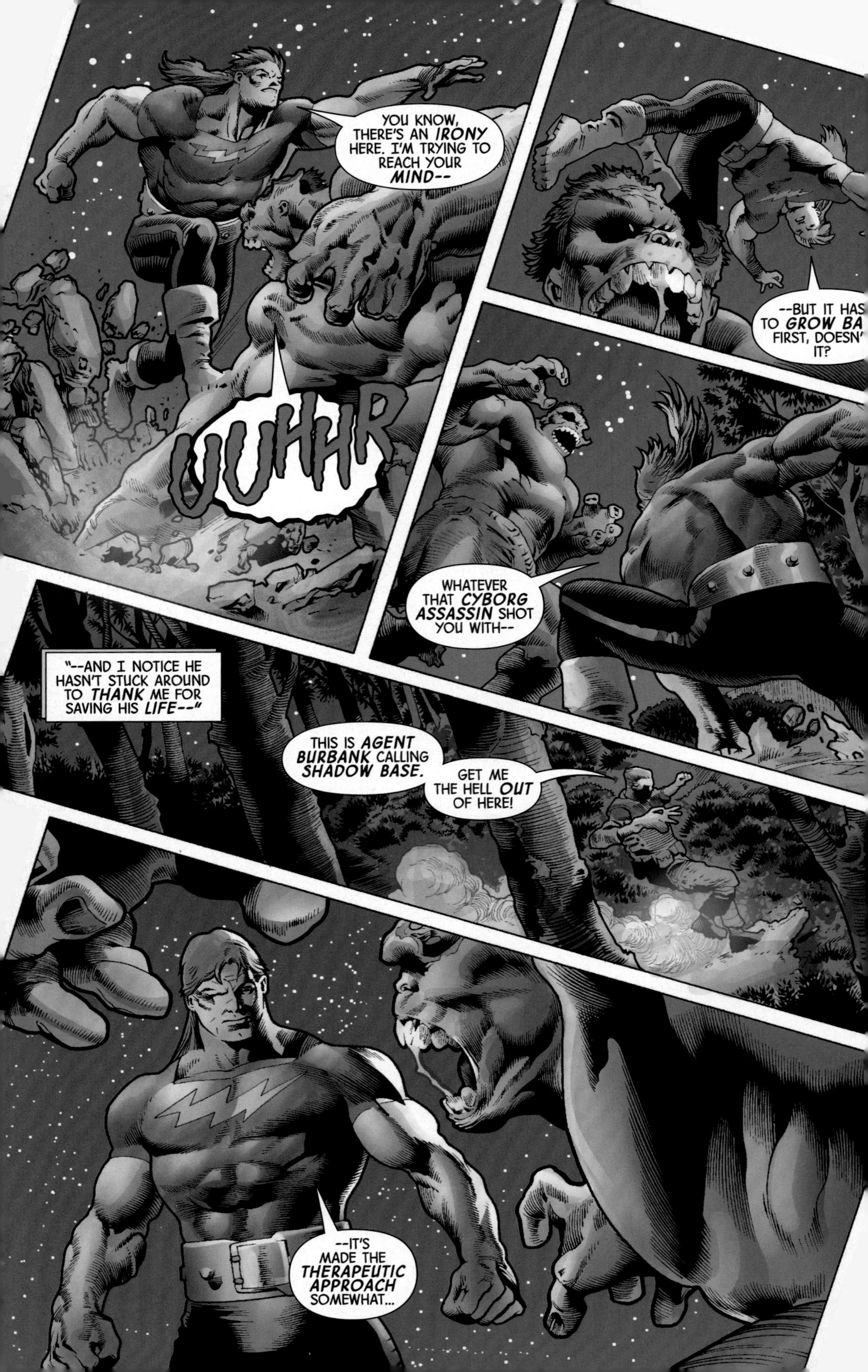

YOU KNOW, THERE'S AN IRONY HERE. I'M TRYING TO REACH YOUR MIND--
UUHHR
--BUT IT HAS TO GROW BA FIRST, DOESN' IT?
WHATEVER THAT CYBORG ASSASSIN SHOT YOU WITH--
"--AND I NOTICE HE HASN'T STUCK AROUND TO THANK ME FOR SAVING HIS LIFE--"
THIS IS AGENT BURBANK CALLING SHADOW BASE.
GET ME THE HELL OUT OF HERE!
--IT'S MADE THE THERAPEUTIC APPROACH SOMEWHAT...

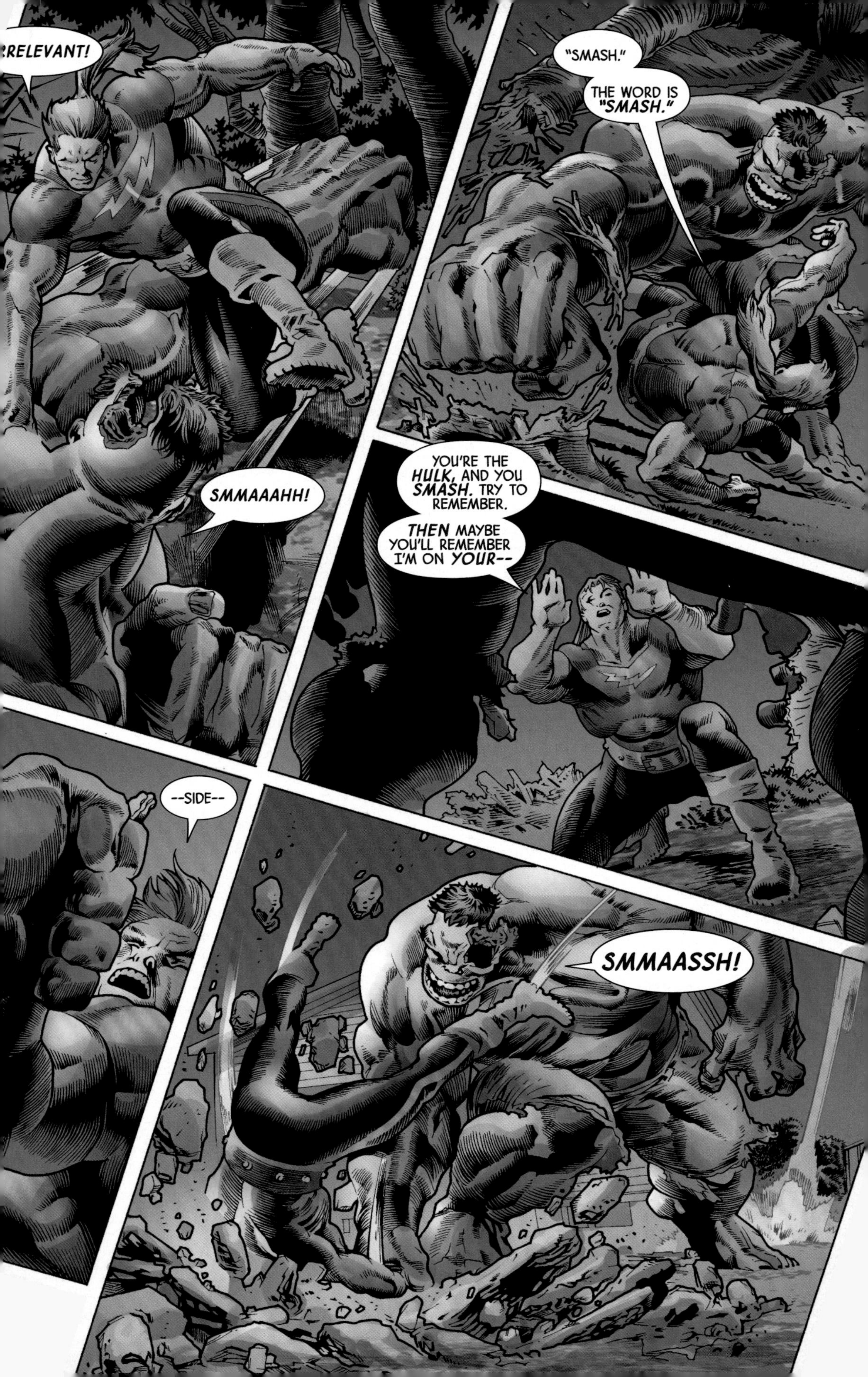
RELEVANT!
SMMAAAHH!
"SMASH."
THE WORD IS "SMASH."
YOU'RE THE HULK, AND YOU SMASH. TRY TO REMEMBER.
THEN MAYBE YOU'LL REMEMBER I'M ON YOUR--
--SIDE--
SMMAASSH!

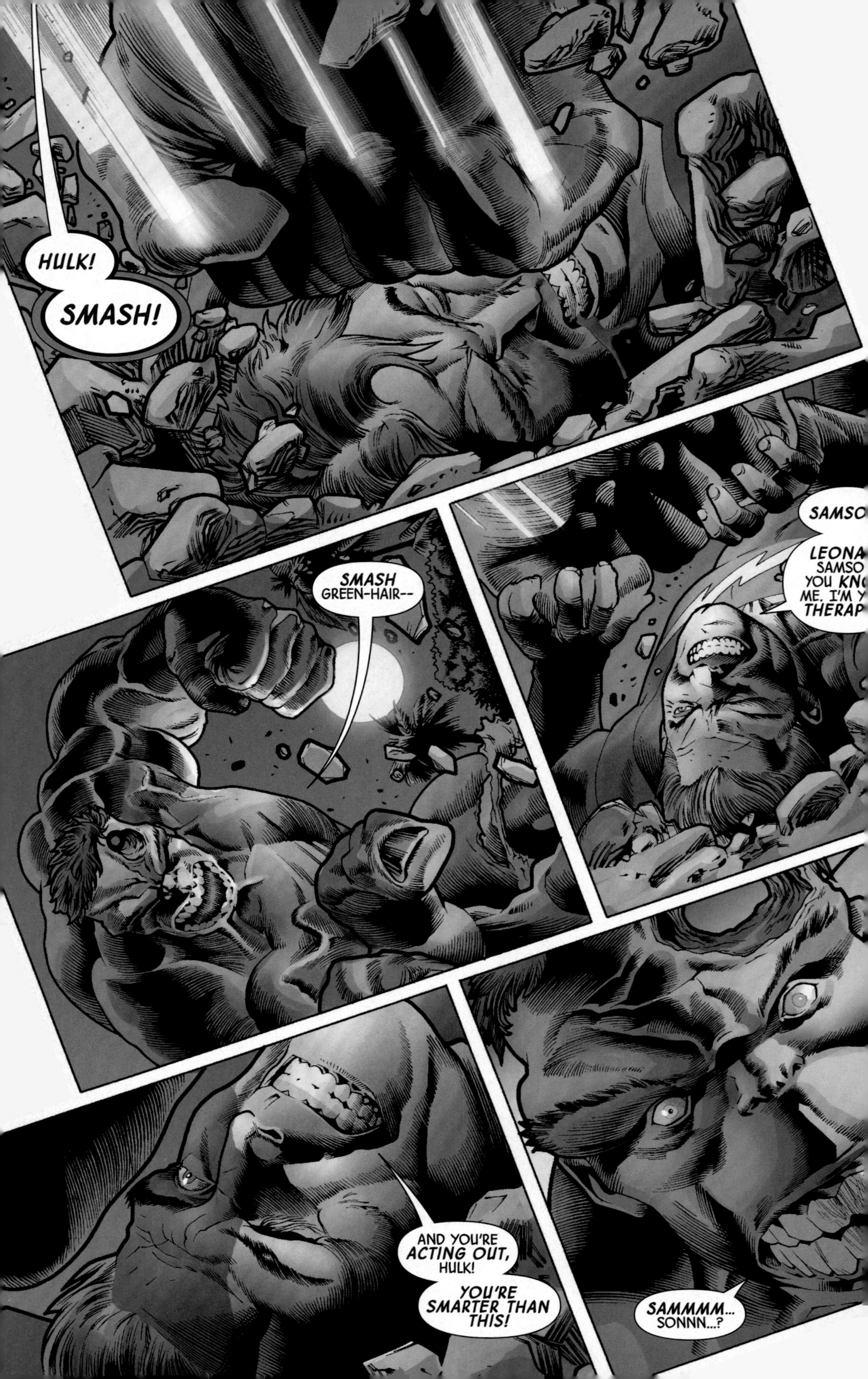
HULK!
SMASH!
SMASH GREEN-HAIR--
SAMSO
LEONA SAMSO YOU KNO ME. I'M Y THERAP
AND YOU'RE ACTING OUT, HULK!
YOU'RE SMARTER THAN THIS!
SAMMMM... SONNN...?

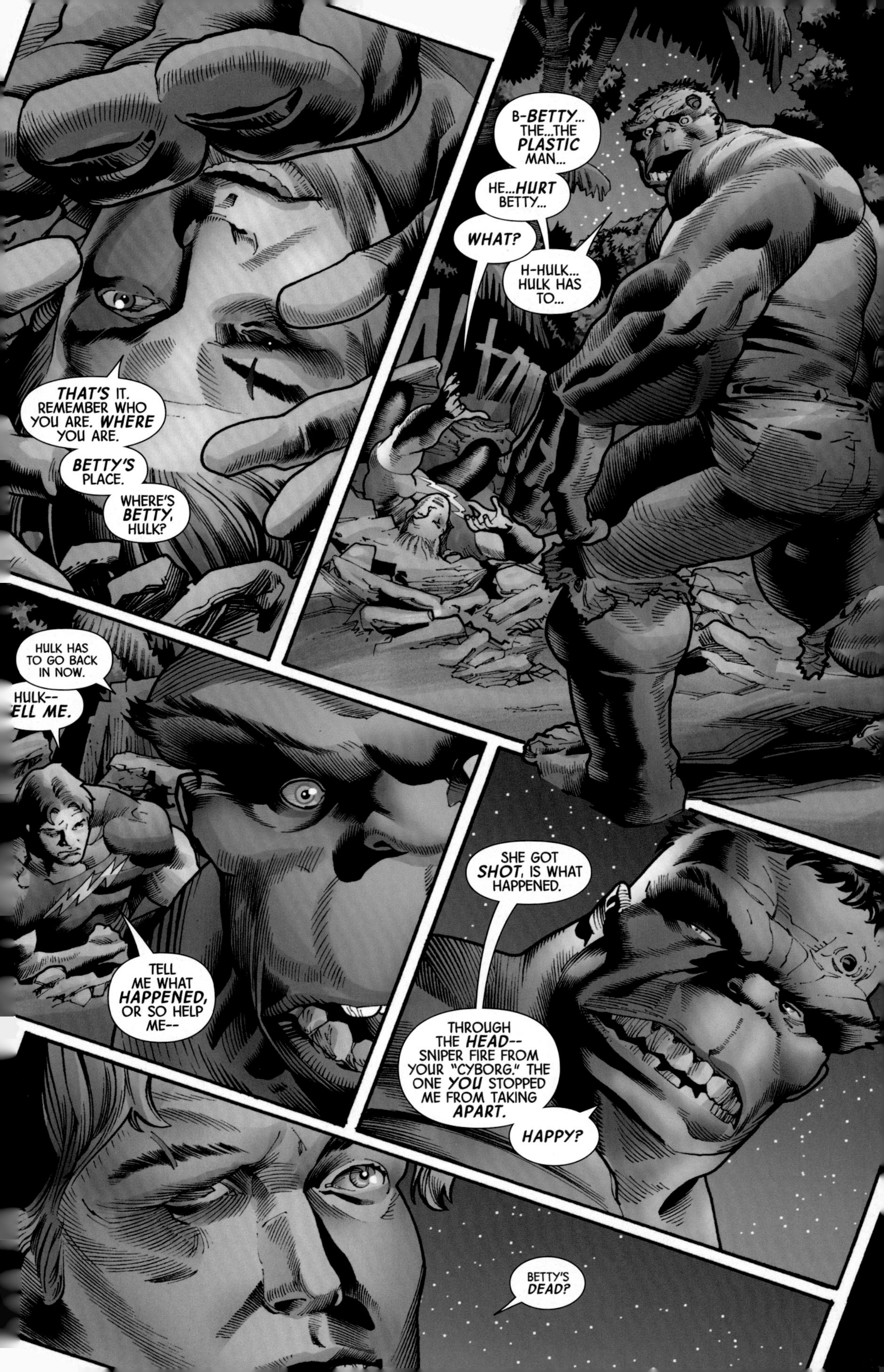
THAT'S IT. REMEMBER WHO YOU ARE. WHERE YOU ARE.
BETTY'S PLACE.
WHERE'S BETTY, HULK?
B-BETTY... THE...THE PLASTIC MAN...
HE...HURT BETTY...
WHAT?
H-HULK... HULK HAS TO...
HULK HAS TO GO BACK IN NOW.
HULK--
ELL ME.
TELL ME WHAT HAPPENED, OR SO HELP ME--
SHE GOT SHOT, IS WHAT HAPPENED.
THROUGH THE HEAD-- SNIPER FIRE FROM YOUR "CYBORG." THE ONE YOU STOPPED ME FROM TAKING APART.
HAPPY?
BETTY'S DEAD?

...BETTY'S *NOT* DEAD?

SHE'S NOT *HERE*.

MY GUESS IS SHE WENT *THAT* WAY WHILE WE WERE *BUSY*.

I *KNEW* BANNER SEEING HER WAS A BAD IDEA...

WHAT *IS* YOUR RELATIONSHIP WITH HIM THESE DAYS? I HEAR *STORIES*...

WE DON'T TALK. NOT IN *WORDS*.

YOU *KNOW* HOW CRAZY BANNER'S LIFE WAS, SAMSON.

AND IT GOT *WORSE* WHILE YOU WERE GONE.

NOBODY SAW--NOBODY *WANTED* TO-- BUT HE WAS SO *BROKEN*, HE SET UP HIS OWN *MURDER*.

"AND ALL *THAT* DID WAS BREAK HIM *MORE*.

"THERE WAS A HULK THAT CAME OUT TO WORK FOR *HYDRA*, YOU KNOW THAT? JUST A BIG BALL OF RAGE AND NOTHING *ELSE*. A WORDLESS *THING* THAT DIDN'T CARE *WHO* IT HURT.

"THAT DIDN'T S[ ] *PEOPLE* AT ALL

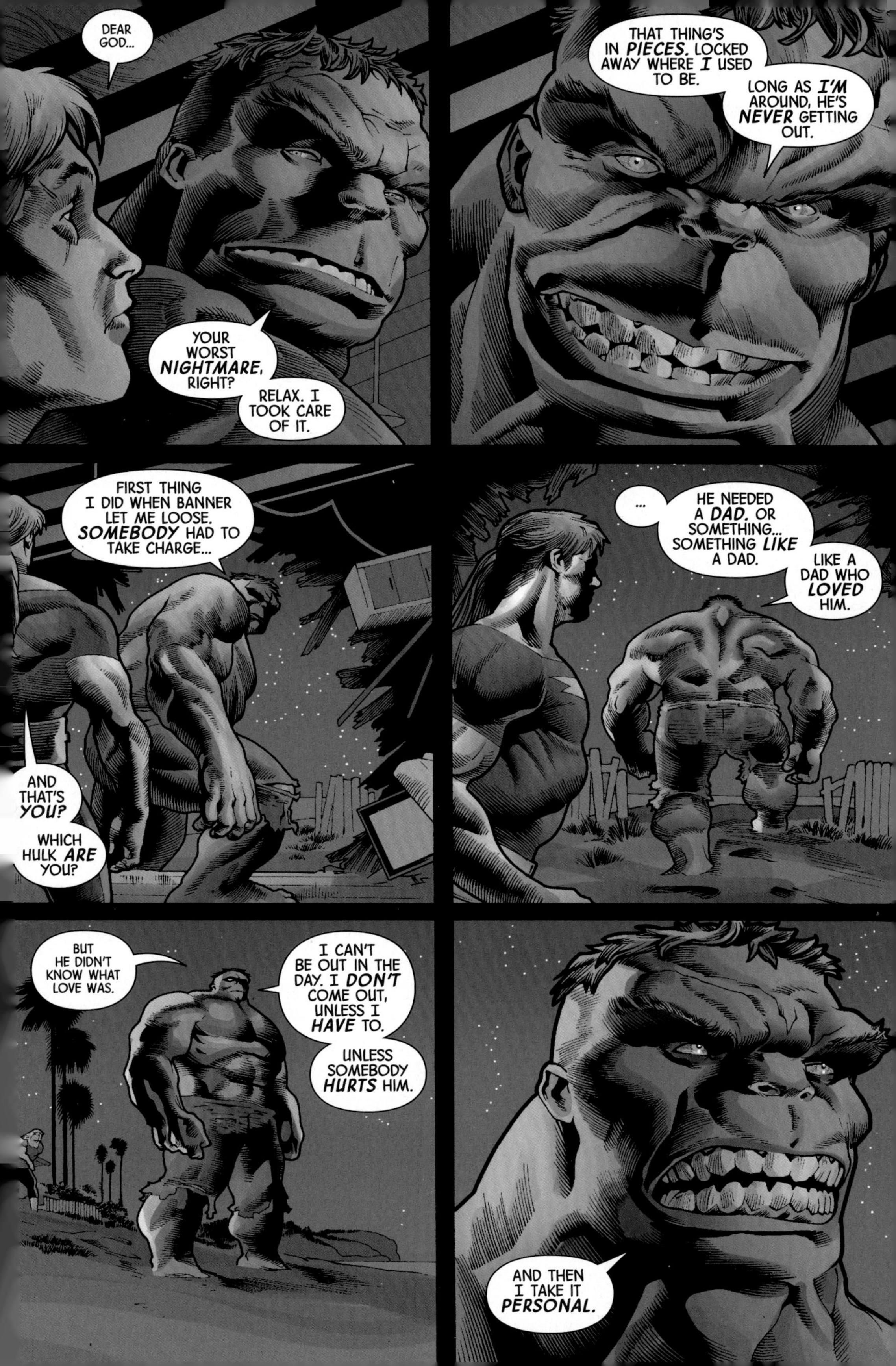
DEAR GOD...
YOUR WORST NIGHTMARE, RIGHT?
RELAX. I TOOK CARE OF IT.
THAT THING'S IN PIECES. LOCKED AWAY WHERE I USED TO BE.
LONG AS I'M AROUND, HE'S NEVER GETTING OUT.
FIRST THING I DID WHEN BANNER LET ME LOOSE. SOMEBODY HAD TO TAKE CHARGE...
AND THAT'S YOU?
WHICH HULK ARE YOU?
...
HE NEEDED A DAD. OR SOMETHING... SOMETHING LIKE A DAD.
LIKE A DAD WHO LOVED HIM.
BUT HE DIDN'T KNOW WHAT LOVE WAS.
I CAN'T BE OUT IN THE DAY. I DON'T COME OUT, UNLESS I HAVE TO.
UNLESS SOMEBODY HURTS HIM.
AND THEN I TAKE IT PERSONAL.

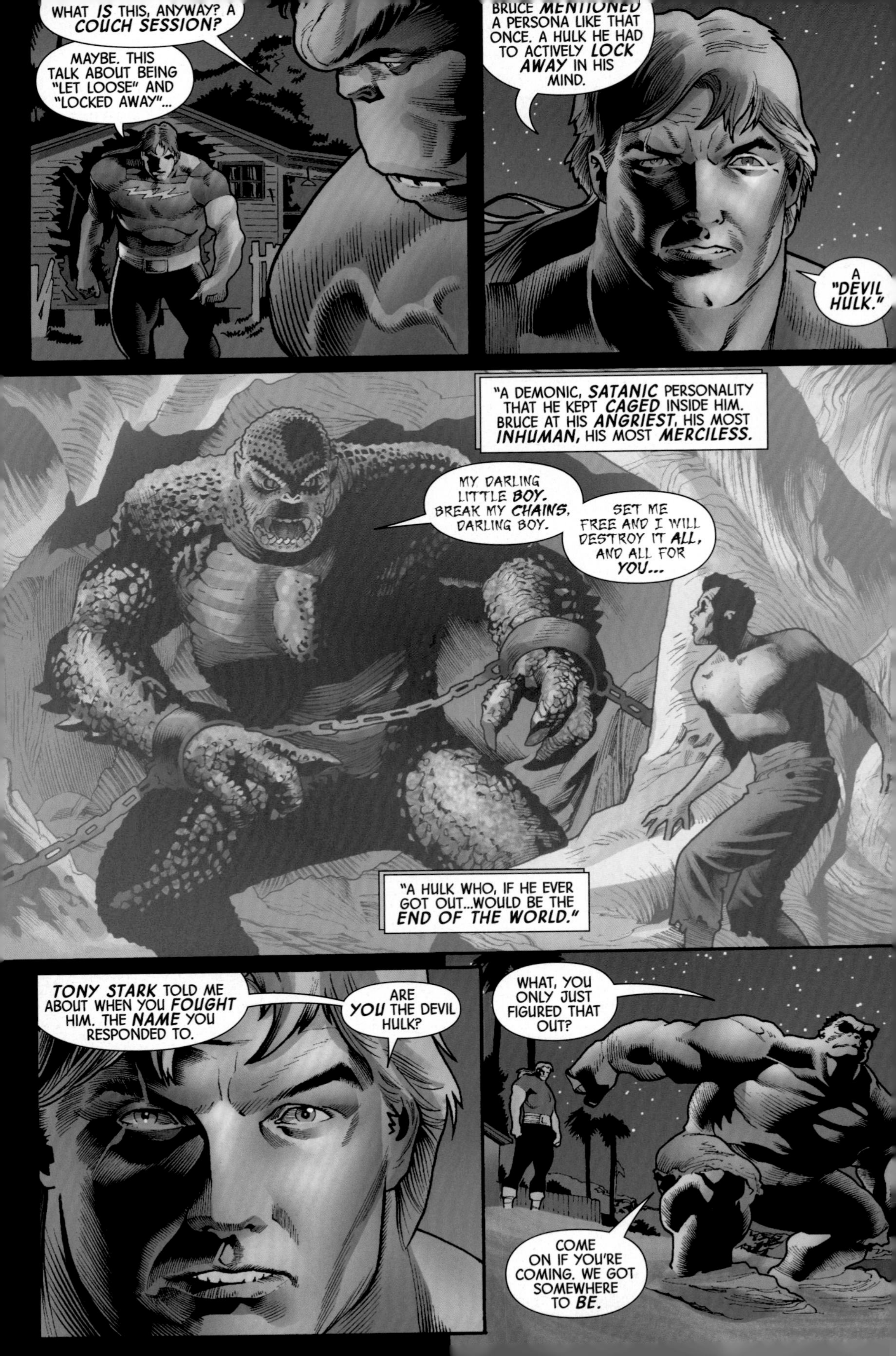
WHAT IS THIS, ANYWAY? A COUCH SESSION?
MAYBE. THIS TALK ABOUT BEING "LET LOOSE" AND "LOCKED AWAY"...
BRUCE MENTIONED A PERSONA LIKE THAT ONCE. A HULK HE HAD TO ACTIVELY LOCK AWAY IN HIS MIND.
A "DEVIL HULK."
"A DEMONIC, SATANIC PERSONALITY THAT HE KEPT CAGED INSIDE HIM. BRUCE AT HIS ANGRIEST, HIS MOST INHUMAN, HIS MOST MERCILESS.
MY DARLING LITTLE BOY. BREAK MY CHAINS, DARLING BOY.
SET ME FREE AND I WILL DESTROY IT ALL, AND ALL FOR YOU...
"A HULK WHO, IF HE EVER GOT OUT...WOULD BE THE END OF THE WORLD."
TONY STARK TOLD ME ABOUT WHEN YOU FOUGHT HIM. THE NAME YOU RESPONDED TO.
ARE YOU THE DEVIL HULK?
WHAT, YOU ONLY JUST FIGURED THAT OUT?
COME ON IF YOU'RE COMING. WE GOT SOMEWHERE TO BE.

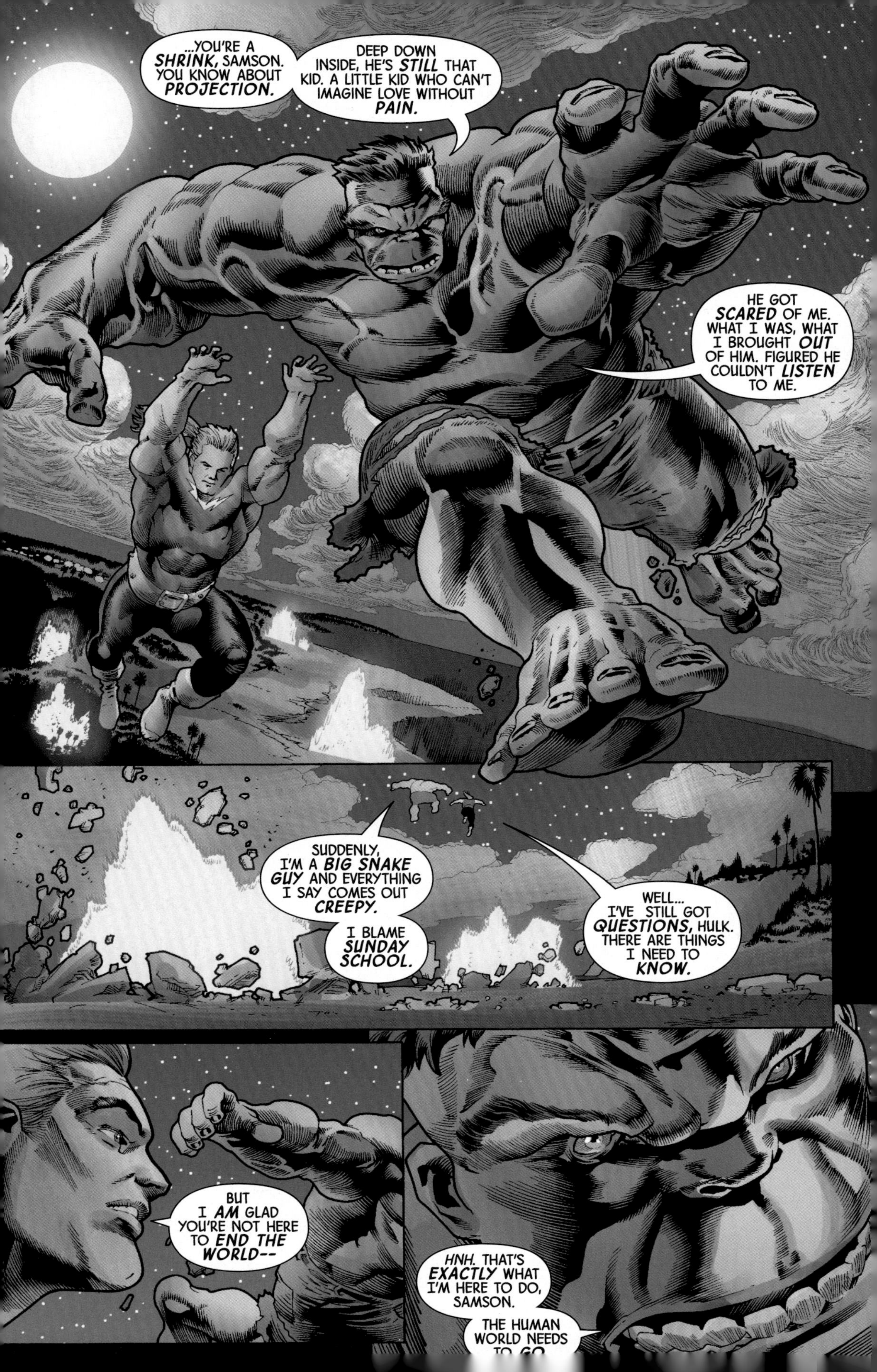
...YOU'RE A SHRINK, SAMSON. YOU KNOW ABOUT PROJECTION.
DEEP DOWN INSIDE, HE'S STILL THAT KID. A LITTLE KID WHO CAN'T IMAGINE LOVE WITHOUT PAIN.
HE GOT SCARED OF ME. WHAT I WAS, WHAT I BROUGHT OUT OF HIM. FIGURED HE COULDN'T LISTEN TO ME.
SUDDENLY, I'M A BIG SNAKE GUY AND EVERYTHING I SAY COMES OUT CREEPY.
I BLAME SUNDAY SCHOOL.
WELL... I'VE STILL GOT QUESTIONS, HULK. THERE ARE THINGS I NEED TO KNOW.
BUT I AM GLAD YOU'RE NOT HERE TO END THE WORLD--
HNH. THAT'S EXACTLY WHAT I'M HERE TO DO, SAMSON.
THE HUMAN WORLD NEEDS TO GO.

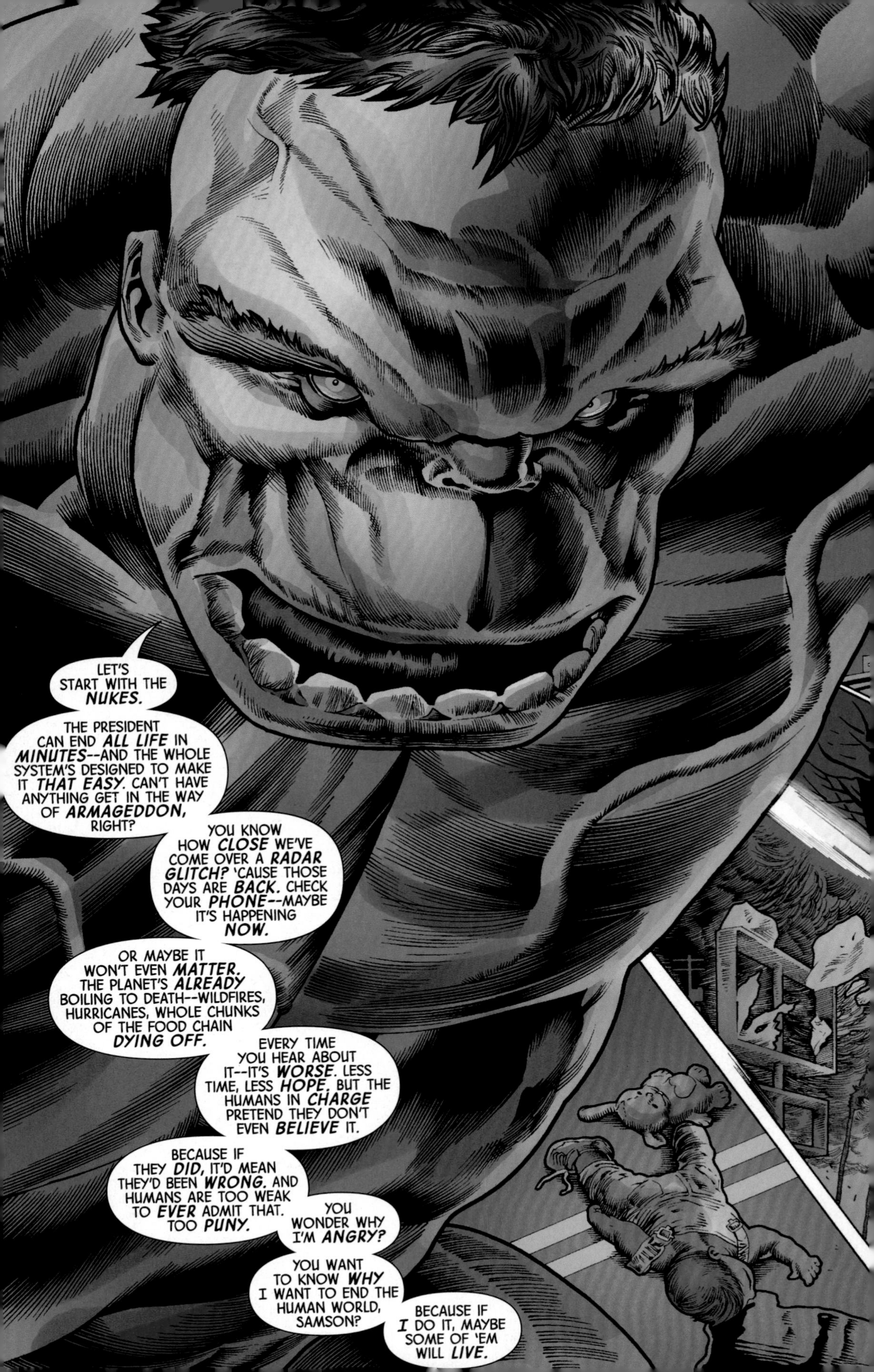
LET'S START WITH THE NUKES.
THE PRESIDENT CAN END ALL LIFE IN MINUTES--AND THE WHOLE SYSTEM'S DESIGNED TO MAKE IT THAT EASY. CAN'T HAVE ANYTHING GET IN THE WAY OF ARMAGEDDON, RIGHT?
YOU KNOW HOW CLOSE WE'VE COME OVER A RADAR GLITCH? 'CAUSE THOSE DAYS ARE BACK. CHECK YOUR PHONE--MAYBE IT'S HAPPENING NOW.
OR MAYBE IT WON'T EVEN MATTER. THE PLANET'S ALREADY BOILING TO DEATH--WILDFIRES, HURRICANES, WHOLE CHUNKS OF THE FOOD CHAIN DYING OFF.
EVERY TIME YOU HEAR ABOUT IT--IT'S WORSE. LESS TIME, LESS HOPE. BUT THE HUMANS IN CHARGE PRETEND THEY DON'T EVEN BELIEVE IT.
BECAUSE IF THEY DID, IT'D MEAN THEY'D BEEN WRONG. AND HUMANS ARE TOO WEAK TO EVER ADMIT THAT. TOO PUNY.
YOU WONDER WHY I'M ANGRY?
YOU WANT TO KNOW WHY I WANT TO END THE HUMAN WORLD, SAMSON?
BECAUSE IF I DO IT, MAYBE SOME OF 'EM WILL LIVE.

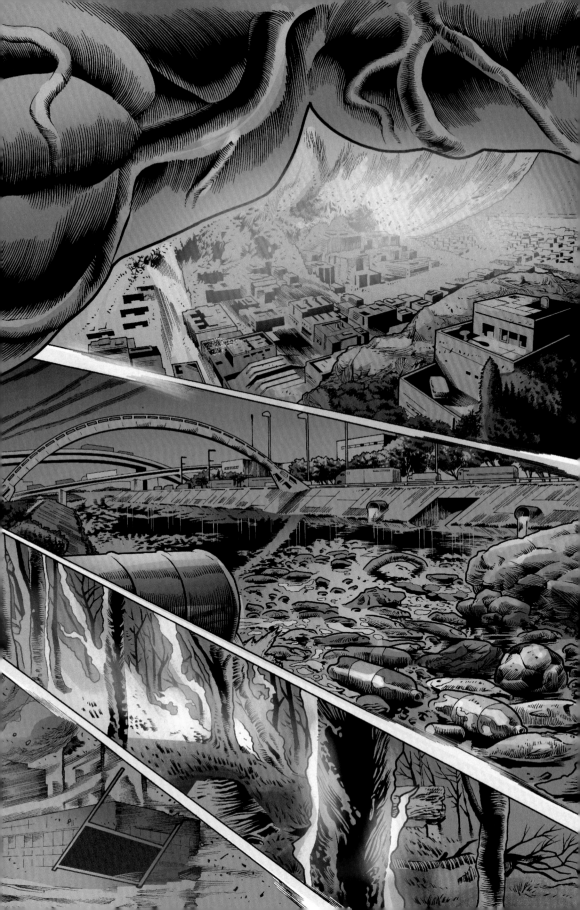

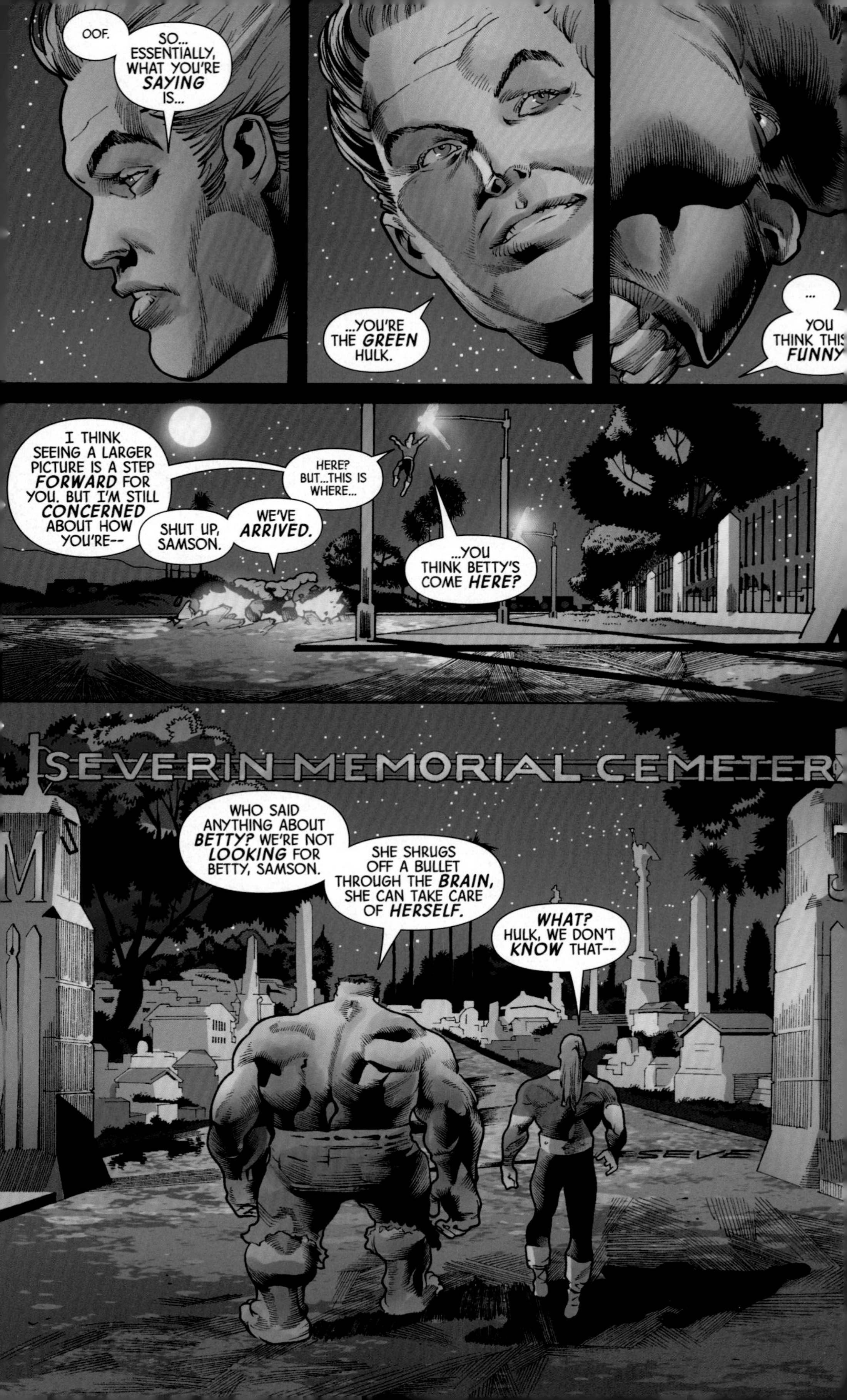
OOF.
SO... ESSENTIALLY, WHAT YOU'RE SAYING IS...
...YOU'RE THE GREEN HULK.
...
YOU THINK THIS FUNNY
I THINK SEEING A LARGER PICTURE IS A STEP FORWARD FOR YOU. BUT I'M STILL CONCERNED ABOUT HOW YOU'RE--
SHUT UP, SAMSON.
WE'VE ARRIVED.
HERE? BUT...THIS IS WHERE...
...YOU THINK BETTY'S COME HERE?
SEVERIN MEMORIAL CEMETER
WHO SAID ANYTHING ABOUT BETTY? WE'RE NOT LOOKING FOR BETTY, SAMSON.
SHE SHRUGS OFF A BULLET THROUGH THE BRAIN, SHE CAN TAKE CARE OF HERSELF.
WHAT? HULK, WE DON'T KNOW THAT--
SEVE

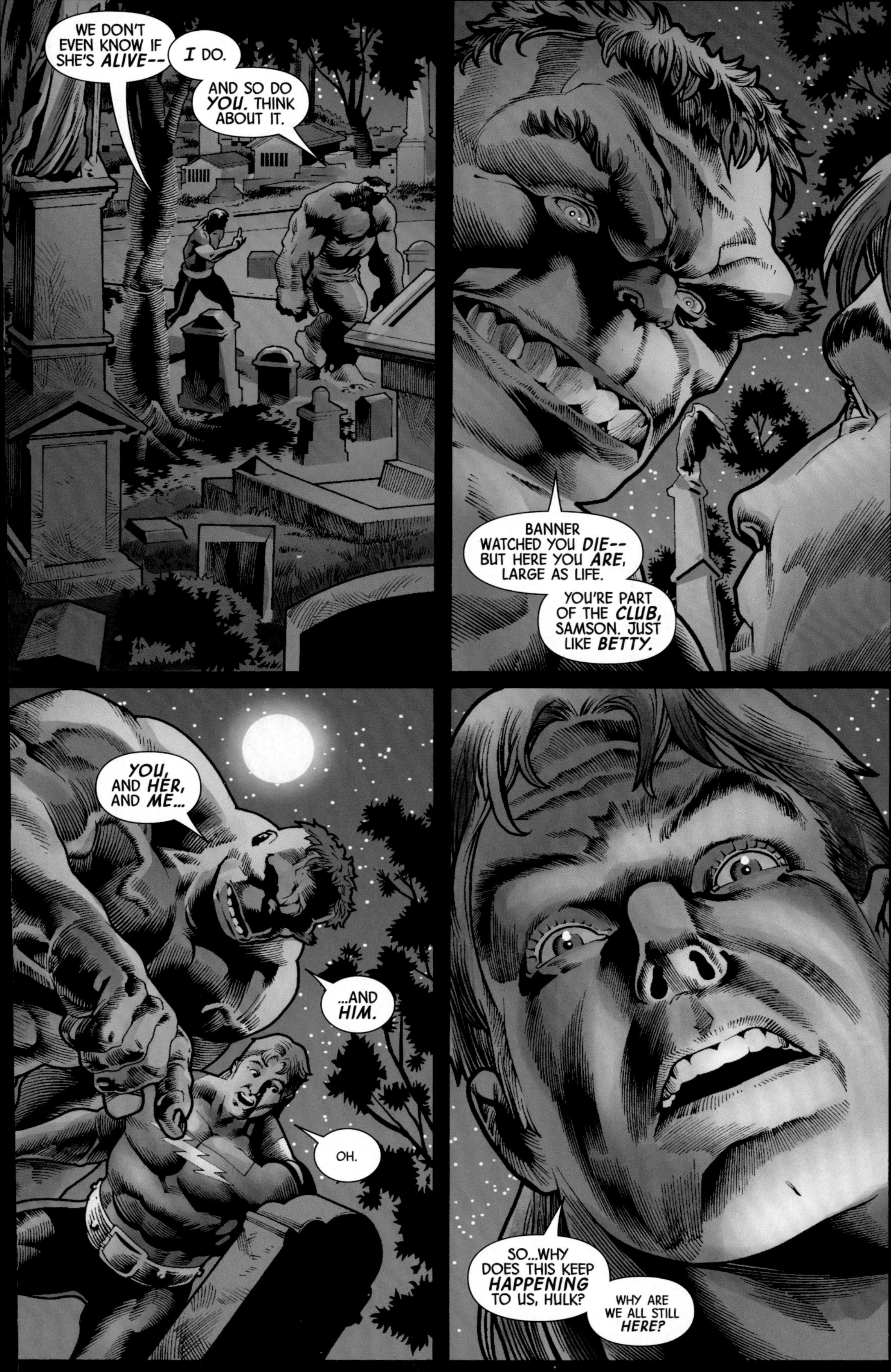
WE DON'T EVEN KNOW IF SHE'S ALIVE--
I DO.
AND SO DO YOU. THINK ABOUT IT.
BANNER WATCHED YOU DIE-- BUT HERE YOU ARE, LARGE AS LIFE.
YOU'RE PART OF THE CLUB, SAMSON. JUST LIKE BETTY.
YOU, AND HER, AND ME...
...AND HIM.
OH.
SO...WHY DOES THIS KEEP HAPPENING TO US, HULK?
WHY ARE WE ALL STILL HERE?

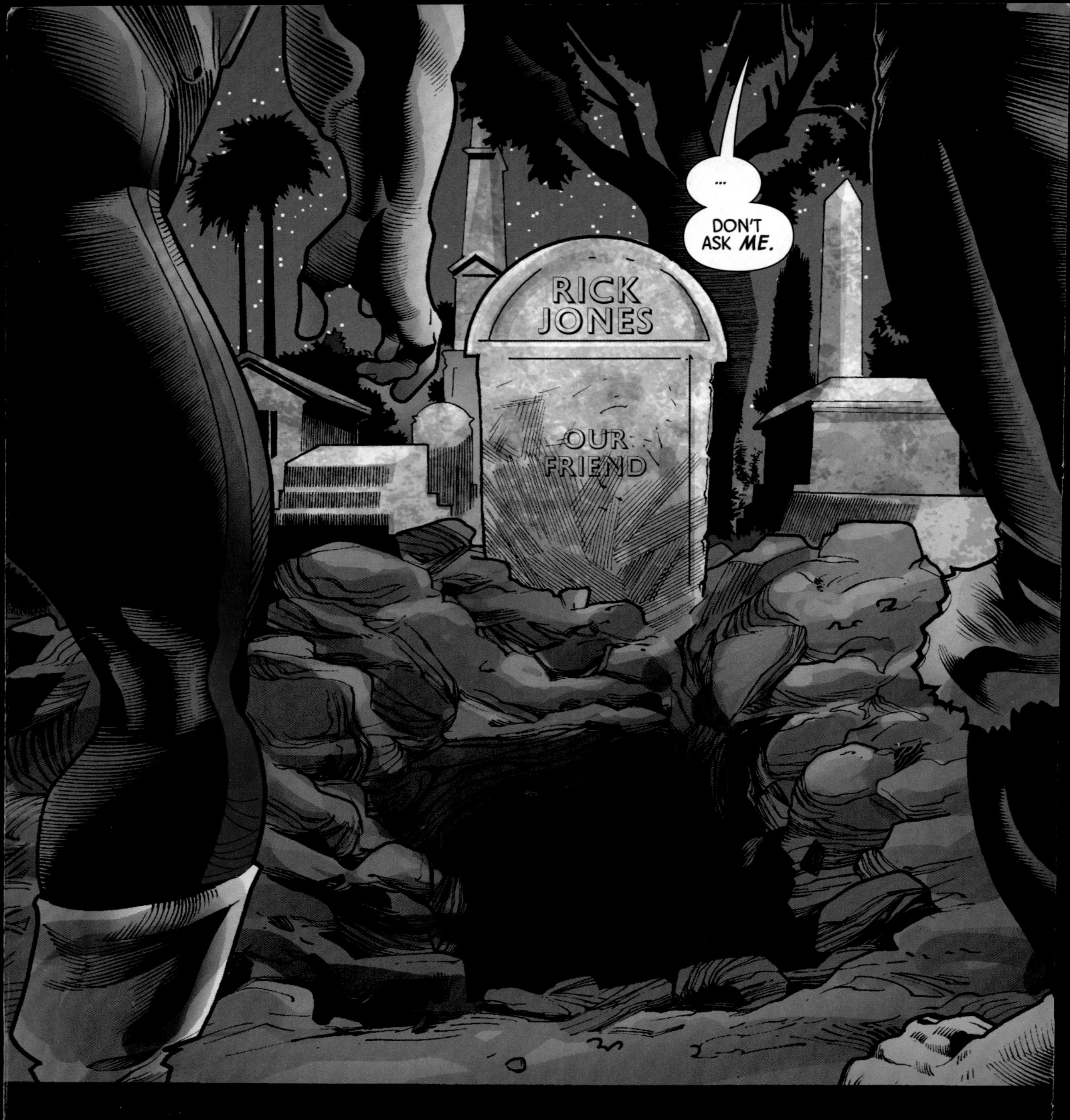
...
DON'T ASK ME.
RICK JONES
OUR FRIEND

THE HOLY OR THE BROKEN

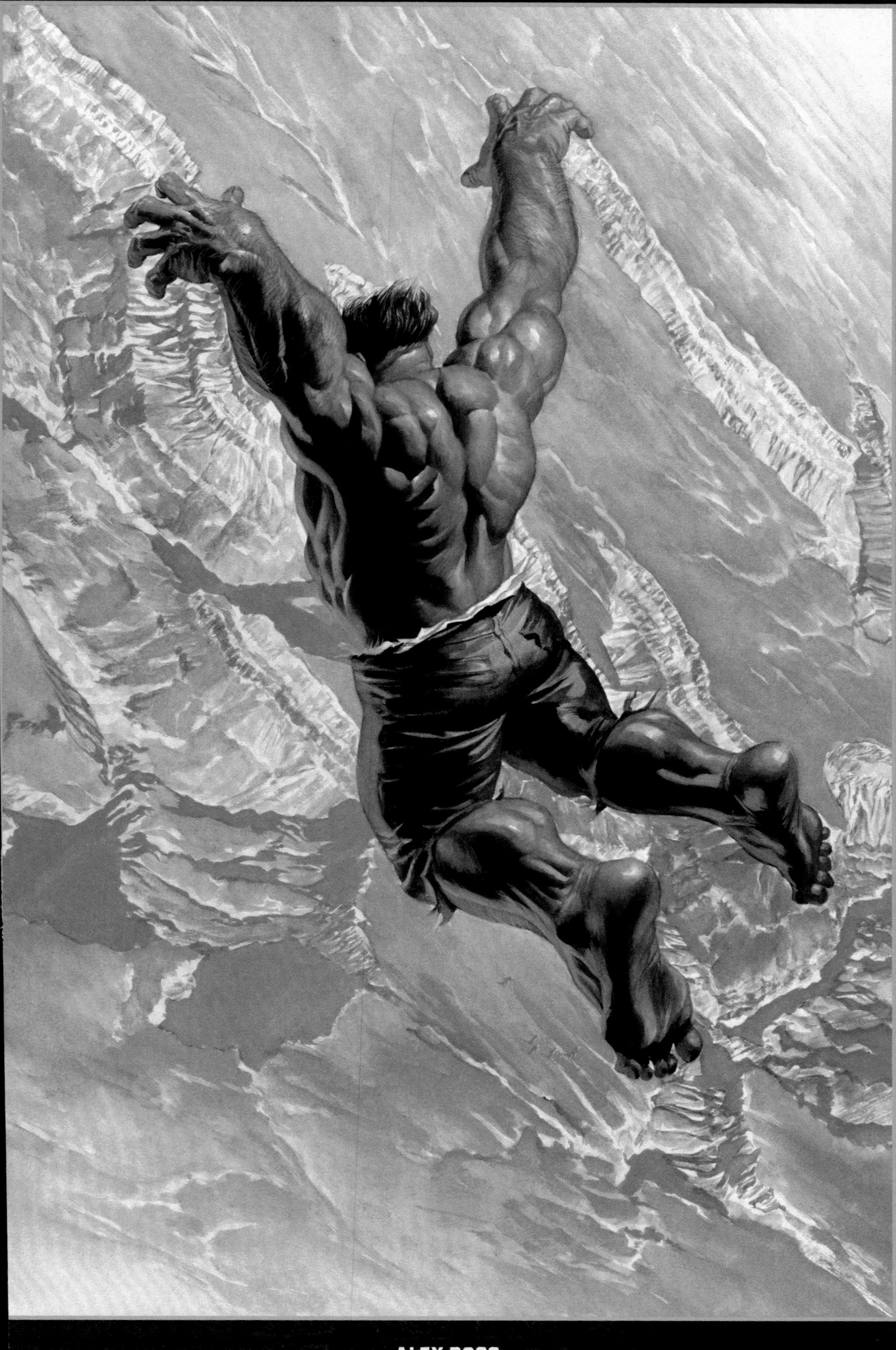

ALEX ROSS
#15 VARIANT

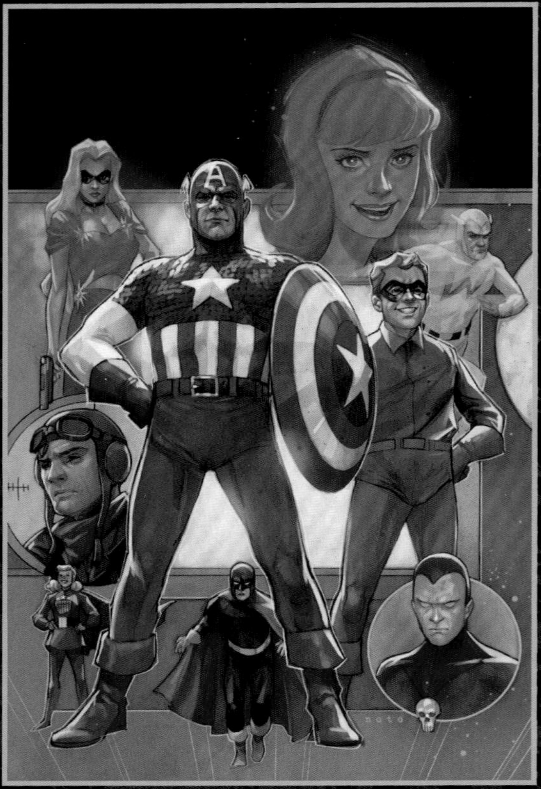

PHIL NOTO
#11 MARVEL 80TH VARIANT

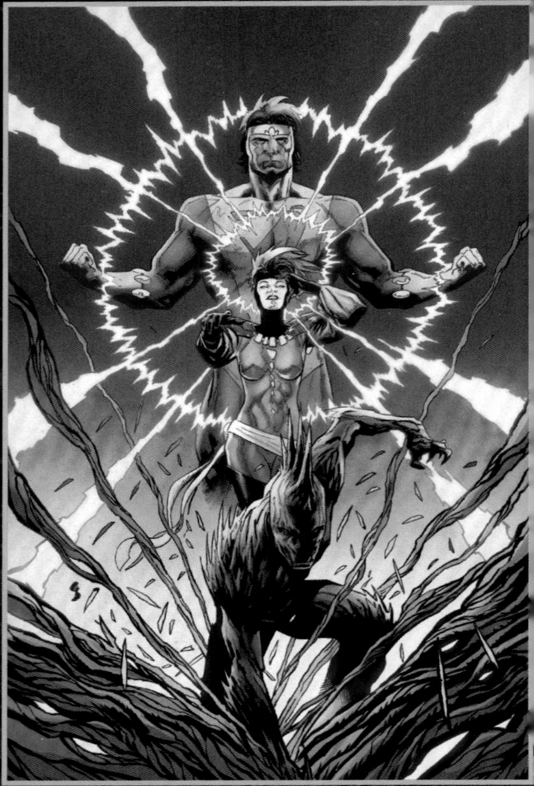

GEOFF SHAW & JASON KEITH
#12 GUARDIANS OF THE GALAXY VARIANT

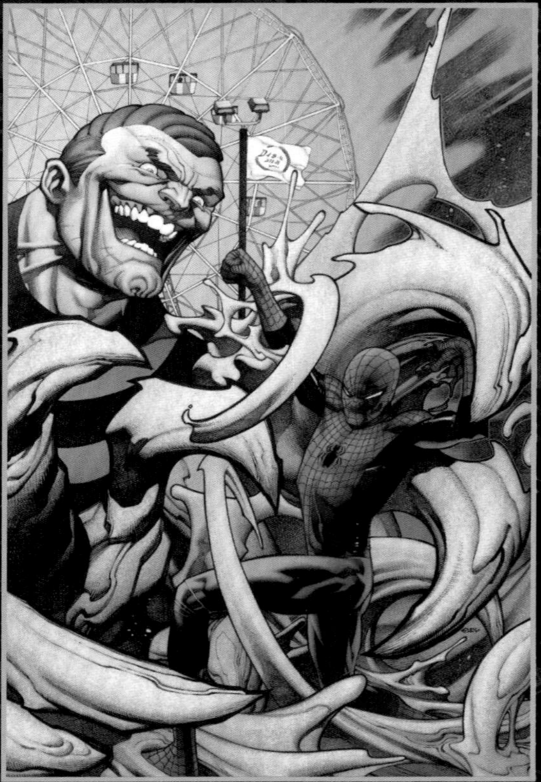

CHRIS STEVENS & MORRY HOLLOWELL
#14 SPIDER-MAN VILLAINS VARIANT